Build and Upgrade Your Own PC

Build and Upgrade Your Own PC

Third edition

Ian Sinclair

Newnes

OXFORD AMSTERDAM BOSTON LONDON NEW YORK PARIS
SAN DIEGO SAN FRANCISCO SINGAPORE SYDNEY TOKYO

Newnes
An imprint of Elsevier Science
Linacre House, Jordan Hill, Oxford OX2 8DP
225 Wildwood Avenue, Woburn, MA 01801–2041

First published 1999
Reprinted 2000
Second edition 2001
Third edition 2002

British Library Cataloguing in Publication Data
A catalogue record for this book is available from the British Library

ISBN 0 7506 57588

For information on all Newnes publications visit our website at
www.newnespress.com

Typeset by Avocet Typeset, Brill, Aylesbury, Bucks
Printed and bound in Great Britain by Biddles Ltd, *www.biddles.co.uk*

Contents

Preface

The mass production of PC chips, circuit boards and accessories of all types has led to the growth of a thriving assembly industry in PC machines. The result is that it has for many years been possible for anyone with facilities for assembling circuit boards into cases to put together PCs with capabilities equal to all but a few modern designs. The sheer number of small-scale suppliers, and the standardization of design, indicates how easy this work can be, using plug-in boards from the lowest cost sources. Construction, in this sense, can mean assembly, and not necessarily much assembly in some examples.

The small-scale assemblers, most of whom can offer machines with high specifications, cannot necessarily offer much more than hardware. In particular, they cannot offer a manual that makes much sense to the first-time user, and even an experienced PC user can be baffled by a new machine if little or no information is available.

This book is a form of manual that will cover the construction of a PC, either from scratch or following the much more common (and more rational) method of buying a low-cost machine from a local assembler, or from other sources such as auctions, and improving it as required.

This book will also be a useful reference text for users of all the machines that can be described as generic, machines which are very closely compatible with standard PC/AT design but with enhanced facilities. If your low-cost PC comes provided with a manual that can be politely described as rudimentary, this book is one that will be useful to you. To avoid making this book unnecessarily long, the construction of machines to older specifications is now relegated to the last chapter because the parts are now quite difficult to obtain, and such machines can be obtained ready-made at very low prices if you shop around. The emphasis in this edition will be on the construction of a machine to modern standards (typically at least an 850 MHz clock speed) or updating a machine of close to this standard to a higher standard (more than 1 GHz clock speed).

To clarify terms, the first IBM desktop machines were known as PC, meaning personal computer. AT means *Advanced Technology*, and the PC/AT type of machine set the standard that is still followed (with many improvements) today. This type of machine is also referred to as ISA, meaning *Industry Standard Architecture*, and the letters EISA (E meaning *Extended* or Enhanced) are also used for the later versions such as the MMX types (the use of the term MMX is now discontinued, since all processor chips for PCs are of this type). We are concerned in this book with EISA machines using processors of the Pentium 3/4, Celeron, AMD Duron, Athlon and Thunderbird (or later) types.

One point that often worries prospective DIY builders is that their machine will be non-standard. The fact is that a home constructed machine is likely to be totally standard, more so than some big-name varieties, and more adaptable to upgrading. Another worry is that some inadvertent action will destroy the whole machine, and this also is a myth unless you make a habit of dropping hammers into equipment. Perhaps we should add the worry that the machine will be damaged in some way by unsuitable software or when a program locks up. As this book points out, the computer clears its memory when it is switched off, and a fault in a program cannot affect any other program that is run after restarting like this. Unless a runaway program has, by a most unusual fluke, altered the contents of the hard drive, no harm will be done. By contrast, the type of program that we class as a virus will often alter the hard drive contents – careless use of the Internet is much more dangerous than building your own computer.

- The most dangerous action, as far as a computer is concerned, is a hard knock on the casing while the hard drive is working.

As it happens, building a PC totally from scratch is usually *more* expensive than buying a machine from some of the small-scale firms, and most private owners take the course of buying only as much as they need of an assembled machine – often a case, PSU, and mother-board only. Many suppliers specialize in this type of *bare-bones* machine, and because the parts are usually standardized, such machines are easy to work with and to upgrade. By starting in this way you can gain a price advantage, because there is no way that you can buy components cheaper than an assembler who can buy in bulk. The casing, for example, that costs you £55 may have been bought for less than £10 each, but only in container loads. You may, however, feel that you can use the monitor, casing, keyboard and some other parts from an older machine that you are currently using, but only if the machine is not *too* old.

The point of assembling your PC in this way is that you can also upgrade for yourself, avoiding the high costs that are so often associ-ated with changing hardware. A second-hand computer, after all, depreciates like a second-hand car. Once again, though, you need to know a fair bit about PCs to know what can, and cannot, be upgraded. Since the actions of upgrading are almost identical to those of constructing from scratch, the snags of upgrading are discussed in a separate chapter.

Another route which is now significant is to buy machines that have been discarded by local authorities and other corporate users. The more a local authority or nationalized service complains about lack of money the more computers they appear to scrap (not sell), simply because they are not the most recent models. These machines are found at auctions and at car-boot sales, often at very low prices. Some are older 80486 types which are almost useless, others are almost new Pentium machines which have been used in networks and which may lack a hard drive. Prices of £50 to £100 make this a very encouraging start and one which is much cheaper than buying all parts separately.

Another possible reason for building your own is to make a machine to a high specification but without items that are irrelevant to your needs. You might, for example, want to build a machine with the fastest processing speed attainable, but without the DVD drive, scanner, CD-R/RW, Webcam and other accessories that would almost certainly be loaded on to such a machine if you bought it ready-made.

The aim of this book is to provide information for anyone taking any of these routes, because no manuals will be available. Since many readers of this book are likely to be experienced in electronics, some aspects of computer circuitry and disk recording are explained in more detail than would be relevant to the reader with no electronics background. Other than these paragraphs, the book is intended to be used by newcomers and experienced users alike, either in computing or in electronics.

• Since the effects of construction and upgrading cannot be judged without the essential software, the essentials of installing Windows *Me*, and Windows XP, the operating systems that are most suited to the home constructor, are also included, along with a section on printers. For details of how to use Windows, see the various *Pocket Books* and *Made Simple* books from Newnes.

I am most grateful to August One Communications Ltd for Windows *Me* and Windows XP discs for evaluation. I am also grateful to AMD Inc. for permission to use some images from their excellent website devoted to the construction of a PC using the Athlon processor.

Ian Sinclair
March 2002

Chapter 1

The PC machine

This and most of the following chapters are intended primarily for the prospective assembler of a modern fast PC, whose experience has been in either electronics construction or in computing. The text is, however, also an essential guide to anyone who is constructing a PC with no previous electronics experience and possibly very little experience with a computer. If you are already well experienced in computing and want to experience the joys of self-assembly then read this by all means, but be prepared to skip some explanations that are intended for the newcomer to computers.

Before you start

Before you start to build your own computer, you need to know a few facts, and the answers to what we call FAQs (frequently asked questions).

The first point that you need to be clear on is that there are limits to DIY. You are not expected to build a monitor, keyboard, mouse or printer, and there are no kits of parts available for constructing these items. Assembly work is limited to the main processing unit, and one good reason for this is safety. There are no exposed high-voltage points in the main processing unit, and assembly is limited to plugging and fastening circuit boards and other units into place. The other main reason is that standardized parts are readily available only for the main processing unit.

If you intend to assemble the whole computer system, including keyboard, mouse, monitor, printer and other accessories such as scanner or digital camera, you will pay much more for the privilege of doing it all yourself than you would if you bought a package from PC World, Mesh, Time Computing or Tiny Computers (now part of Time Computing), to give just four well-known sources. This should not come as a surprise because the same applies to many other DIY projects, particularly cars. You will never have the advantage of getting the low prices on single components that can be obtained by someone who can order in thousands.

You might, of course, already have a keyboard, mouse, monitor and printer and possibly other devices as well, and want only to build the main processing unit. In this case, because there are few suppliers of this item of hardware by itself, you might very well make a cash saving. You might want a machine that is not so elaborately specified as the models that are on sale, or one that incorporates items that are not usually part of a ready-made machine.

- Many modern packages that are sold at prices of around £700–£1000 are intended for a user who has nothing, and who needs a complete machine with printer, scanner, digital camera and all sorts of other accessories. If this applies to you, then such a package is your easiest route into computing. If you don't need all the bells and whistles, or if you have items such as a monitor and keyboard already, then the advice in this book will save you money and time.

Selling an old computer to help finance a new one is seldom economic, because a second-hand computer, unless it is a very recent model, is difficult to sell, and prices are low despite the values some sellers hopefully put on their old machines. If your 'old' computer is not too old you are always likely to be better off by upgrading it rather than selling it and building a new machine.

- If you also want a better keyboard, a larger monitor, and possibly a better printer as well as the main processing unit, then forget the idea of doing any construction for yourself, and buy a package at the best combination of specification and price that you can find.

Words and meanings

If a self-build computer is to be your first computer, or the first you have encountered for some time, then you need to know some of the language of today's computers and the way that these words are used. If you are already using a reasonably up-to-date PC, then you can skip over this part.

To start with, the type of machine that we now describe as a PC is one that is modelled on the IBM PC type of machine that first appeared in 1980. The reason that this type of machine has become dominant is the simple one of continuity – programs (also called *software applications*) that will work on the original IBM PC machine will work on later versions and will still work on most of today's PC machines using Windows *Me* or Windows XP Home (possibly using the *Accessories* – *MSDOS Prompt* menu item for running pre-Windows programs).

By maintaining compatibility, the designers have ensured that when you change computer, keeping to a PC type of machine, you do not necessarily need to change software (programs). Since the value of your software is much greater than the value of the hardware (the computer itself) this has ensured that the PC type of machine has become dominant in business and other serious applications. Other machines that are not compatible with the PC (or with each other) have less choice of software, more expensive components, and self-building is actively discouraged.

- Windows 2000 is much less tolerant of older hardware and software, and so is much less compatible than older versions of Windows – it is, however, a recommended step up if your computer already uses NT4. If you have previously used Windows 98, then the upgrade option is Windows *Me*, not Windows 2000. If this is your first computer you should opt for Windows *Me*. The most recent version of Windows at the time of writing is XP and the Home version is the one recommended for most users. More details of Windows XP will feature in Chapter 10.

Figure 1.1 The original IBM PC computer. This used a 5¼ inch floppy drive with no hard drive and only 64 Kbytes of memory, but it set standards that eventually most of the microcomputer industry would follow

Compatibility works only one way, however, and most of the (Windows) software that is being written now will not run on older machines, though a lot of old-style MS-DOS programs will still run on a new machine. The main benefit of a long-established design is that components are remarkably cheap and reliable, and that the layout of machines is more or less standardized. Though you can build or buy an old-style machine for a low price, it is well worth the small amount of extra cash to construct or buy a PC machine that is reasonably up to date in design. This allows you the luxury of being able to use any software written for the PC, not just the older programs. You should aim at least for a machine that can run Windows *Me*, and if your computing interests are mainly for business purposes, possibly sharing or networking the computer, then preferably you should go for one that can run the later version Windows XP Pro. Chapter 10 contains a brief guide to installing Windows.

- It is very difficult now to build a machine to an older specification because the parts are simply not available except by dismantling older machines. You cannot, for example, easily find a hard drive smaller than 20 Gbytes now. Do not be tempted to build using second-hand hard drives (or any other mechanical component second hand). Even purely electronic components can be so out of date that a modern version of Windows cannot make use of them.

Explaining the words

If you have been using a computer or, at least, keeping up with the magazines, the following will not really be applicable to you. On the other hand, if it is all rather a mystery and you feel that the magazines are aimed at experts rather than at beginners then you might find this section of explanations useful.

The CPU: First of all, the actions of a computer are all regulated by the *processor* or *CPU*, a microchip which is quite large and is cooled by a block of finned metal (a *heatsink*) with a clip-on fan. The speed at which this processor works is important and is controlled by its clock pulses, electrical impulses that repeat at a very high speed. Some CPUs used to come mounted on a board with the fan attached – these are referred to as slot-fitting processors because the board has a set of electrical contacts along its long edge that attach to a slot fitting in the *motherboard*. Slot fitting is no longer used and will not be featured in this book. The fan is essential because a processor gives out as much heat as a 60 W lamp bulb.

Clock rate: The *clock rate* of a processor is measured in megahertz (MHz), meaning millions of clock pulses per second, and you can expect to use clock rates of 800 to 2000 MHz (1000 MHz = 1 GHz, 1 gigahertz) for modern machines. Because modern machines are so fast, the unit of the GHz is more often used now, and a typical machine would have a clock rate of about 1.5 GHz. The same units of MHz are used for specifying other rates, like the clock rates that are used in the linking connections (buses) between the CPU and other chips. A typical bus rate is 100 MHz for the older chips, 133 MHz for average machines, faster (266 MHz) for more recent designs.

Motherboard: The processor is mounted, along with other important chips, on a *motherboard*. This motherboard has slots to hold other boards, variously described as *daughterboards*, or simply as boards or cards, that add other actions to the computing actions of the motherboard. The motherboard with all of its slot-fitting cards is mounted in a case that contains the sealed power supply unit (PSU). Several different varieties of motherboard were in use at one time, but all home-assembled machines now make use of the type of motherboard referred to as ATX.

Chipset: The processor is a very important chip, but it can't do everything. On the motherboard you will find a set of other chips that control how data signals flow to and from the processor. The performance of your computer depends as much on this chipset as it does on the processor. There are several such chipsets with brand names such as Triton (from Intel), SIS, Ali, VIA and Opti. The chipset that you get is fixed by the type of motherboard you buy — there is no option for changing the chipset the way that you can change the processor.

Sockets: At one time, all CPU chips fitted into a socket, typically using several hundred pin-contacts. For some time, there was a fashion for processors that were already fitted onto a board that plugged into a slot, but these are now obsolete. All modern processors fit into a socket and though sockets for different types of processors may look identical they are not electrically compatible so that you have to take care that you are fitting the correct type of processor into the socket on the motherboard.

OS: The processor actions are controlled by the *operating system* (OS), a program that is responsible for the whole system, ensuring that memory, disk drives, monitor, sound card, keyboard, mouse, etc., all act together. For most readers, this OS will be some version of *Microsoft Windows*.

Applications: The *applications software* items are the programs that you make use of. These programs will call on the operating system whenever they need to use any routine actions such as working with disk files, printer, keyboard, monitor, mouse, and so on.

GUI: At one time, an operating system required you to type in commands, and though you can still use such systems (such as MS-DOS and LINUX) all modern PCs provide a *graphical user interface* (GUI) which almost eliminates typing commands in favour of using the *mouse* to select images (icons) or menu items and clicking a button to start an action. The PC GUI is *Microsoft Windows*, and the most recent versions at the time of writing are Windows *Me* and Windows XP, though Windows 98 and the older Windows 95 are still in use. Windows 2000 is not a natural upgrade from Windows 98 in the sense that it will necessarily work with the hardware/software that you use with Windows 98. Windows *Me*, first demonstrated to the public in April 2000, is the best option for any PC user who is upgrading or building. Windows XP Home version is a natural upgrade from Windows *Me*, but it requires the user to activate it by contacting Microsoft. An unactivated copy can be used for only 30 days, and once activated, Windows XP cannot be installed on another computer. It is not clear at the moment whether it could be reinstalled in the event of a hard disk crash that required a new hard disk to be installed. Activation is a feature that does not endear XP to self-constructors and upgraders who might change the hard drive frequently.

Memory: All programs, whether operating system or applications, need *memory* to work. The program instruction codes are stored in memory while a program is running, and memory is also used to store the data of a program and also temporary items (such as words you have cut from a word-processor document, or the carry-over in a piece of arithmetic). Memory is supplied in small daughterboards that fit into slots on the motherboard.

Bytes: The unit of data is the *byte*, which is 8 bits, with each *bit* being either 1 or 0. This allows a single byte to store a code number that can be between 0 and 255. This range is enough to allocate a number code to each letter of the alphabet, each digit (0 to 9) and each punctuation mark, so that word processing can be carried out using a byte for each letter. A more complicated system, using up to 8 bytes per number, is used for working with numbers in arithmetic.

The byte is a small unit of data (corresponding to the storage space for one typed character) and for practical purposes we use the larger units of Kbyte (Kilobyte, meaning 1024 bytes), Mbyte (Megabyte, meaning 1024 Kbytes or 1 048 576 bytes) and Gbyte (Gigabyte, meaning 1024 Mbytes). The reason for using the factor 1024 rather than 1000 is that 1024 is an exact power of 2 (it's 2^{10}), and the whole scheme of counting digitally is based on powers of 2.

- Memory for a modern PC is measured in Mbytes (megabytes) and typical values nowadays are 128 Mbytes to 512 Mbytes. Though adding memory enhances performance, machines that use the 'home' versions of Windows cannot use more than 512 Mbytes of memory, though the professional versions of Windows will allow much more to be fitted and used.

RAM: The memory in a PC is usually called RAM (random-access memory), to distinguish it from other types. All memory allows random access, and the name is an old one that has been retained to mean memory that can be written, read and rewritten, because everyone uses it. The important distinction is that RAM is cheap and easy to make in large sizes, but it does not retain information when the computer is switched off. There are many different varieties of RAM and it's essential to buy RAM that matches the motherboard and processor that you will use.

ROM and CMOS-RAM: The *hard drive* is used to hold information when the computer is off, and there are two types of memory that will also retain data. These are *ROM* (read-only memory) which is used to retain data that the computer needs to get started, and *CMOS RAM* which holds changing data, such as the date and information on the hard drive, because it uses a small battery to keep the data memorized. Both of these are small sizes of memory, very much smaller than the main RAM.

Hard drive: The *hard drive* is another essential part of a modern computer, and is used to store the operating system and all your applications. The main memory of a PC operates only while power is applied, and some method of storage is needed to store the bytes while the machine is switched off. The hard drive uses magnetic storage, which does not depend on a power supply, but which is much slower to use than the electronic memory.

- The word drive is used as a reminder that this is a mechanical component that uses an electric motor to spin a disk. All drives are liable to mechanical wear and tear, and their life is inevitably shorter than that of purely electronic components.

When hard drives first became available for small computers, a storage capacity of 32 Mbytes was a luxury, but the normal size nowadays is 20 Gbytes or more. Prices have now fallen to such a level that it is not a real economy to buy a small hard drive even if you can find one. Large-capacity hard drives cannot be used in old PC machines. Despite the capacity differences, hard drives are nowadays all the same physical size.

Floppy drive: The *floppy drive* uses removable disks which can hold up to 1.4 Mbytes each. These are used for short application programs and for small amounts of data.

CD-ROM: Larger amounts of data are catered for using the *CD-ROM drive*, together with CDs that can store up to 700 Mbytes. The CDs that are used for a PC employ exactly the same methods as the music type, so that you can play a music CD on a PC that has a sound card and loudspeakers. You can also fit a *CD-R/RW* drive that will create CDs, so that you can hold large amounts of data or music on a disc that you have created for yourself.

- A few music CDs are now being produced that are deliberately designed so that they will not play in the CD drive of a computer. If you buy such a CD, return it and ask for a refund, so that the music industry will understand that they have no right to choose how you want to play CDs.

DVD: A more recent development is the *digital versatile drive* (DVD). This uses the same disc size as the CD drive, and can read existing CDs. The difference is that the DVD can use more closely packed data and also use both sides of the disc, so that it can, in theory, cope with up to 17 Gbytes of data. The more usual size is around 4.5 Gbytes. DVD reader drives, with software for displaying movies, are reasonably priced, but the DVD recordable drives (which write as well as read) are still expensive at the time of writing, and look likely to remain so for some time. Worse still, there are two competing formats (like the early VCR days with Beta and VHS), so that you

risk spending a lot on a format that might disappear soon. The use of
DVD recordable drives to replace the VCR seems less likely now than
the use of large hard drives.

Sound: Modern PCs come with a *sound card*, whether you want one
or not. Sound is useful if you want it, annoying if you don't, but there
is no obligation to use a sound card if it is fitted. Sound in digital
form uses a large amount of memory and hard drive space, so that
your computer will be considerably less cluttered if you don't use
sound. On the other hand, you will miss the full impact of *multimedia*
programs (using text, sound and pictures) if you omit it. A sound
card is essential if you wish to work with sound inputs from old
recordings, transcribing the music on to CDs, or if you wish to work
with the modern MP3 music files.

Peripherals: The main casing of your computer contains many
sections that deal with the data. There are, however, other units that
cannot be contained inside the computer. Three obvious examples are
the keyboard, the mouse and the monitor. These devices are peripherals, something outside the main casing, and other peripherals are the
printer, the scanner, the loudspeakers and possibly devices such as a
Webcam or a digital camera. These peripherals have to be connected
to the computer by cables that run from connectors called *ports*.

Ports: *Ports* are the connections between the main section of the
computer and the other units (the *peripherals*). Strictly speaking, a
port is a circuit that allows signals to be transferred and (if necessary)
changed in form, but the name is just as often used for the connectors. The usual set of ports consists of a single parallel port for a
printer, two serial ports for modem or mouse, a keyboard port, a
mouse port and a monitor port. A separate mouse port is omitted if
the serial port is to be used for the mouse. The latest computers use
a more recent type of port, the universal serial bus (USB) that can
replace all of the other types. This is useful only if all of your equipment (monitor, keyboard, mouse, printer, scanner, etc.) uses USB. If
you are upgrading a motherboard and retaining items such as these
you need to ensure that the ports that you need will still be available.
At the time of writing, a new standard for USB (USB-2) is now established for connecting to peripherals that require fast data flow, such
as digital video cameras.

Modem: The *modem* is the device that connects your computer to the telephone lines and so to the Internet. A modem can be internal or external, and the favoured system nowadays is the internal type because it is cheaper and does not need another external connecting cable and mains supply. You should go for the fastest modem that you can get, which nowadays means the type labelled as *V90*. A modem will need a connecting lead to a conventional BT telephone point, and this will be packaged along with the modem.

● Many low-priced modems use software to carry out actions that are performed by hardware in more costly units, and this intensive use of software demands a fast processor and can cause memory conflicts. The modem is the device that triggers the majority of problems when the most recent versions of Windows (such as Windows 2000 and Windows XP) are being installed.

There has been a lot of publicity about using WAP-enabled mobile phones in place of modems. The system works, but is no faster than the use of a mobile, and very much more expensive. If you are considering it, ask yourself if you have ever had a mobile phone conversation that did not break up at some point, and how much it would cost to be online for an hour or so.

Modern PC machine

A modern PC type of machine is currently identified by the following points:

1. It uses a microprocessor which is an Intel Pentium, Intel Celeron, AMD Duron, Athlon, or Thunderbird, or a compatible chip from these or other manufacturers.
2. It uses a program called MS-DOS or PC-DOS as a master controlling system (an operating system), to enable it to load and run all other programs.
3. It has enough hard drive and memory space to run Windows 98, Windows *Me* or Windows XP.

Decisions

Some decisions about your computer have to be made early on; others can be left until later. As in any other DIY project, you have to be crystal clear about what you want; otherwise you will almost certainly end up with something you do not want.

The most important decision concerns the type of computer you are constructing. It's a PC, of course, because you can't get components to build any other type, but for what purposes will you use it? One use might be word processing because you need to write reports, articles, sermons, notes, books or whatever. It might be database use, because you need to keep track of several thousand items in a mail-order catalogue or points in a sports league or references in newspapers. It might be a spreadsheet because you need to keep tables of items in a way that allows you to work out totals and averages, or it might be a bookkeeping or accounting program for your business needs.

If your plans are for a machine with serious uses, meaning some word processing, keeping accounts, perhaps editing the parish magazine, then you can build a machine of modest specification at fairly low cost. If, on the other hand, your needs run to games with fast graphics, editing video or digital photographs, and working with sound, then you need a particularly fast machine with a lot of memory.

- Either type of machine can cope with the Internet, because this depends much more on just one component, the modem, than anything else. You certainly do not need the latest whizz-bang model if your main aim is to use the Internet or e-mail.

You might, of course, decide that you want to construct a reasonably capable machine that can cope with most normal actions, with some word processing, some work with still images, some sounds, and Internet use, without going to extremes such as paying £400 for the processor unit alone. This is reasonable enough and you need to know that any modern machine can cope as long as you are not expecting it to run the latest and most demanding software. For such a machine, a processor price of under £100 is reasonable.

Whatever your needs are initially, once you have experienced the advantages of working with the computer, and adapted your methods to the use of the computer, you will want to make it work harder for you. You are likely to buy other main items of software, and you are also likely to want to use the programs that are collectively called *utilities*.

The point about adapting your methods is important. Any task that you have previously done by hand usually needs to be done quite differently by computer. The computer forces you to work in a different way, but as compensation it allows you to work with greater freedom. You can make corrections and alterations easily, for example. Try typing an article and then inserting a 20-word amendment in the middle of the work. This is simple, routine stuff when you use a word processor, tedious and awkward when you use a steam typewriter. Try using a card index to produce a list of all UNF-threaded bolts in size 6 with cadmium plating and hex heads – it's easy with the computer running a database, but you must have organized the information correctly in the first place, and not as you would for a card index. When users feel disappointed with the use of a computer, the reason is almost always that they are trying to make the machine work in the way that they formerly worked with pen and paper.

Whatever you bought the machine for in the first place, you are likely to find that you have many more applications for it after a year or so. This is when you may come up against restrictions that seemed unlikely when you first bought the machine. You may need more memory to run larger programs, more disk space to store them, faster actions, and a better monitor. If you chose wisely initially you should find that your machine is capable as it is, and even if you went for the minimum that you could get away with, wise planning will ensure that you can easily upgrade the machine to do what you want. This sort of action is also covered in this book.

Remember, however, that a computer is rather like a hifi system – upgrading can be continued forever and eventually the gains are too small to notice. You have to ask yourself continually if an upgrade really fulfils a need or whether it simply allows you to use a more elaborate version of a program that serves you perfectly well at the moment.

- One problem that has been with us since small computers became available is *bloatware*. This means software that comes out in a new, enhanced and much larger form each year. You have to decide for yourself when the software that you use provides you with all you need and if a new version that is twice the size and runs at half the speed is really more useful than the older version.

Over the last year or so, it has become customary for computers to be offered for sale that are faster, and with more memory and disk space, than anything that has gone before. At the same time you see advertisements offering add-on devices that were hitherto either unknown or very expensive and specialized. Examples of such items are digital cameras, CD-ROM recorders and scanners. At the same time, software has also become more demanding, needing faster processing and more disk space.

- Many computers that are currently on offer are grossly overspecified for the requirements of the average serious user, because they are aimed at the user who wants fast-acting games and video displays.

This is a rat race that you cannot win and, if anything, the home constructor is better placed than anyone else. Anyone who buys a complete computer system today can expect to find that in a month's time it will either be offered at a lower price or it will provide an upgraded specification for the same price. If you have built your own machine, you will be much better placed to know how to upgrade and whether or not an upgrade is needed.

- Just to put all that in perspective, there are computer users all over the country who are perfectly happy with machines that have only a tiny fraction of the speed, memory and disk size of today's offerings. Their secret is that they are happy with the software that they are using and do not need any upgrade to the computer to use it. Their problem, however, is that if they need spares for their machine they may be quite unable to find any.

The important decision, then, after deciding what *type* of software you want to run is to decide on the make and version of software you want to use. For example, the well-known graphics program *Corel Draw* is currently at version 9, but you might find (as I did) that version 6 suits you just as well, and can be bought for a fraction of the price. I find *Word-97* indispensable for typesetting my books, but if your needs are more modest you might be perfectly happy with *Word-6* or even *Word-2* (there were no versions between these, despite the numbering). These older versions will run happily on machines with much less memory and hard drive space than the latest versions. It is better, however, to use a modern version of Windows rather than an older one.

- In addition, the requirements that are often quoted for running Windows assume that you will be running several large programs simultaneously and transferring data between them. If you don't do this, then you can get by with a slower machine and less memory.

The third decision is harder to make. What will your future demands be? For example, if you are content to make use of your existing word-processing software, will you always want to type the words? There might come a time when you decide that you want to use word dictation software, speaking your thoughts directly into a microphone and watching the words appear on screen. This, however, demands much more of the computer, and is a prime reason for wanting a fast processor, more memory and more disk space. Another possibility is that you would like to convert all your old home video into digital form and record it on CD rather than transcribe it on to VHS cassettes. This sort of requirement also demands faster processing and large amounts of memory and disk space, as does the recording of sound.

If, on the other hand, you feel that you will not be tempted by new whizz-bang software and you are quite content with something that has already served you well, or which is modern but not too demanding, then this also points you in the direction of a machine that need not be in the top rank of the fast and furious.

- After all, if you have assembled your own computer you will also know how to upgrade it if you ever need more than it can supply in its original form.

Expanding the machine is not confined to simply increasing its memory and its ability to deal with more complex programs. Add-on boards exist for virtually every purpose for which a computer can be adapted and the PC machine forms an excellent basis for experimental work for anyone with experience in electronics. The current add-on fashion is fast video boards, allowing you to edit your camcorder tapes or work on video images from TV or from a video recorder. Similarly, you can capture Teletext pages, compensating for the short-sighted design of TV receivers that makes no provision for attaching a printer. You can also use your PC along with a digital camera and colour printer to replace the tedious business of buying films that have to be developed and printed, with no editing facilities. This, however, requires a good printer and good graphics-editing software.

A less-trumpeted aspect is control engineering, using analogue–digital converter cards, allowing the PC to act as part of a control system for process engineering, environmental control and so on. Similar add-on cards can also be used to make the PC part of a security system with the advantage that the response can be altered by programming the machine for yourself. You can also couple in devices such as bar-code readers and printers to make the PC part of a data system. All of these actions are too specialized for this book, but you should be aware that they exist and if you are interested, look out for books that deal with these topics. For some of these actions you do not need the latest and fastest type of PC, and in many cases the requirements are *very* modest.

The results of these decisions will all be relevant to the parts you choose for your computer, and you also need to take into account any parts that you want to recycle. For example, if you are retaining a monochrome printer, there is little point in having the capability to work with colour images that need huge amounts of memory. If all your software is on a hard drive of reasonable size (and which is nowhere like full) then why buy a new one? On the other hand, you might find that, even if you are used to a monochrome printer pack, you might wish to consider replacing it with a colour one because very few manufacturers now sell monochrome printers – and these generally are laser printers. We will look at more of these types of decisions later.

The components

> **NOTE**: If you intend to use Windows XP Home Edition, which was at the time of writing the most recent version of Windows, you must make sure, when you buy hardware or software, that the items you buy are XP compatible. This will save you a considerable amount of time and expense later when you come to install Windows. See Chapter 10 for more details. You should also ensure, if you are upgrading a computer, that you carry out all your hardware changes *before* you install Windows XP Home Edition.

A basic PC system consists of a main casing that contains the power supply in a sealed box, the motherboard with a graphics card, and the disk drives, along with a separate keyboard, mouse and monitor. The contents of the main casing are the components that lend themselves to DIY assembly, and the monitor, like the keyboard, mouse and printer, is bought as a single, separate, item. A modern monitor will be a 17-inch or 19-inch colour unit capable of much higher resolution than a TV receiver. At the time of writing, several suppliers are offering 19-inch monitors, with the luxury option of 21-inch conventional monitors or 17-in flat-panel types.

The main advice here is to avoid working with the older components. The 8088, 8086, 80286, 80386 and 80486 microprocessors are now completely obsolete and though there are millions of PCs working happily with these processors, they are not capable of running the mainstream of modern programs, particularly Windows *Me* and XP. Even the more recent Pentium-1 and Pentium-2 types of machine are by now too restricted in speed to run modern software. Windows *Me* and XP need a machine which is initially as capable as you can afford, and which can easily be upgraded, particularly with more memory, later. You will handicap yourself if you build using old components (if you can find them) unless you are simply practising for a later effort.

The assembly of a PC machine from scratch is, if anything, easier than making a working model from old-style Meccano, with the difference that you start with a full kit of bigger parts. The comparison is not entirely fanciful either, because a PC is put together using bolts of standard types, and circuit boards that plug into position; no elaborate tools are required nor is vast experience needed. What you need to know is what parts you need, where to buy them and how to put them together. You do not need to know how to solder, and the highest order of electrical work you will be called on to do will be to connect up a standard mains plug. The main requirement is to know that the parts you are buying will match up with each other correctly.

 The tools you need are mainly screwdrivers, preferably in the smaller sizes, and both plain and crosshead (Phillips) types. A pair of pliers is also useful though seldom essential, and tweezers are useful for retrieving small bolts from inaccessible places. Other than these you need common sense (square plugs do not go into round holes) and some motivation (such as lack of money or just fascination with computers). One useful point about assembling your own PC is that you can do it one step at a time. If cash is limited, you can buy one part each month until you complete the assembly.

- On the subject of cost, assembling a complete PC outfit from scratch is always going to be more costly than buying a new machine made from the same parts and bought from the cheapest sources after some shopping around. The lowest-cost suppliers of components are almost always going to be small-scale mail-order suppliers or stallholders at computer fairs and because they work on lower margins than the others they are more vulnerable to problems like slow payers, worried banks and strikes in delivery services.

Because of this, you should always assume that such a supplier is unlikely to be a permanent fixture, and you should not part with real money. If you pay using a credit card (either in person or over the telephone) you have the protection of the credit card company. If the supplier vanishes overnight you will not lose because your card account will not be debited. There is no other way of paying that is so secure. Watch out, however, for firms that levy a surcharge on the use of a credit card, or that insist on fast and expensive delivery that can almost double the price you pay for a single component.

- Note that if you use a debit card (like *Switch* or *Connect*) you have no more protection than if you handed over cash. Stallholders at computer fairs will seldom accept credit cards because of the surcharges that this involves, though they will always take cheques backed by a bank card.

Remember that mail-order suppliers will usually add a charge for courier delivery that will put anything from £6 to £15 on to your costs (and with VAT added over and above the carriage charge). You can avoid these costs if you can buy at a computer fair or from a local assembler. You do not need to build from scratch, however. You can use the casing and power supply from an old (but not *too* old) machine or buy a package of modern parts that will start you off at a lower price than you would pay if you bought each part individually.

- If you have a good local computer shop, make this your first call when you are looking for components. Many such shops are run by enthusiasts who have vast experience in assembling and upgrading hardware, and who know all the snags that can arise. You may also find that the prices you are asked are no more than you would pay from some mail-order supplier (allowing for carriage and possibly credit-card surcharges), and you have the advantage that you can see the goods before you buy. Another advantage is that you can get prompt attention if a problem arises with anything you have bought.
- The same is true if you have a regular monthly computer fair at a town near by, because the same stallholders will appear each month and they are usually knowledgeable, friendly and helpful. After all their customers are mainly those who upgrade and build their own machines.

Looking for mail-order suppliers is easy if you subscribe to magazines such as *PC Shopper* or *Micro Computer Mart*, whose advertisers include many that specialize in parts for the DIY assembler. Do not confine yourself to these, however, because shopping around is important, and you may find bargains from suppliers who make no claims to cater for the assembler but who nevertheless hold an immense stock of PC parts at low prices.

- A few hours spent with these magazines can save you much hard-earned cash because you learn what the going price is for everything. You can also check out delivery charges.

All of this refers to standard desktop machines. Portable (laptop) computers are quite another problem because there is no standard design, the parts are costly and difficult to obtain, and you need a ten-year apprenticeship as a sardine-packer to be able to work on them. There are many buyers of portable machines, but fewer serious users who would not be as well served with a notebook and a pencil.

The essential bits

The essential main bits of a PC are the casing (with power supply), the motherboard, graphics card and the disk drives. To check that a machine is working you also need a monitor, but since this is bought ready-made and can outlast several computers we do not count it, or a printer, as part of a DIY project.

Do not on any account attempt to convert a TV receiver into a monitor, or convert an old monitor into something suited to a modern PC, unless you have very considerable experience of working on TV equipment, and a set of circuit diagrams that you can use for guidance. Note in particular that any monitor must use an earthed chassis.

Monitors from other types of machines will not necessarily be suited to a PC computer, though a few are adaptable if, and only if, you know how. Be particularly careful of monitors, particularly large-screen monitors, offered as bargains. Some of these work with non-standard graphics boards which must be supplied along with the monitor, because they cannot be connected to a standard VGA board, but you cannot be sure that your software (and that includes Windows) will be able to use such a monitor correctly, if at all.

CASE

The case or casing contains the power supply unit (PSU) that converts the mains voltage (220–240 volts AC, and dangerous) to the low (and safe) DC voltages that the computer uses. The PSU is always the

Figure 1.2 The shape of a typical monitor. Slim monitors with a flat screen are now available, but are still very expensive compared to the older type

type referred to as *switch-mode*. The output voltages are so low that they present no risk of shock, but you should be careful to avoid placing metal tools on to live contacts because enough current could flow to cause overheating and start a fire. The power supply unit is usually sealed with all the mains voltage parts inside and only a switch connection to the outside, along with space for the mother-board, a set of shelves, called *bays*, for disk drives, various LED indicators and switches, and a lot of empty space.

The most useful, and most common, type of casing is the small (mini or midi) tower construction. An alternative is the desktop type, which is also the cheaper. Do not be tempted by miniature slimline cases, because they are more expensive and often difficult to work with if you want to add more disk drives and cards. Tall, full-size tower-block types are easy to work on, but they are cumbersome, more expensive, and may be difficult to house in a small working space.

Casings once came in two types, AT and ATX, as well as a variety of shapes and sizes. The AT type of case is now obsolete, and all modern computers use the ATX motherboard layout. Beware of special offers of very cheap cases that turn out to be suitable only for the old AT layout.

- If you buy from a local shop or a computer fair, check out the noise from the fan in the PSU. Some fans are so noisy that they make working with the machine an irritating experience. The more expensive cases should be fitted with fans that are reasonably quiet. The fan on the processor may also be noisy.

The back of the casing also has a set of six or more openings, usually temporarily covered by metal strips. These openings are at the *expansion slot* positions, and each time you expand the capabilities of the computer by adding a card, one cover plate will have to be removed to allow a connector mounted on the card to project outside the casing. These metal strips are each located by a single screw, usually of the crosshead Phillips variety. Do *not* use the machine with strips removed unless there are connectors to replace them, because this will upset the fan-driven airflow inside the machine. The front panel of the casing has cutouts covering bays for CD and disk drives, and also a panel of switches and LEDs. Some recent designs make provision for some connections (typically for audio or video equipment) to be made at the front of the casing.

- On some modern casings, the covering strips may be attached, and you have to break small metal tabs to release a strip. Do not break off more strips than you need. Older casings had strips that were secured by screws.

The casing will also contain a small loudspeaker which will beep when the machine is starting (*booting up*) and which provides a few warning sounds. It will also contain a *reboot* switch for use when nothing else will release the machine from a software lockup (when pressing keys has no effect). This reboot switch should preferably be housed at the rear of the casing so that it cannot be operated by accident, but it's more usual to find it at the front. If the reboot switch is at the front it should be recessed so that it is not so easily pressed accidentally.

At the rear of the empty casing you will also find the mains connectors for the PSU. One of these is the mains input, the other is a mains output which on older designs was controlled by the switch on the casing, and used mainly for the power connection to the monitor. On modern ATX casings this mains output is live as long as there is a mains input, it is *not* controlled by the computer's switch. Also within the PSU is the cooling fan for the whole computer. A separate miniature fan is used to cool the processor, and this can be noisy because it runs at a high speed.

Modern ATX casings have a PSU that is 'soft' controlled by Windows. This means that the main switch works on a standby (or *suspend*) system, so that when you opt to shut down Windows the whole machine goes into standby. The power is shut down to a low level, and the computer stops working, but it can be switched on again either by using the main switch or by actions (which you can select for yourself) such as pressing any key, moving the mouse or receiving a message over the modem. You are not forced to use this system, and my own preference is to switch the whole machine off at the mains when I have finished for the day.

Your choice of casing and other items is dealt with in more detail in Chapter 2. Choosing the correct casing for your computer is very important because it can decide whether or not you can easily upgrade your computer if and when you need to. You need to decide on your choice of motherboard and CPU types before you finally select a case.

Many of the mail-order suppliers sell unbranded cases. These may be excellent, but you cannot inspect them in advance and in particular you cannot tell which may have a noisy fan. Of the brand names that appear in the UK, the most commonly advertised are:

Advance	Antec	Aopen	Aptima
Aqua Wave	Arowana	Casetek	CGA
Chenbro	Chieftek	IDL	KME
Lian-Li	Nautilous	Pro Series	Samcheer
Songcheer	Suntek	Task	Vision

- Note that you may need to look for a case that is marked as approved for the type of processor you intend to use, particularly for the faster types such as Pentium-4, Thunderbird and Athlon. Approval in this sense means that the layout of the case, the power output of the PSU and the cooling are all suitable for a high-speed processor. Advertisements for cases seldom mention whether they are suitable for the faster processors, though if the advertisement for a case mentions a 300 W or higher PSU then it is likely to be intended for a fast system.

MOTHERBOARD

The motherboard, as the name suggests, is the main printed circuit board of any PC machine and it carries the CPU, memory and any other boards (or cards) that are added. It is a multi-layer board, and you must *never* drill it or cut it because the tracks that you see on it are only the surface tracks, with others hidden between layers. The motherboard contains the main microprocessor chip (the CPU), and the type of CPU that is used determines to a considerable extent the performance of the computer.

At the time of writing, low-cost motherboards use the Intel Celeron or the AMD Duron chip, and the faster motherboards can use the Pentium-4, Athlon and Thunderbird chips as well as the slower types. Several types of motherboards can use any of the AMD chips (Duron, Athlon, Thunderbird) but you will need a different type of motherboard for the Pentium chip, and a different one again for Celeron. You should not consider using a motherboard, no matter how cheap to buy, with a CPU whose number indicates an earlier design, such as the 80486, 80386, 80286, 8086 or 8088. Even the Pentium-2 and Pentium-3 are now completely out of date and almost impossible to find except on old machines.

● The motherboard contains sockets for all the important main units such as the processor and the memory. Motherboards, dealt with in more detail in Chapter 2, are supplied now only as the *ATX* type.

The motherboard has a socket for the processor, and your choice of socket type commits you to the type of processor you can use. In general, all the AMD processors use the same type of socket referred to as Socket-A. Using such a motherboard therefore allows you to upgrade from one type of AMD processor to another very easily. If you decide to use an Intel processor, you have to settle on either Celeron or Pentium right from the beginning because you will not find a motherboard that can accept both.

- The older Socket-7 boards are now obsolete, but you can still find some available, though it would be foolish to start building a new machine around such a board.

In addition, the motherboard contains the slots for memory, and once again, the types of slots determine what type of memory, and how much of it you can use. Modern motherboards allow for the standard 168-pin DIMM (D for dual) units to be used, and these can be fitted individually. For example, you could achieve 128 Mbytes of memory by one 128 Mbyte DIMM, and you could expand to 256 Mbytes by adding another such DIMM. A more recent and more expensive form of RAM, called RAMbus, may be specified for some motherboards.

As well as the main CPU and the sockets for memory DIMMs, the motherboard contains all the other supporting chips (the *chipset*) and the connections (or bus) between the CPU and other sections. The other notable feature of the motherboard is the provision of *expansion slots*, sockets for cards that are plugged in to expand the use of the machine. The main type of slot for this purpose is called PCI, and most motherboards will provide four or more PCI slots. Some motherboards may provide one older type of slot, ISA, usually for an old modem. All modern motherboards will also provide at least one AGP slot for a fast graphics board, even if a graphics interface is already provided on the motherboard. These points are also considered in more detail in Chapter 2.

All motherboards now include *ports*, usually two serial ports and one parallel, as part of the board, with short cables to connectors mounted on the rear of the casing. The parallel port is used to connect the printer, but the serial ports are seldom used nowadays. Modern motherboards also feature the USB ports, usually two, and in the near future when the faster USB-2 design is standardized, this may be the only type of port that is fitted. In the past, ports were added separately by plugging cards into expansion slots, but the modern way is to use on-board ports so that the motherboard needs fewer slots. The slots connect to the processor, and the set of connections is called a *bus*.

The motherboard will also contain the connectors for cables to the floppy drive(s), the hard drive(s) and the CD-ROM drive(s) — note that you can have up to two of each device if you have the space to put them into your casing.

Table 1.1 is a list of known manufacturers of motherboards at the time of writing. Only a few of these manufacturers export to the UK, in particular Abit, ASUS, Gigabyte, Intel, MicroStar, Supermicro, and Tyan.

Table 1.1   Manufacturers of motherboards

2the Max	AAEON	ABILITY Electron	Abit
Acer	Achitec Corp. Ltd	Acorp Electronics Corporation	Acouire, Inc.
Acro Computer Corp.	Acrosser Technology Co., Ltd	Activel	Adlink Technology, Inc.
Advanced Integration Research, Inc. (AIR)	Advanced Jenn Bao Enterprises Co., Ltd	Advantech Co., Ltd	Alcom Group (Micron Design Technology Ltd)
American Megatrends, Inc. (AMI)	American Predator	Ampro	American Sunshine Technologies, Inc.
Amjet	Amptron International, Inc.	Antec, Incorporated	AOpen
Appro	Aristo	Arvida Technology Ltd	Ask Technology Ltd
Aspen Systems, Inc.	ASUS	Atima	A-Trend Technology Corporation
Auhua Electronics Co. Ltd (Sukjung)	AVT Industrial Ltd	Azza	BCM Advanced Research, Inc. – see GVC
BIOSTAR	Caliber	California Graphics USA Distribution	Chaintech
Chicony	Commate	Computrend	Computer Technology System Corp.
Concord	Cycle Computer	DataExpert Corporation	Diamond Flower Electric Instrument Co. (USA), Inc.
Diamond Micronics	Digicom Group	Domex Technology Corporation	DTK Computer or Advance Creative Computer Corp.
Edom International Corp.	EFA Corporation of Taiwan	Elitegroup Computer Systems Co. Ltd	Elpina
ENPC Technology Corp.	EpoX	Espco Computer (Eagle Motherboards)	EUPA Computer
Eurone Taiwan	Expert Computer International, Inc.	Famous Technology Co. Ltd	FIC

First International Fine-Pal Company Ltd. Computer		Fittec	Fong Kai Industrial Co. (FKI)
Freetech	Freeway	Fugu Tech Enterprise Co., Ltd	Full Yes Industrial Corp. (FYI)
Gomlight Computer Ltd	Genoa Systems Corp.	Gigabyte	Global Group
Global Circuit Technology, Inc.	Global Legate (Zaapa)	GVC Group	Houston Technologies
HSB Laboratories	Hsing Tech	Impression Products, Inc.	Intel
Iwill	Jaton Corporation	J-bond Computer Systems	JDR Microdevices
Jetway Information Co., Ltd	Joss	Kam-Tronic	Koutech Systems, Inc. or Kouwell
LAN PLUS, Inc.	Lucky Star Technology Co., Ltd	Matsonic	Megastar
Mega System Co. Ltd	Megatel	Megatrends	Mercury Ltd
Micronics	Micro-Star	MiTAC International Corp.	Mitsuba Corp.
Mitsubishi Electric Corp.	Motorola	MPL	MSI
M Technology, Inc.	Mylex Corp.	MyComp	Mynix Technology, Inc.
NewStar Engineering Ltd	Niagara SMD Technology, Inc.	Nimble Technology Corp.	NMC Peripherals Europe GmbH
Octek	Ozzo or NTC Technologies	PC CHIPS Manufacturing Ltd	PC Partner or VTech Computers Systems Ltd
PC Ware or Alton or PC Quest or PC Max or PC Master	Pine Technology USA	Premio (formerly CompuTrend)	Promise Technology, Inc.
Proside or Mpact	QDI Group	Rise Computer, Inc	Sam-Tec
Seanix	See-thru Data Systems Ltd	Shuttle	Soltek
Sowah	Soyo	Spacewalker	Supermicro
SuperPower	SuperTek	Taken Corp.	Tatung Company of America
Tekram	Taiwan Mycomp Co. (TMC)	Tomatoboards	Totem
Transcend	Tyan	US Logic	Vextrec Technology, Inc. (VTI)
WarpSpeed	Winco	Zida	

PROCESSOR

The processor is the silicon (not silicone, please!) chip that is the heart of the computer, providing all of the computing actions under the control of the operating system. Processors are sold in the form of a large slab-shaped chip that needs a slab of metal, the heatsink, to be clipped over it, along with a fan for cooling. The heatsink and fan are clipped tightly to the socket on the motherboard, so that the chip has to be inserted before these items are clipped on.

You may see references in price lists to *boxed* processors. A boxed processor means a processor with a matching heatsink and fan supplied in the same package. The alternative and cheaper packaging system is described as *OEM* (original equipment manufacturer) and consists of the processor only. This leaves you free to use whatever heatsink and fan you prefer for yourself, but it's up to you to ensure that the heatsink and fan that you use is adequate for the amount of power that has to be dissipated. The amount of power that a typical processor will dissipate nowadays is between 35 and 80 watts.

A fan costs around £10 if it is bought separately, but you will usually want to buy a fan along with a processor unless you particularly want a high efficiency fan or a silent fan. There are two basic types. One type takes its power from the disk drive supplies, the other type from a set of pins on the motherboard. The first type can be fitted on any machine, but the second can be used only if the power supply pins are on the motherboard. The second type is better if you want to make use of the chip temperature monitoring features of a modern motherboard.

- You can buy old types of chips such as the 80486 type very cheaply. Do not be tempted, because you will have great difficulty in finding motherboards and other matching parts, and performance on modern software will be very slow. Even old Pentium-1 types such as the Pentium-60 or Pentium-75 are simply not up to working with modern operating systems and software.

MEMORY

Do not consider installing a memory of less than 64 Mbytes and never fill your motherboard with memory initially, because that makes it very expensive to upgrade later. At the time of writing, memory prices are very low, but you cannot assume that they will always be. DIMMs are now the standard system, and many motherboards provide for up to three DIMMs, so that you can usually upgrade easily to the limit of 512 Mbytes that is set by Windows. Very few motherboards cater for Rambus memory units.

DRIVES AND ROMS

The disk and CD drives are the other essentials, because a computer by itself is as useless as a CD player with no CDs. In computer jargon, the hardware is useless without software. Most of the memory of a computer is the kind described as *volatile*, meaning that it is wiped clear each time the machine is switched off, so that all the instruction codes that the machine needs to do anything have to be stored in a more permanent form. The three most familiar permanent forms are as a chip (a ROM or read-only memory chip), a magnetized disk, or a CD in its drive.

Modern machines use all three of these systems, and your motherboard will contain one or more ROM chips that contain a comparatively small amount of program code. This is sufficient only to allow the machine to respond to the keyboard in a limited way and to operate the disk drives, also in a limited way. The rest of the essential codes, the operating system, are read in (booted) from a disk, usually the hard drive.

The aim of this multi-part storage is to build into the machine just sufficient permanent instructions to read in an operating system that you can choose for yourself. The operating system is something that needs to be upgraded each time the capabilities of the computer are extended and if it were in ROM form it would require the ROM chips, see Figure 1.3, to be replaced. This action of using a small section of code to read in the rest of the operating codes is called *bootstrapping* (from the old myth of lifting yourself by your own bootstraps) or *booting*, and the action of switching on a computer is referred to as *booting up*. The smallest portable machines do not use a disk drive, and they keep all of their operating system code in a ROM.

Figure 1.3   A typical ROM chip of the older type. Modern ROM chips are programmable, meaning that their contents can be altered by using commands. This is a risky business, because any error could stop your computer working until a new ROM chip could be inserted

- The main ROM chip is called the *BIOS*, meaning Basic Input Output Services, and this is a good description of what it provides.

BIOS chips can come from a variety of suppliers, and the type that you find on your motherboard determines what additional facilities you may be able to call on. In particular, the BIOS chip works along with a small CMOS RAM memory chip that is used to store machine information such as the date and the machine facilities, using a battery backup so that the information is held permanently as long as the battery lasts. Because this is a form of RAM its contents can be changed at will.

The disk drives are vital to a desktop machine, and all modern machines need at least three – one floppy drive that uses replaceable magnetic disks, one hard drive which uses a set of magnetic disks that are fixed and encased in a sealed container, and a CD-ROM drive. The floppy drive is used so that you can copy short programs (software) that you buy and place on the hard drive, and also for holding your own data. A hard drive has a limited life, so that it is essential to have a copy on tape, on floppy disks or on CD-ROM of everything on the hard drive. At one time it was possible to use a computer with a floppy drive only, but modern programs are too large to fit on a floppy drive, and the drive itself is too slow to allow a program to be run using just the floppy drive. The CD drive is used because the size of modern software is just too much to allow the economical use of floppy disks, and many machines now come with CD drives that allow writing a CD as well as reading it.

The motherboard carries the disk interface circuits that convert the numbers stored in the memory into pulses that can be recorded magnetically, and vice versa. The type of disk interface that is almost universally used at the time of writing is the ATA or EIDE system, the initials meaning *AT Attachment* and *Extended Integrated Drive Electronics*, respectively. You will find two sockets on the motherboard labelled as *Primary* and *Secondary* EIDE connectors, respectively, and the usual arrangement is to connect the hard drive to the Primary EIDE and the CD-ROM drive to the Secondary EIDE connector. Each socket connects to the cable with two plugs that it drives. This allows the primary EIDE connector to work with two hard drives and the secondary one to work with two CD drives (one CD-ROM and one CD writer), or one CD ROM and another hard drive.

- The term ATA has appeared more recently to mean what we all used to call IDE. The reason for the distinction is that this is the more correct name, because SCSI drives (see later) are, technically, also integrated drive types and could be termed IDE.

The card that usually has to be added to the motherboard (usually into a PCI type of slot) is the video graphics card that converts the computer pulses into video signals that a monitor can use. Once again there is a universal standard called VGA or SVGA, and adding this card will allow you to connect up the monitor and see what happens when the computer is switched on.

The faster types of graphics cards make use of a faster type of connection, the AGP slot. Whatever type you use will be fitted with fast memory on the graphics card itself, and nowadays this is likely to be 8 Mbytes or more. Some graphics cards make use of the main motherboard memory, but this is not desirable because it is not as fast as dedicated graphics memory and it reduces the amount of memory available to applications. What happens from that point onwards depends on the software which is the subject of later chapters in this book. Because changing a graphics card is often an upgrading action, it has also been noted in Chapter 8. Table 1.2 lists a selection of well-known manufacturers of graphics cards at the time of writing.

Table 1.2   Manufacturers of video graphics cards

3Dfx	3Dlabs	Abit	Aopen	Asus
ATI	Creative Labs	Elsa	Excalibur	Geeforce
Guillemot	Hercules	Leadtek	Matrox	MSI
nVidia	Prolink	Riva	Sparkle	VideoLogic

FLOPPY DRIVE

The floppy drive on modern machines is the 3½-inch type that has been used for many years and which is also used on other types of computers (Macs, for example). There is no particular reason to prefer one make of floppy drive to another, and you should look for a low-price unit. Do not be tempted by the expensive floppy drives that can use equally expensive high-capacity floppy disks, because though these disks can be replayed on your drive you might want to exchange disks with someone who does not have the same drive. If you need large capacity removable discs, look at the modern range of CD writers, see later. A CD-R disc holds 650 Mbytes and costs about 50p at the time of writing.

HARD DRIVE

The hard drive is another essential component that needs some tough decisions. Hard drives have developed in capability at the same time as prices have been falling, so that they represent excellent value for money. The price I paid for my first 32 Mbyte hard drive now buys 40 Gbytes of space.

- Do not consider using a second-hand drive, or taking one from a machine you have been using for several years. You cannot tell what life to expect from an older drive and, worse still, the performance of an old drive can be poor. In the extreme you may find that an old drive simply will not work with modern equipment – a really old drive might need a separate interface card fitting to an ISA slot.

For some time now, all new hard drives have used a system called

DMA, meaning direct memory access. On older PCs, a hard drive was read from or written to using the processor as an intermediary. The processor would read a byte from memory and then write it to the hard drive, or read a byte from the hard drive and then write it to memory. This involvement of the processor for each byte made the process slow and also prevented the processor from being used for anything else at the time of writing or reading.

- The DMA system uses the processor only to set up conditions (how many bytes, where from, where to) and then allows another chip, the DMA chip, to do the work. This releases the main processor, enabling it to carry on with its computing tasks, with a considerable benefit in speed.

DMA has now been replaced by *UDMA*, the U meaning Ultra, and if you are building or upgrading you should not consider using an older type of hard drive that is not labelled as UDMA. Your motherboard must be capable of dealing with UDMA, but you are rather unlikely to buy a motherboard (other than a second-hand one) that does not. The only snag is that older operating systems might not be able to make full use of UDMA.

Nowadays, do not consider using any hard drive that is not to the ATA-100 standard, permitting very faster transfer between the drive and the motherboard. This type of drive is essential if you are going to use applications such as digital video editing that handle a large amount of data at a very high speed. Even if you are not considering such applications at the moment, it is likely that you'll find that slower forms of transfer become obsolete, and it's never a good idea to be saddled with obsolete equipment.

CD-ROM DRIVE AND DVD

A CD-ROM drive, considered a luxury only a few years ago, is now a standard item for a PC. When CD drives were introduced, it was to allow multimedia software (text, images and sound) to be run, because this would have been impossibly clumsy if floppy disks had to be inserted and removed at frequent intervals. Nowadays, the CD-ROM drive has become essential because operating systems and applications software packages have become so large that large numbers of floppies are needed for distribution, and the CD represents a much cheaper and more secure way of holding programs. The price of a CD-ROM drive is now so low that it makes no sense to construct a machine without one because, apart from anything else, all modern software, including Windows, is distributed on CD-ROM.

CD-ROM drives are graded by speed, and because the speed of a CD is not constant (it spins faster when reading the inner tracks than when reading the outer tracks) the figure of comparative speed is used, with the audio (music) CD taken as a standard. A CD-ROM drive that operates at 4×, for example, will spin four times faster than a music CD. Speeds of 24× are now common, but though higher speeds are possible, they are not necessarily much of an advantage. A speed of 36× is as fast as most users need.

The more recent CD-R/RW drives will write as well as read. They can read any normal CD as well as the types they create for themselves. The CD-R discs can be written, but not rewritten, and though you can add data to such a disc until it is full, you cannot then rewrite it with other data. The CD-RW, by contrast, can be written and rewritten like a floppy, though the process of rewriting is clumsier unless you use modern software such as the excellent Click'N Burn, noted later. The snag is that the CD-RW disc costs around £1.50 at present, with the CD-R type costing around 50p (though some high-street suppliers still try to charge much higher prices). These prices include the 'jewel box' that contains the disc. Packs of CD-R discs can be bought at a lower price in the flatter plastic cases which are ideal for posting, but such cases do not fit well into the CD stacks and drawers that are used for CD storage.

Advertisements for CD writer drives quote two or three speeds. For the CD-R type, the two speeds that are quoted are the read speed and the write speed (always lower), so that a CD-R drive quoted as 6×, 2× will read at 6× and write at 2×. The CD-R/RW types of drive that can use any type of disc quote three speeds, the first for reading, the second for CD-R and the third for CD-RW.

- If you are contemplating writing CDs it would be rather short-sighted to buy an old type of drive that dealt only with CD-R and not with CD-RW as well, but the CD-R type of blank disc is now so inexpensive that you will probably find that you seldom use the RW type. All CD writer drives sold nowadays will work with either CD-R or CD-RW discs.

Note that there are three varieties of CD. The pressed type is mass produced and is the type you buy in shops or find on the cover of magazines. The data is coded in the form of tiny pits in the surface of the disc. The CD-R discs are coated with a coloured dye that changes colour when it is affected by the laser that is used for writing. This change is not reversible, and the lower power that is used for reading does not affect the dye. CD-R discs can be read on any CD-ROM drive or modern music CD player. The CD-RW type uses a much more complicated system of exotic materials whose magnetism and light-reflecting ability are linked. You may find that a CD-RW disc you have recorded cannot be replayed in a music CD player, or even in an older CD-ROM drive on another computer. It will always be replayable on the drive that created it, however.

- Beware of rip-off prices on CD-R discs, usually with the excuse that they are specially designed for recording music.

DVD means digital versatile disc and the name applies to a more modern type of CD that holds very much more information, typically 5–17 Gbytes. The 'normal' speed of a DVD is higher than that of a CD, so that speed factors such as ×6 for DVD refer to much higher speeds than ×6 for CD. DVD players can be use for reading CDs and at the time of writing, DVD reading drives are being fitted to many types of computer packages. These drives can read CDs of all types as well as DVDs, so that it's an advantage to specify such a drive rather than one that handles CDs only. DVD writers, however, are still rare and expensive in the UK, and there is a compatibility problem. See Chapter 4 for more details.

PORTS

All PCs currently come with two serial ports, a keyboard port, possibly a separate mouse port (of the PS/2 type), a printer port and two USB ports. In future, these different connecting devices may all be replaced by a set of universal serial bus (USB) connectors, but that has not yet happened at the time of writing. At present, USB will be found in addition to the other ports, because so much equipment still uses the older types of ports.

- One very considerable advantage of using differently shaped connectors at present is that you can easily see which connecting cable leads to your printer, which goes to the mouse and which is for the keyboard. Using USB connectors, all the leads may have identical connectors, and you have to trace the cables to the devices they connect to if you want to know which is which. Worse still, some units are now fitted with more than one type of USB connector. Windows *Me* lists a set of problems that may be encountered by users of some USB equipment.

On current motherboards, the printer port and the serial ports are linked by short pieces of cable to connectors that are mounted on the case. The keyboard port and a PS/2 mouse port will always be provided mechanically fixed to the motherboard at a position that coincides with a hole in the casing. If you try to match a motherboard to the wrong type of casing this is one problem that you will find quite soon. The USB type of port is mounted either on the motherboard or on a separate card.

- If no PS/2 port is used for the mouse you can assume that a serial or USB mouse is needed. If your present mouse is not a serial type you can buy an adapter that allows a serial mouse to be used on a PS/2 port, and you can also buy adapters for using a PS/2 mouse on a serial port.

OPERATING SYSTEM

Your computer is useless without an operating system. If you buy a PC it will quite certainly come with Microsoft Windows *Me* or XP, and you will most likely want this operating system for your own machine.

If you do not have the Windows *Me* or Windows XP disc, only the disc(s) for an older system such as Windows 98 or Windows 95, you can still install one of these older systems and upgrade later. This is an advantage, because buying a copy of Windows 98 for installation on a hard drive that has no operating system currently installed (an OEM copy) is more costly than buying an upgrade disc for use on a machine that is already running Windows.

- Legally, you should not be running the same copy of Windows on two machines, but if you are scrapping an old machine when you commission the new one there is no problem about this.

What do you need?

To start with, you need the components. If you want to buy as you go, start with the casing and the motherboard, then add the processor and the memory, always checking with the supplier that these parts will work together correctly. You can then assemble this lot together and fit it all into the casing, and then add drives. Unless your motherboard contains a video graphics port you will then need to add a graphics card. This makes your PC ready for its operating system, so that you can check that everything is working. Once you have checked out Windows and set it up, you can add other cards (such as sound, video player, scanner interface, etc.) as you please.

- The golden rule is to check that everything works as soon as you have a functioning PC, and don't add any more until you are certain that what you have so far is all working.

Don't forget incidentals. A motherboard needs to be placed on mounting columns, so either the motherboard or the case should be supplied with these columns and matching bolts. The motherboard should also come with cables for connecting hard drive, floppy drive and CD-ROM drive. Some motherboards will also contain connectors for the monitor.

- It is always a good idea to lay items out where they will eventually fit, to check that you have everything lining up correctly.

Drives – hard, floppy or CD – need mounting bolts, and these should be packaged with any new drive. It's most unlikely that you will have spares in your toolkit, because the bolts are a size that you won't find in the local ironmonger's shop. For the record, these are 6-32 UNC × 0.31 or metric M4 × 0.7-6H. Do not attempt to use self-tapping or any other bolts that are not a perfect fit.

Make sure that you have the correct matching cables before you start any installation. Match up the cable connectors to make certain that you know which cables are used for which task, and learn to identify the Pin 1 side of a cable by looking for the red stripe or other identifying mark that runs along one side of the ribbon-shaped cable. The corresponding Pin 1 position is printed on to the connectors on motherboard and drives, or is otherwise identifiable from drawings that come with these items.

You need only a minimum of tools, and you can expect to get by with a small conventional screwdriver and a small Phillips screwdriver. A pair of pliers can come in handy, but nothing more elaborate is needed unless you want to be a martyr and do things like making up your own connecting cables.

With the essential bits in hand you can connect up a working PC machine in under an hour, though it will not necessarily do everything that you want. From that stage, however, you can add other facilities by plugging in additional circuit boards, called expansion cards, to extend the capabilities of the machine. You can also plug in additional DIMM memory units, because whatever you do with a machine is likely to require more memory sooner or later unless you start with as much memory as the motherboard can take. At the time of writing, memory is not expensive but don't buy until you really need to, unless you feel that the price is so low that it can only rise. The price of memory has fluctuated considerably in the past, and may do so in the future.

Planning

A bit of advance planning helps considerably to make construction easier. Make sure, first of all, that you can identify each part. This is particularly important for cables because, until you get to know them, one ribbon cable looks pretty much like another. Note that the hard drive cable uses more strands than the floppy drive cable and this applies also to the CD-ROM drive (read or write).

Make sure that you read over the manuals that come with the motherboard, hard drive and other bits. This may be a pain because such manuals often look as if they are translated rather badly from Chinese (very likely, as these items are almost always made in Taiwan), but there is always useful information and often useful diagrams.

- Look in particular for restrictions and warnings, such as a mother-board being unsuitable for some types of processor or even for some types of operating system.
- Do not buy a motherboard you have never seen advertised, from a supplier that you know nothing about – there are some badly designed and badly made motherboards around, and reputable suppliers do not import them.

The order of assembly is an important aspect of planning. Each time you bend a motherboard you risk breaking the delicate printed lines of metal that connect the chips on the motherboard. A motherboard in its case is supported on a few pillars, and it can bend quite alarmingly when you insert connectors or expansion cards unless you can place one hand under the board to support it.

- The risk of bending the motherboard makes it sensible to place the main items into the board before you place the motherboard in the case, because when you can put the motherboard on a flat surface you are not likely to bend it. Some casings have a separate flat steel sheet, or pan, that can be detached to have the motherboard fitted to it.

The biggest risk of bending comes when the cooling fan is clipped over the processor. The processor itself needs no force – the socket type uses a ZIF (zero insertion force) holder that the chip drops into and is then secured by moving a lever. Clipping the fan to a socket-fitting processor, however, requires pressing down the fan really hard while the spring clips located in the socket are placed over the fan casing.

- The best way of tackling the addition of a fan to a socket-fitting processor is to place the motherboard on a flat surface, lying on the black plastic material in which it came wrapped. This material is slightly electrically conductive to minimize any risk of damage to chips if an electrostatic voltage were to be generated by rubbing the motherboard along any surface. You can then press down hard to engage the clips that hold the fan in place with little risk of bending or otherwise damaging the motherboard.

My own preference is also to insert all the drive cables while the motherboard is on a flat surface. This has the added advantage that insertion is much easier, because when a motherboard is in place it can be quite difficult to find the correct way round for each cable, and also quite difficult to hold a connector and insert it without exerting undue force on another connector. The position of these connectors on some motherboards is such that you cannot hold the cable ends easily because of the PSU box above them.

The most difficult item is usually the PSU connector which is at the end of a short and stiff cable that leads from the PSU. The insertion of this connector is therefore impossible until the motherboard is roughly in place. You can usually perform the task more easily if you put the motherboard in position, but left unbolted. You can then support the motherboard under the connector and take time to ensure that the connector is the correct way round. Once this connector is in place you can bolt down the motherboard – all this is described in detail later in Chapter 7.

Finding components

There are three main sources of components for DIY computers, local computer shops, computer fairs and mail-order suppliers. A quick flick through magazines such as *Computer Shopper* or *Micro Computer Mart* will show that the prices of components bought by mail order look low, but you have to remember the cost of carriage, which can be out of proportion if you want just one small item. Whereas, a few mail-order suppliers will take orders and payment over the Internet, often with the incentive of no carriage charges, so that this can be a useful option if you already use a computer with an Internet connection. This is a particular advantage of buying on the Internet if you can. While some suppliers will levy a surcharge if you pay by credit card – my instincts are to avoid these particular suppliers – buying with a credit card provides protection that is not available if you use any other form of payment such as debit card or cheque.

Obviously, ordering over the Internet means that you cannot inspect the goods closely until you receive them, and you need to be quite sure of what you are buying because many mail-order suppliers will impose a 'restocking' fee if you return an item that you ordered but have had second thoughts about.

• You should look for mail-order sources that have lengthy, clear descriptions of components, and if you are in doubt, ask for more details when you are ordering. If you are ordering using a supplier's website, print out the specification and read it carefully before you place an order.

Local shops have the considerable advantage that you can see exactly what you are getting, and can even take a look at manuals and diagrams before you buy. You might pay extra for this, but this is not inevitable, and it can be very comforting to know where you can return an item that turns out to be faulty, and possibly get some help or advice. Do not, however, expect to buy the time of an expert for the amount that you pay for a small item – it's another matter if you are paying out several hundred pounds. That said, local shops are usually run by enthusiasts who will offer guidance and will frequently go out of their way to help you.

• No two shops are alike, and you cannot expect the same level of attention in a large shop as you can in a small one where every customer counts.

Computer fairs are an increasingly popular way of selling hardware components. In addition, you can find components that are not readily available in other outlets, such as out-of-date components. Though it's unlikely that you want to build a PC with a ten-year-old design, this can be handy if you want to repair an old machine before disposing of it.

• Computer fairs also allow you to see the goods and to get information. The stallholder at a fair is likely to be knowledgeable, and can assist you in making a choice, and you can also readily compare products and prices between several suppliers.

At one time, the fear of computer fair purchases was that the supplies were of dubious quality and origin, and that the supplier might never be seen again. Nowadays, computer fairs are run by reputable companies who take some responsibility for vendors, and you can see which stalls show a name, address and telephone number and which show only a mobile number (avoid these!). Goods are in their original packaging, so that you aren't likely to be sold out-of-date items in plain boxes.

As always, however, you need to exercise some caution, and one good way is to pay by credit (*not* debit) card. Many vendors will take credit cards, and the advantage (not available if you use a debit card) is that the goods theoretically belong to the credit card company until you pay the bill. This means that if the goods are faulty, the credit card company will take responsibility. There aren't many traders who will refuse to change an item when the credit card company is conducting the negotiations. Remember that you may be surcharged for using a credit card.

Avoiding laptops

There's just one last point. All of this is about the full-scale desktop or tower case computer, not about laptops, portables or palm-top machines. The plain desktop type PC is a standardized design so that you can fit components from a huge range of suppliers in the confidence that all will fit and work.

This is not true of any miniature machines, which exist in the legendary 57 varieties. Each manufacturer has a different layout and uses custom-built components extensively, so that there is no market in interchangeable components. The only exception is the supply of small hard drives for replacement purposes. There is no source, other than taking a trip around the computer markets in Taiwan, of sets of components that you can buy to make your own laptop. In any case, you need a ten-year apprenticeship as a sardine packer before you feel confident enough to try it.

FAQ section

Q Can my computer possibly be as good as one that I buy as a package?
A Yes, because you will probably be using the same parts. If you buy high-quality parts, it's quite possible that you can assemble a better machine than one on offer in your high street. It will certainly suit you better.

Q What about maintenance? If I buy a complete machine there is at least a telephone number I can ring to listen to music for a time until a voice answers.
A If you have built it you have a better chance of being able to maintain it than someone who has never opened the casing. After all, you have unlimited access to the manufacturer.

Q If a part is faulty what do I do?
A Contact the seller and ask for a replacement in the usual way, just as you would if you bought a spare drive belt for the vacuum cleaner and it snapped.

Q What about installing Windows?
A If you had Windows on your old machine you should have the original installation CD or floppies. A copy of Windows is licensed for one computer only, but provided that you are not using the old machine and the new one as well with the same copy of Windows you are not doing anything illegal.

Q Don't I need some sort of specialized skill?
A Nothing spectacular. If you have ever used a screwdriver then you are fit to tackle a computer, because the bits all slot into place and are fairly distinctive.

Q Can I get any help on the Internet?
A Yes, many people are prepared to take time to help you if you clearly describe the problem. If your knowledge is limited, say so, and helpers will try to avoid being too technical. There are some websites devoted to blow-by-blow assembly instructions with illustrations, such as the superb AMD site that shows how to assemble a computer using the Athlon chip.

Finally in this introduction, computing has enriched the English language with a large number of new words and new uses of old words. If these are new to you, Appendix A contains a glossary with full explanations, and some have been explained already in this chapter. Note that the word *disk* is used to refer to a magnetic computer disk, and the more familiar *disc* is used for CDs. This distinction has become important now that the CD format is used to distribute software, replacing the use of floppy disks.

Chapter 2

Casings

The casing of a computer is its most obvious hardware aspect, often labelled as boring by people who should know better (if you want bright transfers you can apply them yourself, or you can buy a casing that is brightly painted). Choosing a casing is not so simple as you might expect, and the price difference between the cheapest and the dearest can be considerable, more than the price differences between other components.

There are several good reasons for making the choice of casing with care:

1. An unsuitable casing could make it almost impossible to expand your computer later, forcing you to build another machine.
2. An unsuitable casing with poor cooling can prevent you from upgrading to a faster processor at some later date.
3. Some casings are very much better designed than others, allowing easier access to components and making upgrading easy.
4. The casing contains the power supply unit, and some of these have fans that are so noisy that they inhibit you from using the computer.

The differences between case types are also important, and two main patterns are currently on sale – desktop and tower. Of these, the tower is now more common.

Desktop and tower styles

The two basic shapes of cases are the desktop and the tower type. The desktop is the conventional box whose height is much less than its width. The case sits on the desk, often with the monitor placed on top. It has a hinged lid that makes it easy to get at the insides (once you have heaved the monitor off it) and the layout is usually quite easy to work on. If this is the way you like to work, make sure that the top of the casing will not be dented when it carries the weight of a monitor. Placing a large monitor (17 inches or more) on the top of a desktop casing is not advisable.

A full-scale desktop casing is around 14 inches wide by 16 inches deep by 6½ inches high, but there are many other varieties of various descriptions such as small-footprint, minicase and so on. The full size of case was needed in the early days when the main board (motherboard) was large and when a small disk drive implied a 5¼-inch full-height unit. Nowadays, slimmer casings can be used, often because motherboards are smaller and disk drives are slimmer. Typical case shapes are illustrated in Figure 2.1.

Many manufacturers now use as standard a tower-block form of casing in which the casing rests on its 18-inch by 7-inch base. The tower type of casing comes in three sizes, mini, midi and full tower. The full-tower design is intended for large server machines that need a large number of hard drives and are linked to other machines through a local network that uses cables. Because such a machine is for professional purposes it's most unlikely that you will be building one for yourself, though you might feel that the large casing allows you almost unlimited expansion. After all, it can be placed under the desk or table.

The mini tower is a popular size. It sits easily on a desk with room for a monitor alongside, and this places the monitor usually at a better height for the user. What you need to be sure of is that a mini tower will allow you room for expansion. There is usually room for a second hard drive, but the space for drive bays (see later), particular the 5¼-inch type, is limited. This is not good news if you want to use

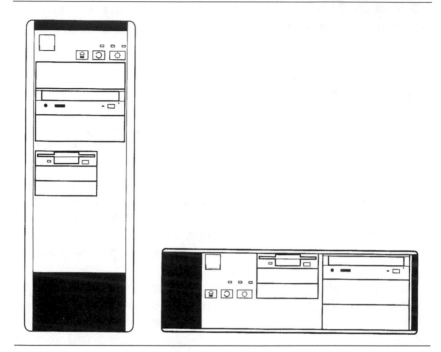

Figure 2.1   Two typical modern case shapes

a fast CD-ROM, a slow CD-R/RW writer and a tape backup all on
one machine. Though you can buy extension bay units that connect
to the main computer through a parallel port, this is not a desirable
way of expanding unless there are no other options.

The midi size is deservedly popular because it offers room for
expansion, takes up very little more desk space than the mini tower
and offers a good number of drive bays. This is the case size that every
manufacturer can supply and you can, with advantage, compare the
layout of several different makes.

For many purposes, however, the mini tower is attractive, and
many commercial machines use this form and size of case. If you
decide on this type you will want to ensure that your chosen case is
easy to work with, not hiding any important part of the motherboard
under the PSU box. The lack of space can be a problem, and on some
designs in the past it has been very difficult to carry out even
straightforward expansion actions like increasing memory because of
the limited space inside the box. Another insertion action, of cards
into expansion slots, can sometimes be impeded by the size of the

casing to the extent that some expansion slots cannot be used. Much depends on the design of the motherboard as well as that of the casing.

The casing is not just something that should concern you if you are building a machine for yourself. The casing that a manufacturer has used for a machine determines quite critically what you can do in the way of adding new facilities and replacing the motherboard. Since a computer design can be considered as fairly new for only a few months, it is important to be able to upgrade a machine easily. Even if you are starting with buying a machine that is by modern standards obsolete, you should not neglect the case design, because it may make the difference between being able to upgrade cheaply by replacing a motherboard or expensively by having to replace everything. The quality of the case is often the best way of deciding between two clones of unknown name and almost identical appearance. No matter how neat and tidy a small casing may look, it is not necessarily something that you will congratulate yourself about later.

- The snag is that until you have built one computer, you are not likely to know what might be a disadvantage in the design of a case, because it takes experience to know what to look for. By way of consolation, there are no really bad cases, but some are very much easier to fit boards into than others.
- You should not undertake the construction of a machine nowadays that does not use a power supply of at least 300 watts, with cooling adequate to run a processor at up to 2 GHz. Any specification lower than this will make it difficult to upgrade later if you start with more modest requirements.

What should you look for in a casing? A metal casing is important, because a metal casing greatly reduces the radiation of radio interference from the computer. Some big-name manufacturers in the past have used plastic cases and been obliged also to use metal sheets internally to comply with radio interference regulations. You should not attempt to upgrade a machine that uses a case of this type because it probably does not meet modern standards on radio interference (RF emission).

- Cast aluminium casings are now available, offering lower weight and better heat dissipation, but at a considerably higher price than the normal pressed steel type.

Using a pressed steel case is a much less costly solution, and the best form of case for easy working is either the midi-tower type or the desktop flip-lid type which allows easy access to the interior simply by pressing two catches and lifting the lid up on its hinges. The snag with the desktop type is that the raised lid often gets in the way, and unless you can remove it while you are fitting boards into the case, this makes working with this type of case more difficult.

Finally, there is the problem of fan noise, and that's something you can assess only if you can connect the power supply to the mains and get the fan running. This is by no means simple on modern units (because the power supply does not switch on fully until its remote-control leads are shorted, usually by connecting to a motherboard and clicking the ON switch). You may have to take a supplier's word that the fan is not too noisy, or you may be fortunate enough to have a complete computer demonstrated that uses the same casing.

The really objectionable fan noise is often due to the processor fan rather than the main PSU fan. The fan is usually attached by four self-tapping screws into the fins of the heatsink, and one way of reducing the noise is to remove the fan from the heatsink and relocate it slightly – a shift of half a millimetre along the fins may be enough to reduce the noise, removing the unpleasant rattle and leaving only the whine. Another possibility, applicable to any type of fitting is to use another heatsink and fan combination – but you would have to be sure that the replacement was quieter. For a machine in which the fan is lying horizontally inside the casing an effective solution is to mount the fan on a sort of subchassis of rubber. One such useful scheme is outlined on the website:

http://www.ec.se/personal/hansf/noise.htm

but you should remember that you use this at your own risk. This method separates the fan from the heatsink to which it is normally attached, and the risks are that the space between the fan and the heatsink might be too large for efficient cooling, or that the rubber mounting detaches from the heatsink fins so that the fan drops off. If the fan is vertical, this latter danger is greater.

- Some suppliers offer the option of a quieter fan with a processor and heatsink. Remember that if you find the fan too noisy it is an almost impossible task to remove the fan and heatsink from the processor, so that unless you can replace the fan with a quieter one on the same heatsink you are stuck with what you've got. If you are building a fast PC with a processor clock speed of more than 1 GHz, you need to be careful that the fan is adequate for cooling. Good cooling is more important than quiet operation, though both can be achieved.

BAY TYPES AND NUMBER

The overall size of a casing is not quite so important as the space for internal components, and one of the most important of these considerations is the number of disk drive bays (Figure 2.2).

Bays are the rectangular spaces that are used to contain drives. They can be *internal* with no access from the front panel (as for a hard drive) or *external* (as for a floppy or CD-ROM drive), and they come in two standard sizes, 5½ inch (wide) or 3¼ inch (narrow). The position and number of these bays determine how easy or otherwise it will be to expand your drive provision.

- Do not confuse an external bay with an external drive. An external bay allows access from the front panel of the computer, but the drive is contained in the computer. An external drive is held in a separate casing and connected to the computer usually through a fast parallel port (of the ECP or EPP type, see later) or by a USB connection.

A disk drive bay of the older conventional sort (Figure 2.3) is a shelf which is intended for the older type of 5¼-inch disk drive, and is used nowadays mainly for the CD-ROM, CD-R/RW, or DVD drive. Such a drive will slide into the bay from the front and be secured by screws at the side of the bay. The piece of casing at the front of the bay is usually a clip-on plastic portion which can be discarded when a floppy disk drive is fitted into the bay. A good case should offer at least two such bays, and at least two other smaller bays that will take a 3½-inch drive – one will be used for a hard disk drive and the other for the main floppy drive. There will also be two or

Figure 2.2   Side view of a modern ATX case showing PSU and bays

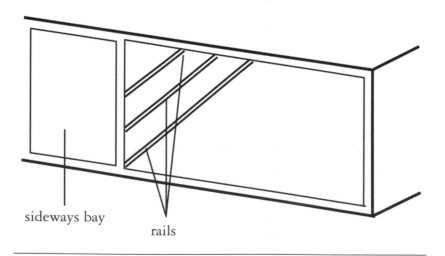

Figure 2.3   Typical older-style 5¼-inch bays as seen from the front

more internal 3½-inch bays with no front panels that can be used for hard drives.

The internal bays are usually of the 3½-inch size, and some mini casings provide only one for the main hard drive. Larger cases provide for two such bays, and often more. If more than one bay of this size is provided they should be reasonably close to each other, because if you want a second hard drive you need it to be placed where the data cable and the power supply cable can both reach easily. Believe it or not, this is not true of all casings. It's most unusual to find a 5¼-inch internal bay.

Many cases are poorly supplied with external bays. Some midi-tower cases offer up to three external bays of the 3½-inch size (but not necessarily the means to fix the drives in place!), desktop cases often have only one. The 5¼-inch drive provision is usually for two drives, of which one will almost certainly be used for a fast CD-ROM or DVD drive. Desktop machines usually offer two drives of this size either side by side or one over the other, a relic of the days when your up-market PC had two 5¼-inch floppy drives and no hard drive.

In general, the mini-tower type of machine is most likely to be limited for drive bay space, as you would expect, but you should not assume that moving to a midi tower will necessarily offer more. Sometimes there are more bay covers, but the space behind one or more may be impossible to use because of a diagonal strut or other metalwork. If this strut can be removed without weakening the case, then the bay can be used, but you will seldom find any printed advice on this point.

- You may see an old machine on offer at the price of a new casing, and feel that this provides the ideal basis for building a machine. This is seldom so. These cases will always be of the old AT type, and may even be of the older large AT rather than the modern Baby AT type. Worse still, the machine may be from a 'famous name' manufacturer who has a used a non-standard layout of motherboard and casing, making it impossible to use the casing with modern standard components.

As always, it boils down to making an inspection if you can, and asking a lot of questions (or looking at a diagram) if you are ordering by mail. As a consolation, there are no really nasty cases, but some are much better than others in terms of having no rough edges that will cut you, a quiet fan, lots of space to work in, and enough bays to let you use more drives later on.

The importance of drive bays cannot be overestimated. You might think that one 5¼-inch bay would be enough, but items such as tape backup drives, DVD drives and read/write CD drives need this size of bay, and there may be many other add-ons that are as yet under development that will require these fittings some day. If your case is lacking in drive bays and you need more drives then you will have to buy a larger case and start again. The only other option is to add new drives externally until the next time you rebuild.

- Another important point is that if you buy a larger casing, the power supply within it usually provides more connectors. This also is important if you are likely to add other drives.

The older type of large casing looks very empty when the lid is raised or cover removed, because modern motherboards are so much smaller than their predecessors. This makes more room for clipping other accessories, and it is not an advantage, as noted above, to opt for a small case unless you are very short of desk space. The conventional set-up of a PC machine is to use the flip-lid case to support the monitor, with the keyboard in front of both. The cables that are supplied will usually allow for other configurations – for example, I have the main cases for two machines on a shelf under the desk, with only the monitors and the keyboards on top. This confers the advantage that I can look downwards at the monitors without needing to jack up the chair to an unreasonable height. A tower form of casing also allows for more versatility in placing the units.

The back of the casing should allow for at least as many slot openings as the motherboard uses, or, if possible, more. The number of the slots on the motherboard governs the number of add-on boards that can be used, and though you can easily estimate how many you need now, it is less easy to guess how many more you might want in a few months' time. The number of slot positions in the casing determines how many boards can be used along with connectors that protrude from the back of the casing (Figure 2.4) and though several boards do not need connectors, it is always advisable to assume that each board will need to have a connector. On modern machines the demand for slots is less and you may find new motherboards with very few slots provided, mainly PCI slots.

Figure 2.4   Rear of a modern case, showing the power plugs and connectors plugged into sockets in slots

- Do not assume that all the slot positions on the motherboard will have matching cutouts on the casing. It's quite usual to find that one slot cannot be used, and if you have opted for a motherboard with several ISA slots it's usually one of these that is unusable.

The hardware that comes attached to the casing is also worth looking at. There will always be an on/off switch and often a reset switch. The reset switch is almost always at the front of the casing, though most users would prefer it to be at the back, well out of the way of fingers to avoid being pressed accidentally. There should also be LED indicators for power on and, usually, another to indicate when the hard disk is reading or writing. The leads that are connected to these switches and LEDs are fairly well standardized.

The small loudspeaker which is used to provide warning notes is built into the case, and provided with leads that should reach the corresponding connectors on the motherboard. The location of the loudspeaker is not fixed, and different manufacturers are likely to place this component in different positions, but usually near the front of the case. The loudspeaker is of portable-radio standard: and is used only for warning beeps. Provision for sound on modern machines is made by way of a separate sound card with external loudspeakers.

- Most modern cases provide for another fan to be fitted at the front to assist cooling. Not all suppliers can provide a fan to fit this space and it is not needed unless you are building a machine of very high performance, with a processor speed of more than 1 GHz. A much more welcome development is the use of a quiet fan on the PSU and another on the CPU. Modern motherboards designed for fast computers will use other fans built on to the board to cool critical chips.

Finally, the floor of the casing has pillars that will support a motherboard. Very often there are more pillars than the motherboard needs, and there may be some mounting holes on the motherboard that do not correspond to pillar positions. This is seldom a problem because provided the motherboard is well supported it does not need to be bolted down in many places. At least one of these pillars should be the type that is fitted by metal screws on to both the casing and the motherboard. The others can be plastic pillars that locate by clips.

- Note that many modern motherboards have a separate section (floor pan) that is used for motherboard mounting, and which can be detached to make this action much easier. This is a feature that is well worth having, because it makes assembly much easier.

Ease of construction

Once you have decided on the type of casing and its format, you have to make judgements about how easy it will be to assemble components into it. Once again, this is a matter for inspection of a casing or an accurate drawing. The casing fixes the position of the PSU, the drive bays and the motherboard, and you need to know what parts of the assembly will be difficult to reach when the motherboard is in place. This is not an easy matter unless you have seen several PCs with their covers off, and you simply have to use your imagination (though it helps if you have a paper template of the motherboard that you intend to use).

- The principles are simple enough. No part of the motherboard that you need to reach for initial insertion or for expansion should be inaccessible.

Unfortunately, that's a gospel of perfection, and you have to make concessions if you want a small casing. Even on larger casings, you are likely to find that some part of the motherboard will be covered by either the PSU or a drive bay. Designers have to make compromises, and most will have ensured that the memory slots and expansion slots are easy to reach. Remember that the motherboard and the casing will have been made by different manufacturers so that there is no certainty that they will match perfectly. It's important to be able to reach the memory slots easily, and modern cases and motherboards are all good in this respect.

Inevitably, some parts will not be easy to reach, and the usual victim is the backup battery which keeps the small amount of CMOS memory alive (so that the internal clock keeps time and retains data settings for drives when the computer is switched off). This battery may last five years or more, and when it expires it is more likely that you will want to build a new computer rather than insert a new battery into the old one.

The connectors for drives and the PSU connector are also items that can be difficult to reach once a motherboard is bolted down, so you have to ensure that all connectors are thoroughly in position before you secure the motherboard. This is not as easy as it sounds, because it's often difficult to avoid disturbing the cables when you are working.

Power supply

The power supply unit (PSU) is in a sealed casing within the main case, and this also contains the main cooling fan. The PSU box is prominently marked with notices that it must not be opened by unqualified personnel. Observe this warning, and, if you must open the box, first make certain that the machine is unplugged from the mains, that all cables have been disconnected, and that it has been switched off for at least ten minutes to allow capacitors to discharge.

The standard rating for the PSU was at one time 200 watts, and this was adequate for any self-build machine. Higher power is needed now because modern processors, multiple hard drives and the large amounts of memory that are now fitted need more power. The standard rating is now 300 watts, and if you are contemplating upgrading to a processor of 2 GHz, or higher, speed then you should consider a 350 or 400 watt power supply. The power supply box also carries the main switch and the casing fan, and it is connected (in the UK) by a standard three-pin rectangular socket of the type known as a Euroconnector. The plug end of this will be attached to a cable to which you can fit, or have fitted, a standard three-pin mains plug. The mains plug should carry a 3 A fuse – do not on any account use a larger rating.

Power supplies are, as noted above, now normally rated at 300 W. This provides for a 5 V supply at 30 amps, with +3.3 V at 28 amps (for the CPU), +12 V, 15 amps and −12 V and −5 V at 1 amp each. This should be adequate for even the most heavily extended machine and for most users is much more than is needed, but the techniques that are used allow a 400 or 500 W unit to be built at virtually the same price of the older 200 W type. The power output cable uses a 20-pin plug, though many also provide the two 6-pin type of plugs that were used to fit the old Baby AT type of motherboard.

The PSU outputs are in the form of a set of cables, one of which is terminated in the connector that plugs into the motherboard. One point to watch is the number of power supply plugs for drives. Many PSUs allow for only four of these, and this limits you to a floppy drive, a hard drive, a CD-ROM drive and one other. This is likely to be a bottleneck for expansion, because you may want to fit tape backup, a CD-RW drive and other devices that are at present in the development stage.

The standard type of power plug is a four-pin type that is used for both hard and CD-ROM drives, but you may also find at least one smaller connector. Some 3½-inch floppy drives use these smaller connectors, but the larger type is preferable because you can always use an adapter if you need the smaller type of connection, whereas you cannot easily find an adapter that will convert the smaller type of plug to fit the larger type of socket.

Figure 2.5   PSU with cables for drives tucked underneath

The number of these drive supply cables (Figure 2.5), limits the number of drives that you can use, and this can limit your ability to expand. Sometimes the supply to the processor fan is taken from one of these PSU cables, and if the number of cables is limited you may find that you are unable to fit a second hard drive, a CD writer drive, or a tape backup drive. You can buy a Y adapter for a power cable that allows two units to be connected to one cable, but you have to be certain that the supply can cope with this. A sound principle is to use the Y adapter to supply units that are seldom, if ever, running at the same time (such as tape backup and CD-R/RW drive).

There is no standard for the number of drive cables, and a reasonable minimum is six, allowing for expansion to a second hard drive as well as supplying floppy, CD-ROM, processor fan and one other unit. You are not likely to find this number of PSU cables in a mini-tower casing, and even midi-tower units may be a connector or two short of this number. This is a point that you need to take up with the supplier if you are concerned with your ability to expand.

At the input end of the PSU box you will find two connectors of the Eurosocket three-pin type (Figure 2.6). The one with visible pins is the input, and you plug the cable from the mains socket in the

room to this input. The other has no pins showing, and it connects
to a plug that may be supplied on the end of a cable for the monitor.

A matching plug is seldom supplied for the builder who wants a
different layout. Few electrical shops stock such plugs, and they are
best obtained by mail order, using firms such as *ElectroMail* or
Maplin. The ElectroMail reference number for a suitable straight
plug is 4.89-251 and the Maplin code is HL1GS. Business users with
an *RS Components* account can order using the same code as for
ElectroMail.

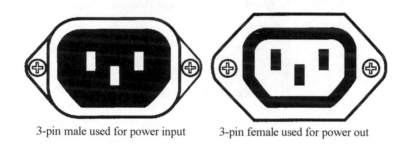

3-pin male used for power input   3-pin female used for power out

Figure 2.6   The Eurosocket and plug fittings

My preferred use for the Eurosocket is to make up a cable using the
Eurosocket at one end and a four-way distribution board at the other.
The monitor, printer, scanner and loudspeaker supply plugs all
connect into this distribution board, ensuring that all are off when
the supply to the computer is off. On older casings, this will also
ensure that everything is turned off when the computer itself is
switched off, but on modern machines you need also to turn off the
supply to the computer. Another solution is to use distribution
boards that have built-in switches, allowing you to switch off peripherals even if the computer is used on standby.

- If you have some experience of power supply units on other electronic equipment, note that the computer power units are of the
  switching type, and specialized knowledge is needed to deal with
  them if trouble arises. The one servicing exception is replacement
  of the main reservoir capacitor − this is usually the culprit if the
  unit fails after being switched off and on again several times in
  quick succession.

Fan

The fan that is positioned on the rear of the PSU box is the main fan for the whole computer, and you should dust it at intervals to ensure that it does not clog up. The processor has its separate fan, and most motherboards have a temperature monitoring system built in so that they will shut down the system if the processor temperature exceeds a preset amount. Modern motherboards usually have a built-in fan for at least one of the large chips (usually the North Bridge chip), and this is all wired into the motherboard; you do not need to do anything to connect it.

The main fan can be noisy, and at one time silencing kits could be bought that cut the speed and hence the noise of the fan. This was, however, at a time when computers were simpler and did not need so much cooling, and I would not advise the use of such kits on a modern type of machine. Careful choice of casing may help in reducing fan noise, because casings of different manufacture may use different PSU and fan types. Remember that the noise of the processor fan may be the predominant cause – you can check this by running the machine momentarily with the processor fan disconnected (but do not keep the machine running for more than a few seconds in this state).

• Quiet fans are now available as an extra, but so far this option is difficult to find in the lists of UK suppliers. The quieter type of fan is a tangential type (as used on fan heaters) and it is bulkier and of a different shape than the conventional propeller fan.

Cooling and fan noise problems

The use of processors running at speeds of more than 1 GHz, and, at the time of writing, threatening to run at more than 2 GHz, makes the topics of cooling and fan noise more important than they used to be. At the moment, my 850 MHz Duron system displays a processor temperature of 39°C. This is regarded as decidedly cool by modern standards, and the current advice is that your cooling system should keep the processor temperature below 50°C, with the danger point at 60°C, when the system should shut down to avoid damage. This is all easier said than done, because it's quite easy to keep a processor cool in a room whose temperature is, say, 15°C or less, but it's quite another matter if you have a room in which a sunny day can cause the air temperature to rise to 30°C or more.

Normally, when you buy a processor, a suitable heatsink and fan cooling unit will be supplied with it, and you should make certain that this is part of the package otherwise you should add suitable units to your order. It is advisable, when you order a processor and cooling unit, to state what motherboard you intend to use (unless, of course, you are buying a motherboard at the same time). The reason is that there are a few motherboards that are not compatible with some types of cooling blocks, because there are components on the motherboard that get in the way of fitting their heatsink and fan unit. I use an ABIT KT7A, and there are several types of heatsinks and fans that could not be fitted into the space available.

One possible reason for wanting to specify a cooling block separately from the processor is that you intend to overdrive the processor and you find that the existing cooling is insufficient, allowing the temperature to rise dangerously high. Another reason is that the fan that you have been using is distractingly noisy, as many are, and you want to change to the use of a much quieter fan unit such as the Papst.

Changing an existing cooling block is by no means easy, due to the use of heatsink compound between the processor and the heatsink. At one time this would be a heatsink grease which does not tend to solidify and which allows comparatively easy removal of the heatsink from the top of the processor. Current practice is to use a compound that comes coated on to the surface of the heatsink and which melts into a good conducting layer when you start using the processor. Separation of the processor from its heatsink can be very difficult in such a case, and there is a high risk of damaging the processor.

- Note that the heatsink is not intended to make close contact with the processor over all the surface, only over areas that are intended for cooling. Some processors have spacing blocks built in to avoid the heatsink touching the wrong portions of the processor. You must on no account try to remove or reduce the thickness of these blocks.
- If you are building or upgrading for yourself, but running the processor at its normal rated speeds, you need not get into the awkwardness of using alternative heatsink components. If,

however, you are experimenting with overclocking a processor (and therefore forgetting about any sort of guarantees or warranties) then you can remove the heatsink compound that is coated on to the heatsink surface, and replace it with a good heatsink grease such as is sold by Maplin. There are several websites devoted to overclocking techniques that show how this can be done, but it's not really a topic that we should cover in this book which is intended for the average user rather than the avid hunter of high-speed processing.

The main fan that is built in to the power supply unit can, in theory, be replaced by a fan of higher specification, but I do not advise any reader to do so because this involves breaking the seals on the PSU. If you are happy to work within the PSU sealed box, then it's up to you, but you are on your own. A better option is to change the whole PSU for one that incorporates a much quieter fan, providing that the new PSU is of adequate power (usually 300 W or more nowadays) for supplying your motherboard.

This makes it very important to specify, when you buy a casing, that you intend to use a high-speed processor. Apart from anything else, you will be specifying a casing with a 300 watt (or more) PSU, and the fan of that PSU should be able to cope with the volume of air that has to be shifted through the casing. What you cannot normally specify is how quiet this fan will be. Currently, you can buy aluminium casings with quiet fans in the PSU portion, but these are very expensive compared to the normal pressed steel items, and you would go to this extent only if you were particularly keen on good heat extraction with low noise. The use of cast aluminium will in itself contribute to cooling, so that such a casing could be a good investment if you intend to upgrade later to an even faster processor.

A third method of cooling is an intake fan, mounted at the front of the case. Cases do not normally include this item, but they nearly always provided the mountings for such fans, which you can buy separately. The main thing to watch for is that the fan connector can be plugged into either a socket on the motherboard or into one of the power sockets used for internal drives. You should also check that the air throughput of the input fan is less than that of the fan in the PSU, because this is the recommendation of fan suppliers and users. In other words, the air inside the casing should be at a slightly lower pressure than atmospheric.

Front panel

The front panel of a casing features one or more switches, indicator lights, and the bay plates. The main on/off switch is nearly always a push-button type on the tower type of casing, though a rocker switch at the right-hand side of the case is more common on the older desktop type of case. Modern cases often have a plastic cover that can be removed to show the bays and other items (Figure 2.7).

Some units provide only the mains switch, but others have a second push-button that provides a hardware reset. This should preferably be made difficult to press accidentally, because a hardware reset will close down the machine without the refinement of ensuring that you can save any open files. A few machines in the past have placed the reset switch at the rear to avoid accidental operation, but few modern casings provide this refinement. A reset switch is useful for the occasion when the machine has locked up (usually in the middle of an Internet connection) and nothing else has any effect.

The indicator lamps are intended to show what is active, and the minimum is two, one to show that power is on and the other to show that the hard drive is working. The hard drive indicator may have to be connected to the motherboard by a cable that will be supplied along with the casing. We'll look at the other connections such as the loudspeaker leads and the standby power connectors later. You will find all these connectors bunched together at the front of a new case, and they are usually labelled (rather than just colour coded) to indicate which is which.

- There is not usually any provision for showing that a second hard drive is in use, and the drive lights for other drive types (floppy, CD) are carried on the casings of the drives themselves.

The rest of the front of the casing is given over to the external drive bays, and a typical count for a midi-tower case is two 5¼-inch and one 3½-inch types, with additional internal 3½-inch bays for hard drives. On a new casing, each external bay is covered by a plate that is clipped into place. When you install a drive, the cover plate is unclipped and should be kept in a safe place, and the drive is inserted from the front of the case. The exception is when more than one external 3½-inch bay is supplied and a hard drive is used in one – the cover plate is then left in place because there is no point in exposing

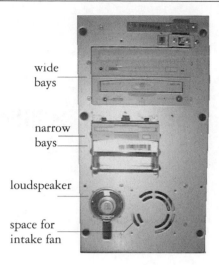

wide
bays

narrow
bays

loudspeaker

space for
intake fan

Figure 2.7   The front of a case with the cover panel removed

the end of a hard drive. You may need to remove the plate, however, if this is the only way of ensuring that the hard drive can be mounted on the slots that are provided.

At the rear of the casing there will be a large number of slot covers, allowing, if you have chosen well, for as many slots that your motherboard possesses. Each slot is initially sealed by a plate that is secured by a small screw (a Phillips type), and when a plate is removed and a card is slotted into the motherboard its connectors will protrude through the space that is revealed. Some casings may provide other fastenings for port connectors that are wired to connectors on the motherboard.

On a new casing, you may have to separate the slot covers and some covers over the positions of sockets on the motherboard. These are held by small metal tabs that can be broken to release the covers.

Chapter 3

The motherboard and its fittings

The motherboard is the main board that contains the microprocessor, its support chips and the main system memory. The illustration of Figure 3.1 shows the outline of the modern type of motherboard for a Socket-A (AMD) type of processor. You can identify which way round the motherboard fits by the positions of the ports (parallel, serial and USB) that will push through slots in the rear of the case.

The motherboard is the main item in any DIY computer project, and a good choice of motherboard will allow you easily to install more memory or a faster processor without needing to take the board out. Motherboards are not of uniform quality, and at least one design in the past has been reported as being faulty to the extent of working only with selected processor chips.

This type of information cannot be obtained from a book, because a book cannot be continually updated. It is only by reading magazines that continually test and check components that you can find where problems are arising. The consolation is that reputable suppliers also become aware of shortcomings in a product, and will often withdraw a product or do not keep it in stock. Another useful function of magazines is updating. It is unusual for a month to go by without a new motherboard being announced, and from time to time suppliers will offer package deals, such as motherboard and processor

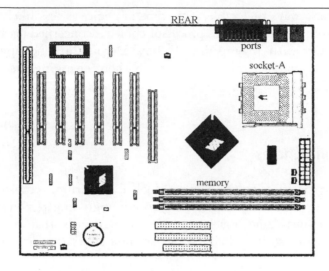

Figure 3.1   A typical motherboard for a Socket-A processor

or motherboard and 128 Mbytes of memory, that represent a considerable saving on individual prices.

New motherboards usually appear at the same time as upgraded processors, and sometimes you will learn of a new processor first because a motherboard is being advertised that accepts it. By contrast some manufacturers of motherboards always seem to be behind the provision of processors.

- The slots and ports on the motherboard always face to the rear of the computer, and the keyboard connector must also be at the rear, but otherwise the position of components is not fixed, nor are the precise dimensions. One point to watch is that the mounting of motherboards can sometimes be slightly too far from the rear of the case to allow boards slotted into the motherboard to be screwed down to the case.
- It is vitally important to choose a processor and motherboard together, with a view to being able to upgrade by using a different processor in the same motherboard later. At a time when new designs appear on an almost weekly basis, it is difficult to offer any hard and fast advice, but if you want to start in a relatively modest way and upgrade to a very much faster machine the type of motherboard that offers a Socket-A connection for an AMD processor is

in many ways preferable. This type of choice is less likely to box you into a corner as far as processor choice is concerned because you can start with a comparatively slow Duron chip and upgrade to faster Duron or Athlon chips later without changing the motherboard.

Specifications

The first specification that you will look at concerning a motherboard is the provision for processors. If you are upgrading remember that some 'famous-name' machines use motherboards that are totally incompatible, so that their casings are unusable for normal motherboards.

Processor provision is not so simple. For the home constructor, the ability to take a wide range of processors is valuable because it allows you to go for fast processors at low prices. If, for example, you use a motherboard that is intended for Pentium-3 and Pentium-4 processors, you are committed to that type – you cannot start with a low-cost Celeron chip in such a motherboard and then replace it with the Pentium-3 or Pentium-4 later.

- You may be able to buy some CPU chips over the Internet, and because what is sold as a new CPU in the UK is often an older type in the USA, prices, even allowing for import duty and VAT, are often very attractive. Be careful, however, because some US outlets are not permitted to export computer chips, and if what you get is not what you expect it can be difficult to return it.

The Celeron has, after a poor start, become a chip much used by self-build experts. The early versions lacked any cache memory and were slow, particularly compared to the AMD K-6 processors of the time. Later Celeron chips were much better and for some purposes could challenge the performance of the Pentium-2 types. It is surprising, in fact, that Intel did not use a different name, because the perception of the early Celeron as a slow chip persisted for several years.

- For the home constructor, there is a lot more sense in specifying a motherboard that uses the Socket-A fixing, because it provides for a wide range of types and speeds of AMD processors. For example, I am currently using a machine with an ABIT motherboard and a Duron 850 processor, but I can easily upgrade to a faster Duron, Athlon or Thunderbird processor using the same motherboard.

A quick flick through magazines will show that there are many manufacturers of motherboards, and many of the mail-order suppliers will be able to offer the products of up to ten manufacturers. This looks like a very wide choice, but on close inspection you may find that only a few match up to your requirements. At one time, most motherboards where intended for Intel processors only and very few could make use of the AMD chips. Now there is excellent provision for AMD and Intel alike.

The rest of this chapter is therefore concerned with the features that you need to look for in a motherboard, and which can be crucial in making up your mind to spend a sum between £40 and £200 on this item.

● Some motherboards are intended to be used with dual processors. These are intended for network server machines running Windows NT, and there is absolutely no advantage in using such boards if you are using ordinary applications with Windows *Me* or XP, though you can use them with Windows 2000. Only a few applications can make use of both processors.

Very fast processors (1.0 to 2.0+ GHz)

Many applications for a computer do not require the fastest possible combination of processor, motherboard and memory that can be obtained. Most of this book is dedicated to the construction or upgrading of machines to a reasonable standard rather than to the fastest that can be obtained, but this section deals with the faster chips, those working with a clock rate of 1 GHz upwards.

I must repeat at this point that if you want to use a very fast processor then you need to buy a suitable casing with a power supply of *at least* 300 watts rating, a motherboard that will be well matched to the processor you pick and memory that is fast enough to work with the FSB rate of the processor.

It's quite pointless to get involved in details of processors here, because new, faster models appear on almost a monthly basis. What we can do is to point out the type of processors that give you good value for money for upgrading or building from scratch, and we can leave it up to you to decide exactly which one you want. You can be quite certain that the most recent and fastest model of any chip will be set at a price that will deter the home constructor, and by waiting just a few months you may be able to buy such chip at a much more reasonable level. It's very different from the mass manufacturer of PCs who can get a very good bargain on a new chip, and virtually name his price on the older ones.

As far as the value for money is concerned, the Duron range from AMD is always outstanding, and the lower speed versions such as the 850 MHz I am currently using are excellent. There are now several Duron types that operate from 1 GHz upwards and which are more advanced in design and construction than the older models. The Duron, however, is now being phased out.

Celeron chips from Intel have in the past offered good performance for their price and the more recent versions are based on Pentium-3 technology and the faster types have performance that runs close to Pentium-4 levels.

Where out and out performance counts as well as price, it's difficult to avoid choosing the AMD Athlon and Thunderbird processors. The Thunderbird in particular is a good choice if your motherboard supports a 266 MHz FSB with DDR memory. At the top of the list for power comes the Athlon XP type of processor, whose clock ratings are not a good guide to their speed. AMD indicate this by numbering the processors in a way that indicates relative speed, for example the 1.53 GHz Athlon XP is labelled as XP 1800.

CHIPSET

A prominently quoted feature of a motherboard is its *chipset*. The processor by itself is not enough to carry out all the computing tasks (though this might change eventually), and it needs a set of chips that are at almost the same level of complication to assist it. These chips are a package that is referred to by name or type number, and the chipset is almost as important in determining how fast your computer will run as the processor itself.

At the time of writing, the most frequently used chipsets are from Intel, Via and Ali. It is pointless to list specific types here because by the time you read this these would have been replaced or supplemented by other later designs, and you will have to decide for yourself whether the level of performance that is implied in the price of a motherboard with some new chipset is what you really need. Unless you must have the fastest possible, it is usually possible to settle on a motherboard that contains a chipset with reasonable performance. What you cannot do is to select a motherboard and chipset independently, because the chips of the chipset are permanently attached to the motherboard rather than plugged into sockets.

The trouble is that neither chipsets nor processors by themselves determine performance – it's the combination of chipset, motherboard design and processor that is the dominant factor, and some actions (like Internet browsing) are always slow no matter what speed your hardware can theoretically achieve. Remember that though you may be able to change your processor easily, the chipset is soldered in place and is not replaceable.

- You should check that a motherboard specification specifically states that it can use the processor you want. A vague statement, for example, about using any Socket-A processor in the range 800 to 1400 MHz is not good enough.

EXPANSION SLOTS

The expansion slots on the motherboard, illustrated in Figure 3.2, are the connectors that hold and make connection to expansion boards. This follows the system used on the original PC machine and featured even earlier on the Apple computers of the late 1970s. The need for slots arises from the need for expanding the facilities of the computer. If you want to add a modem, a sound card, or any of a host of desirable add-ons that each require slot space for a controller card, then these expansion slots are how such add-ons are connected into the computer. Once you have filled all of the slots your expansion capabilities are sharply brought to an end, because there is no easy way of providing for further expansion.

Your only option then is to use expansion systems that act through the USB connector. This can be a very attractive option, such as if you

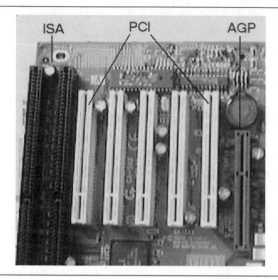

Figure 3.2   Motherboard expansion slots in detail showing three types

need more hard drive space that is not available internally, but the older type of the USB (USB 1.1) is rather slow for this type of expansion. By the time this book is in print, USB-2 will be available for a faster types of equipment, and the older USB peripherals can still be used with USB-2. Another option is to use the parallel port, using an adapter which still allows the printer to be used. This is not always a feasible scheme, because parallel ports on the older machines are strictly one way, and only a two-way parallel port can be used for this type of expansion for external drives. In addition, devices which connect to the parallel port in this way are often more expensive than those which simply slot in internally.

- Note that a modern motherboard may have only two types of expansion slot, plus slots for DIMM memory.

Except for the few motherboards that incorporate graphics on board, you will see quoted the number of PCI, ISA and AGP slots, usually in that order. A typical set of numbers is 5/1/1, and you seldom find more than one AGP slot because only one graphics card is ever likely to be used. The number of PCI slots is important for modern expansion cards, most of which can obtain a useful speed increase by fitting to the faster PCI bus slot. ISA slots are used by many older expansion cards, particularly where high speed is not important, but such cards have not been supplied for some time now, and many motherboards do not now provide any ISA slots. If you are taking expansion cards, such as a sound card, extra port card, modem, or other interface card, from an older computer then you will need sufficient ISA slots for these. If, on the other hand, you are building from scratch you can use a motherboard with no ISA slots.

All of this is complicated by the fact that not all slots may be usable. On one machine I built, an internal modem card fitted on an ISA slot, but the width of the card made it impossible to use the neighbouring ISA slot. On some layouts, slots may be made inaccessible in other ways, so that it is always useful to specify more slots than you think you are likely to use.

On a machine bought in bare-bones trim, you may find that only one of the PCI slots will be occupied, usually by a sound card, and the graphics card will be fitted in the AGP slot. Some motherboards supply one combined slot that will take either PCI or a more specialized type of connection. All of the motherboard slots should be in positions that correspond to openings in the casing at the rear which are normally covered.

A PCI local bus slot uses a much higher clock rate, usually fixed at 33 MHz, than the older ISA slots. It can operate suitable cards at a more advantageous speed and with 32-bit data handling. The AGP slots normally operate at 66 MHz, but you will find very much faster AGP slots indicated by the speed figure ×4. Both PCI and AGP slots can be run at higher speeds by manipulating the jumpers on some motherboards, but you then run the risk that cards using these *over-clocked slots* will not operate correctly.

AGP slots are used for very fast graphics boards and currently practically all graphics boards are intended for an AGP slot. At one time most graphics boards were PCI fitting, but the fact that the faster AGP boards were being produced at virtually the same price killed off the older type.

BUS SPEED

The internal bus of a PC is the set of connections between the processor and the other chips in the chipset. This should not be confused with the buses that feed the PCI slots, which operate at much lower speeds. For many years, the main internal bus of a PC machine operated at a speed of 66 MHz, and memory was arranged to be able to respond in time.

The usual specification for memory speed was 70 ns, with ns meaning nanosecond, one thousandth of a millionth of a second response time. The faster processors currently require a bus speed of 133 MHz or more, and so they require faster memory chips.

Motherboards often allow a range of bus speeds to be set, ranging from 66 MHz to more than 133 MHz. Though some users have claimed an improvement in performance by 'overclocking', using a faster processor clock or bus rate than the processor is intended to use, you should not attempt this unless you are prepared to lose the processor in the experiment. There are several websites that contain detailed instructions on overclocking, along with horror tales about difficulties that you may encounter.

PROVISION FOR MEMORY

Currently, all motherboards cater for memory using DIMMs, a type of board with memory chips mounted on it and using 168 pins for connection into the memory slots. Advertisements for motherboards will show the type and maximum number typically as 4D (up to four DIMMS). Beware of old motherboards that quote the use of SIMM memory.

The speed of memory is also important. Modern, fast processors require the 100 MHz, 133 MHz or higher bus speed and the memory must use DIMM sets which will be described either as 100 MHz bus or as 60 ns chips, or as 133 MHz bus speed chips for faster processors. The fastest processors nowadays use the 233 MHz bus speed.

Whatever may happen in the design of memory units, your motherboard will be able to cater only for the units that were available at the time of manufacture. This makes it important to go for a motherboard that is as up to date as possible. You should also try to leave space for additional memory – do not, for example, fit 128 Mbytes of memory in the form of two 64 Mbyte DIMMs when you could at less cost use a single 128 Mbyte DIMM.

- Some motherboards can use Rambus memory (RDIMM), which is very much faster than the normal DIMM.

ON-BOARD FACILITIES

When the PC was first devised, only the basics were on the motherboard, and everything from video graphics to ports had to be added by way of ISA slots. Over the years, manufacturers have added more functions to the motherboard, and nowadays you are likely to find that all motherboards provide the ports, but what else is available depends on the manufacturer and model.

Four items in particular can usually be added to a motherboard. These are sound, graphics, SCSI interface and monitoring, and though only a minority of boards offer one or more of these, the provision of any of the first three can save you the expense of an additional card. If you feel that a new card gives better performance than the built-in provision, you can disable the motherboard action and plug the card into a PCI slot. The snag is that the manufacturer may have decided that you will not need so many PCI slots if there are facilities built into the motherboard.

A sound interface is useful if you need to use sound, because it saves buying a sound card that might cost in the region of £30 or more. It certainly does not add that much to the price of the motherboard, and if you don't want sound it can be disabled. Conversely, if you do want sound but feel after a while that you want to upgrade to something more suited to your tastes, you can add a sound card in a PCI slot and disable the built-in one. If you particularly need a sound capability that will match CD quality, you should not use a built-in sound interface.

A graphics interface is an essential for any computer, so that a good built-in graphics interface is a boon. You are unlikely to find one on a motherboard costing less than £100, however, and you might prefer to keep your options open by buying a motherboard with an AGP slot and making the graphics card a separate item to buy.

The SCSI interface is rare on motherboards intended for home use. SCSI (small computers signal interface) is a standard that was drawn up many years ago for connecting external devices such as hard drives to a motherboard, and it is still a fast, though expensive, way of interfacing a hard drive and any other item that needs fast signal exchange. Some of the advantages of SCSI have been whittled away by the steady improvement in the (standard) EIDE system that is used on most small PCs, but SCSI is still used in large network server machines with several hard drives. It may also appear, in a more primitive form, as a card used to interface a scanner or a CD-ROM writer drive.

Since this type of interface is likely to appear only on the more expensive motherboards intended for servers, you are unlikely to want to specify it unless you happen to have a SCSI hard drive or other SCSI unit lying around waiting to be used. The outstanding advantage of SCSI is that it allows more than four hard drives to be fitted, something that is not possible using the normal EIDE type of interface. The large drives that are now available in EIDE fitting make the need for more than four drives much less pressing except for network servers. In any case you can now buy a PCI fitting card that offers another pair of IDE connections with each connection capable of linking up to more hard drives.

Unlike these other extras, monitoring is an action that is not intended to replace any add-in cards. A motherboard that is fitted with monitoring can check items like temperature and shut down if a temperature rise threatens the processor. Another typical monitoring action will sense when a hard drive is coming to the end of its life. I have to admit that I have switched off these facilities on my own machine, because I feel that modern computers are so reliable that I don't need the actions (some of which can send out strange messages at times). Monitoring actions are available on motherboards at a range of prices.

● Fan monitoring will switch the system down if a fan (either the main fan or the processor fan) fails. Voltage monitoring will shut down if any of the supply voltages rises or falls to an abnormal level. Intrusion monitoring will disable the system if the casing is removed.

Another aspect of monitoring is the provision of sleep and wake-up actions. With these facilities enabled, after a period of inactivity the computer will shut down power-hungry actions, like the hard drive(s) and monitor, so that it is in a standby state. You can opt to resume (wake up) when any key is pressed or when signals are received along a network, including Internet input from the modem.

JUMPER SETTINGS

Some older motherboards use settings by jumpers, others use autosetting, and though the latter (which sets the voltage by sensing the type of processor) sounds appealing, I prefer to be able to set voltage manually, just in case the autosetting action goes wrong, or if I want to use a processor that was not around when the motherboard was designed. The trend now is *soft setting*, meaning that the settings are made by a software program, specifying either your processor type, or the settings in detail, on a form that appears on your screen when the computer is first booting up. This provides the best of both worlds – allowing you to make all the settings simply by specifying the type and speed of processor, or you can experiment for yourself at your own risk with overclocking if you want to. This system is also much more flexible because it can cater for processors that run faster than anything that was available when the motherboard was designed.

Jumpers are crude miniature switches that are used to link contacts on the motherboard to switch actions in or out, or to allow for options. Each jumper unit normally consists of a row of three small pins with a bridging clip, and the jumper itself, which can be placed over two pins to provide two settings (sometimes three settings if the design provides for the jumper to be removed altogether).

Jumper settings should be correct if you have bought a package of motherboard and processor, but if you have bought separately and the motherboard is not one of the self-adjusting types you will have to make the voltage settings for yourself. Full details of jumper settings and motherboard installation are dealt with in Chapter 7.

Ultra-fast motherboards

If you are building a machine for comparatively undemanding purposes, such as working with text or still images, then you have a wide choice of motherboards available and there's no reason to go for the higher priced types. If, however, you want to run the motherboard in conjunction with a very fast processor (1 GHz or above) then you need a little more care in your choice of board.

In particular you should specify a board that will allow a fast bus rate. Technically this means that the front side bus (FSB) should run at 133 MHz at least, and preferably quite a bit higher. A few can be run up to 233 MHz (provided your memory can match this rate). Another point is that it is preferable to use a board that requires no difficult tweaking or setting of jumpers or switches. Over the years, I have come to prefer motherboards from ABIT and ASUS to any others, and my current system uses the ABIT KT7A (which has four USB sockets). This is a Socket-A board for AMD processors so that it can accommodate the Duron, Athlon or Thunderbird processor, making upgrading simple. The hard drive interface is to ATA/100 standard, which is ideal if you are involved in fast processing, such as converting video.

All modern motherboards are designed to take the DDR type of SDRAM, which has become standardized very rapidly. There are very few motherboards available for Rambus (see later), and these tend to be expensive, particularly for that type of memory. At the time of writing the price of the DDR memory has risen sharply, and since all but the most intensive users will find very little difference between DDR and SDR memory, you may prefer to fit the SDR type in your motherboard.

Another option which is now being pressed quite hard is the use of RAID motherboards. The acronym means Redundant Array of Independent Disks, and it refers to a system in which several hard drives are used with the data split among them and duplicated. The system was devised for business users so that data safety was not compromised if one drive failed. The extra cost and complication does not really justify its use for the non-business user, unless you intend to make very heavy use of your hard drives. One application that comes to mind is video editing, but it's quite likely that you would begin to make do with two large hard drives, each partitioned into two sections, for such applications.

That said, you may need to install more than two hard drives for some applications, but not necessarily with the complications of RAID. This can be catered for by an add-on system such as a PCI card with an extra set of IDE connectors (adding up to four additional drives), or the use of an external drive case connected through USB, or, preferably USB-2. The use of external drives is noted elsewhere.

Table 3.1 ABIT boards for AMD and Intel processors

AMD processors, Socket A (excluding RAID variants)

Type	Processor	FSB	RAM (max.)	AGP	PCI	Onboard	Case
NV7m	Athlon XP	266/200 MHz	1.5 Gb DDR SDRAM	1 AGP 4x	3 x PCI	Audio, graphics	Micro-ATX
KT7A	Duron/ Athlon	266/200 MHz	3 168-pin DIMM SDRAM	1 AGP 4x	6 PCI 1 ISA		ATX
KG7	Duron/ Athlon	266/200 MHz	4 x 184-pin DIMM, DDR SDRAM 2.0 Gb	1 AGP 4x	6 PCI		ATX

Pentium-4 processors, Socket 423

Type	Processor	FSB	RAM (max.)	AGP	PCI	Onboard	Case
TH7-RAID	Pentium 4	400 MHz	2 Gb RDRAM, 4x184-pin RIMM	1 AGP 4x	5x32 PCI	RAID, audio	ATX

Celeron processors, Socket 370 (FCPGA)

Type	Processor	FSB	RAM (max.)	AGP	PCI	Onboard	Case
ST6-RAID	C?	133/100/66 MHz	0/512 Mb SDRAM 3 168-pin DIMM	1 AGP 4	6 PCI	RAID, audio	ATX
VP6	Dual C?	133/100/66 MHz	0/768 Mb SDRAM, 3 168-pin DIMM	1 AGP 4x	5 PCI, 1 ISA	RAID, audio	ATX

Fast memory

The most important memory from the point of view of the user is the RAM. The amount of RAM memory critically determines how fast your computer can run, particularly when you are making use of several programs running together. A computer whose processor is comparatively slow, but which is fitted with a large amount of RAM (128 Mbytes or more) can often outperform one with a much faster processor but a restricted amount of RAM (64 Mbytes or less).

One of the problems that afflicts the self-builder and the upgrader is that the technology of RAM is continually evolving, so that if you have not upgraded a machine for several years you may find that additional RAM to upgrade the memory can no longer be bought, and

the newer types of RAM will either not fit or will not work correctly
in the older type of motherboard.

All the types of RAM currently installed on PC machines are of the
technology that is basically known as DRAM, with the D meaning
dynamic. Dynamic as applied to RAM means that the memory is
volatile and will lose its contents in a very short time, typically
1/1000 of a second. Dynamic memory, however, is very low-cost
memory and it can be used by employing a technique called
refreshing. Refreshing means that the contents of memory are
refreshed at frequent intervals, typically a thousand times per second,
so that data is not lost for as long as power is applied to the computer.
The use of dynamic memory permits the manufacturing of very large
memory units at low cost. The alternative is static RAM (SRAM)
which is faster, but very much more expensive, and is used only for
cache memory in small sizes of, typically, 64 Kbytes and 128 Kbytes.

At the time of writing, the form of RAM abbreviated to DDR
(Double Data Rate) is standard on most new machines, though the
advantages over the SDR (Single Data Rate) are not always apparent,
depending on how you use the machine. One important point is that
the chipset on the motherboard determines whether or not you can
use the latest and fastest technology. There is some degree of back-
wards compatibility in the sense that if your motherboard supports
the fastest modern technology it would probably also accept
memory types that are slower providing that they fit the same
sockets. On the other hand, if you have an older motherboard, there
is very little chance that it will be able to use the most modern types
of memory effectively, though it may be able to use them in the crip-
pled way.

As a guide to the confusing world of memory technology, the
following is a summary of the DRAM types that have been available
in the past few years. This excludes the older types of SIMM memory
which required memory boards to be fitted in pairs, using systems
described as EDO or FPM. The physical type of memory now fitted
uses DIMM construction, meaning that a set of the RAM memory
chips is placed on a board with 168 contacts, and used either by itself
or in conjunction with other DIMM units. For example, if you have
installed a 128 Mbyte DIMM board, you can add another identical
one to make the total memory 256 Mbytes. The design of the motherboard will control the total amount of memory you can use, but if
you are using any of the consumer versions of Windows (as distinct

from NT or 2000) you should not attempt to use more than 512 Mbytes of RAM.

BEDO DRAM: means burst extended data out DRAM. The *extended data out* portion means that the processor can start using memory before the previous command has completed its use of memory, providing a 30 per cent increase in performance. The *burst* portion of the name means that larger blocks of data are used, and this technique also can increase the speeds considerably. The average time required for memory access can be reduced to about 10 ns. The snag with this system is that it is restricted to bus speeds of 66 MHz or less, considerably lower than we use nowadays.

SDRAM: synchronous DRAM is a form of DRAM that will work, synchronized to the clock speed of the bus, at speeds higher than 66 MHz. The established standard for this type of DRAM is PC 100, meaning that it will work at a bus rate of 100 MHz. More recently, the established speed has been raised to PC 133 and this is now the normal rate for these lower machines, with faster machines using memory at a rate of 266 MHz.

DDR SDRAM: Double Data Rate SDRAM is the favoured memory option at the time of writing. The potential speed of this memory is double the rate of normal SDRAM because data can be handled both on the rising side of the clock pulse and on the following side rather than on one side only. DDR chips use 184 pins as compared to the 168 pins of other DRAM types.

RDRAM or **Rambus** is a much more costly form of memory that works in 16-bit units but can run at up to 800 MHz. Though this form of memory has been endorsed by Intel, it has not taken off as was expected, on grounds of cost and the amount of change that would be necessary on motherboard designs.

Chapter 4

Drives

Types and purpose

The motherboard, with all of its chips, provides the 'thinking' actions that you expect from a computer, and the *drives* provide the backup memory and the way of entering data and programs. The earliest PC machines had only a (360 Kbyte) floppy drive, later expanded to two floppy drives, and it was not until the later PC/AT models came along that the user could expect to have a hard drive. The development of CDs for entertainment then led to their use as data backups in computers, using the CD-ROM drive. More recently, we have seen DVD (digital versatile discs) introduced, and drives that can record as well as replay CDs. DVD recording drives for computers have also appeared, but at the time of writing their cost is high, though the cost of a recordable DV disc has now dropped to around £5 for a 4.7 Gbyte disc. DVD writing drives are not a wise buy until a single standard is established.

Drives are needed for two purposes. One is as a way of entering new data, particularly programs, into the computer. Initially, this was the main function of the floppy drives, but they have been superseded now for this purpose by CD-ROM drives, and the use of CDs is almost universal for any amount of data exceeding the 1.4 Mbytes that can be held on a floppy.

● In fact, distribution on a large scale is cheaper using CDs than using floppies, because a floppy can be copied only by writing from a computer or a tape copier, whereas once a master CD is made, it can be copied, like old vinyl gramophone records, by pressing actions, impressing the dot pattern of the master on to hot vinyl discs. As a general rule, CDs of music are cheaper to make than cassette tapes, and DVDs are cheaper to make than video tapes.

The second function of a drive is as a way of supplementing memory. The memory of a PC is fast but *volatile*. Volatile, remember, means that whatever is stored in the memory is cleared when the PC is switched off. It is possible to make a form of memory that will retain data when the power is off, but on the scale that is needed for a PC this would be impossibly expensive, too slow and too power hungry.

Both the floppy drive and the hard drive use magnetic storage because once a substance is magnetized it will retain its magnetism when the magnet is removed. This way, your programs and data are held in the form of magnetic signals on the floppy disk or the hard drive, ready to be copied into the fast electronic memory when you want them. If the data changes, it can be recorded back to the hard drive in its new form, or as a new file. The hard drive is very much faster than a floppy and holds a much larger amount of data. Therefore, it is used extensively, particularly by Windows, as a way of supplementing the memory of the computer – this type of use is called *virtual memory*.

Hard drives

PRINCIPLES

A hard drive is sealed into a metal casing during manufacture, and because this is done in an air-conditioned *clean room*, the air that is sealed in with the drive is clean and free of dust. The drive consists of a motor driving a spindle that is fastened to several discs, called *platters*, made of glass, metal or other hard material, hence the title

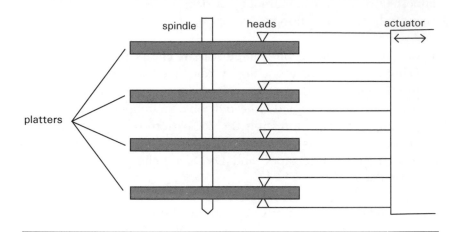

Figure 4.1   Principle of hard drive, showing platters, heads and actuator

hard drive. Each platter is coated with magnetic material on both sides, and each side of each platter is read and written using tiny electromagnets, the heads, each on a lightweight arm. All the heads can be moved together into the axis or out to the rim of their platter. Figure 4.1 illustrates the principles, and Figure 4.2 is a more detailed drawing of the assembly.

Taking any one side of a platter as an example, the disc is revolved by the drive motor for as long as the hard drive is active, and the head is positioned by moving its arm. Passing a current through the coil of fine wire in the head will cause the platter surface under the pointed end of the head to become magnetized, either North or South. This magnetization will persist until the same portion of the platter (the track) is remagnetized in the opposite sense.

When the signal current in the head windings is a set of electrical pulses, some positive and some negative, then the pattern of magnetization on a track of the platter will be dots of corresponding N and S polarity, and if one track is filled the arm can be moved to start another track. The tracks on a magnetic disk are circles, rather than the spiral form used for CDs and, before then, for vinyl gramophone records.

Put like that, it sounds quite simple, and you might think that all that was required was to feed the digital signals of the computer direct to the head of the disk. Such a scheme does not work, first because the computer signals consist of the presence or absence of a

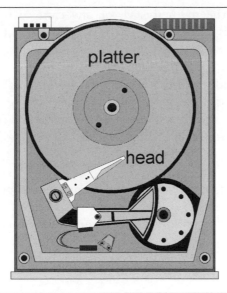

Figure 4.2   An internal view of a hard drive

voltage rather than of alternately positive and negative voltages or currents. The other problem is that magnetic recording is very unreliable if there is a long string of signals of the same polarity (North or South) or if there is one signal of one polarity set in a line of signals of opposite polarity, such as NNNNNNNNNNSNNNNNNNNN. This is a problem that we'll look at in more detail later in this chapter. In addition, the rate at which the processor deals with information is much faster than the magnetic heads can cope with.

All this means that the signals from the computer must be transformed into a pattern of currents that do not contain any very long or very short repetitions, are at a reasonable rate (typically around 15 MHz), and are of sufficient size to magnetize the platter surface so that the magnetization is permanent. This is the task of the *interface* circuits in the hard drive container.

At one time, all the interfacing was carried out by circuits contained on a card inserted into a slot on the motherboard. The snag was that several recording systems existed, and each one required a different card. The later system, IDE, meaning integrated drive electronics, placed all the interfacing circuits in the drive, requiring only a simple piece of circuitry on the motherboard. This way, the manufacturer of the drive can alter the coding system without requiring any change in the motherboard, or any card to be changed. The present system is an extension of the original IDE, hence the letters EIDE.

Reading a platter is just the reverse of the writing process. The platter spins and the head is placed over the written track. The varying magnetism along the track causes varying currents in the wire of the head, and these signals are processed and converted by the IDE interface into the normal digital signals that can then be passed to the computer.

● This principle of converting the computer's digital signals into forms that are more convenient for recording is used extensively for all types of recording systems, particularly for CD-ROM.

HOUSEKEEPING

The electronic circuits of the hard drive are responsible for controlling the speed of the drive motor and the position of the arms that carry the heads, and they will also ensure that when no recording is being done the heads are 'parked', placed over unused tracks on the platters. This helps to prevent damage to the surface of the platter if the drive suffers a jolt while the platters are spinning and the arms are free to move.

● One certain way to damage your computer is to knock it severely while the hard drive is busy reading or writing data. At other times the computer is remarkably immune to such sudden shocks.

All of this, however, does not ensure that new signals are recorded to unused or reused areas or that all the parts of a file can be read. The platters of a hard drive all start unrecorded, but as you add data and perhaps delete some data, various parts of the platters are available for recording but these parts are not necessarily close to each other.

The action of the DOS operating system is to ensure that the platters are used efficiently, that the positions of files are recorded on to a directory track on the drive, and that files are correctly located. In fact, the letters DOS mean *disk operating system*, a recognition of the fact that controlling hard and floppy drives is, and always has been, the most important part of the actions of an operating system.

The use of a hard drive therefore depends on a combination of items, the construction and electronic circuits in the sealed drive itself, the interface that passes signals to and from the drive, and the disk operating system that controls the 'housekeeping' of the drive, keeping track of where each portion of a file starts and ends.

OVERALL SIZE

Early hard drives were of 5¼-inch size so that they could be fitted in one of the floppy drive bays of a PC. Manufacturers then moved to the smaller 3½-inch type when this size of floppy drive came into use, and this also enabled faster hard drives to be constructed because the smaller platters could be spun faster and the heads needed to cover smaller distances. The 3½-inch size has become a standard for hard drives, so that cases allow for more bays of this size than for the larger size.

● The larger capacity sizes of hard drives can also be obtained in SCSI types, requiring an (expensive) SCSI interface. It's most unlikely that any home constructor will want to use this scheme unless several drives (four or more) are needed, and even this is unnecessary now that you can buy PCI fitting cards with two or more IDE connectors.

SPEED AND CAPACITY

The speed and capacity of a hard drive are important factors when you come to select this component for your do-it-yourself PC. One factor that affects the speed of reading and writing is the spin speed in revolutions per minute (rpm) of the platters on their spindle, and is often quoted in advertisements. The lowest speed in general use nowadays is 5400 rpm, and rates of 7200 and even 10 000 rpm are used for the faster drives.

This affects the quoted figure of access time which is used to judge hard drive speed. This is not necessarily a useful figure to use in calculations, but it is a useful comparison of different drives. The access time figure is an average time to move the heads from one track to another, and its units are milliseconds (ms), meaning thousandths of a second. A typical figure for a comparatively slow drive is 11 ms, and for a really fast drive is 6.5 ms. This approximate 2:1 ratio is significant if you are looking for sprightly performance from your hard drive.

The access time, however, is of less importance than the use of a built-in *cache*. The cache is a piece of memory, typically 256 Kbytes in size, that is used as an intermediate store for signals within the hard drive casing. The principle is that moving the heads of a drive is a time-consuming action, but if a whole track is read at a time the required portion of it can be read quickly from the memory. The more the cache can be used, the less need to try to read directly from the platters, and so the use of a cache speeds up transfers, particularly reading. A larger cache, provided it uses really fast memory (much faster than the memory on the motherboard), is a very considerable aid to faster hard drive actions, and cache sizes of 512 Kbytes are used on the faster drives, with up to 4096 Kbytes being used on some of the fastest drives currently available. Another factor that considerably speeds up the drive is the use of faster transfer systems, and a motherboard that provides ATA 100 drive performance will greatly enhance the speed of a disk system.

- Because fast cache memory is expensive, you can expect drives that use a large, fast cache to be considerably more expensive than those which use lesser amounts of slower memory. Caching is also used for the processor itself, with the cache chips placed on the motherboard close to the processor.

Drive capacity means the maximum number of Gbytes that can be stored on the drive, and because no hard drive can function well when it is full, you should always aim to use a hard drive that will operate at no more than three quarters of maximum capacity. The fashionable sizes that are used for PCs nowadays are in the range of 20–80 Gbytes, and you will not save a great deal of money by specifying a smaller drive (even if you can find one). The point is that when a particular size is predominant, every manufacturer mass produces these drives, forcing down prices.

Given that the operating system grows at each new version, that applications software also seems to become more bloated with each issue, and that your use of sound and video creates huge data files, the use of a large hard drive is more likely to be a necessity than an option. Remember, however, that you can use two hard drives on a system, and so if you find that you need more space you can add a second hard drive. You can, if you like, organize this so that the first drive is used for the operating system and the applications, and the second drive is used for data. This type of organization provides a speed benefit, because it cuts down the amount of head movement as compared to the use of one drive in which data and programs are mixed.

● Another useful form of organization is to fit a CD writer, and transfer to CD all the files that you need but which do not have to be kept on the hard drive for instant access.

Drives generally come with a three-year warranty, and with reasonable use should outlive this by a generous margin. A hard drive is, however, a mechanical component, and motor failure is the usual cause of problems. When this happens, you will be very glad that you kept a full backup of everything on the hard drive, because replacing a motor or reading the data from a set of platters when the motor or the head drive has failed can be very expensive, certainly more costly than a new hard drive.

DMA and UDMA 33/66

The older models of hard drive used much the same methods of transferring data to and from the drive as the floppy drives of old (which are more or less still with us). When you read a hard drive, for example, on an older machine, the microprocessor locates each byte and reads it, then writes the byte to memory. This has to be done for each byte of a file, and though some time is saved by reading and writing four or more bytes at a time (using processors of the 386 class or later), this is always a slow process. Worse still, it is a process that uses the main processor intensively, so that it cannot be used for anything else at the same time.

More recent hard drives use the *DMA* (direct memory access) system. These drives make use of a supplementary processor, the DMA chip on the motherboard, to do all the reading and writing work. All the main processor needs to do is to pass the information to the DMA chip concerning which data has to be copied to or from the drive. Once this has been done, the main processor is free again, and the DMA chip handles all the donkey work.

After a few months in which DMA hard drives were the ultimate in speed, the Ultra-DMA 33 standard appeared. This is much the same but faster, allowing data transfers to be done at 33 MHz, about as fast as the design methods of the time permitted. A more recent version is DMA-66, but most really modern motherboards and hard drives will feature the faster version called ATA-100. Nearly all hard drives offered for sale currently are of this type, but you need to be careful about older or second-hand drives that might look tempting pricewise but disappointing as far as performance is concerned.

FAT16 and FAT32

One important factor about hard drives is that the manufacturing techniques have run ahead of the development of operating systems, so that very large-capacity hard drives can now be sold at low prices. When MS-DOS was first adapted for hard drives, a 16-bit binary number was allocated for storing the number of memory units on the disk. This stored number is used in a *File Allocation Table* (FAT) that allocates a number for each unit of data, and the electronics of the hard drive can convert each FAT number into a location on the hard drive in terms of track and sector numbers. A 16-bit binary number can store up to 65 536 units, and if each is a 512 byte sector, that limits total storage to 65 536/2 Kbytes (because 512 bytes is 0.5 Kbyte). This would limit disk storage size to 32 768 Kbytes, or 32 Mbytes, and this was about the maximum size of the first hard drives.

In the early days, this seemed quite adequate, but as programs grew in size and generated large amounts of data, the limit became a problem that was solved by using *clusters*. A cluster is a set of sectors, and if we use clusters of 8 sectors (4 Kbytes) then our number 65 536 corresponds to 65 536 × 4 = 262 140 Kbytes, about 255 Mbytes. This extended the use of hard drives, and the solution was to use a different number of clusters for each size range of hard drive. For example, using 32 Kbyte clusters permitted the use of a hard drive of 204.8 Mbytes, 2 Gbytes in size. This could be doubled again by using 64 Kbyte clusters.

All of this, however, leads to inefficiency. Suppose you need to store ten small items of data, each 128 bytes (such as shortcuts to Windows programs). Each of these has to be stored on a cluster of its own, because otherwise there is no way of finding it on the disk because each item must correspond to a number in the FAT. This made the use of large hard drives inefficient, and one solution in the past was to partition the drive using a utility called *FDISK*, dividing it up before formatting it into a set of drive letters as if there were a set of separate small drives, each with a smaller cluster size. Another solution was the use of Microsoft's *DriveSpace* utility, which could pack each cluster with data and use another reference number to find the position of the data in the cluster.

In Windows 2000, Windows 98, Windows *Me*, Windows XP, and on the later (1997 onwards) version of Windows 95, the FAT32 system has been available. As the name suggests, this uses a 32-bit FAT, allowing the storage of numbers up to 4 294 960 000 and so greatly extending the size of disks that can use reasonably small clusters. The maximum disk or, more correctly, partition size that can be used is 32 Gbytes. If you use any later versions of Windows that include FAT32, you can convert a hard drive that has used the FAT16 system to use the FAT32 system, without the need to reformat the drive and lose the data. The (OEM) version of Windows 95 that used FAT32 was not made available to individual users, only to manufacturers, because it did not contain any utilities for preserving the data on a drive.

- Windows 2000 and Windows XP offer a third system, NTFS (NT Filing System), that is incompatible with the older FAT16 and FAT32 systems. Utilities are provided to allow you to convert your existing drive(s) when you change to Windows 2000 or XP. You should not convert a drive to NTFS unless you are quite certain that you will never need to use it again with the FAT32 system. The advantages of using NTFS are that it will support the use of disks up to 2 Tbytes (terabytes), which is 2048 Gbytes, it provides better file security and it uses the disk space more efficiently.

Large hard drives

When the second edition of this book was written, a large hard drive meant something of more than 5 Gbytes. The demand for storage space has increased enormously since then, and the two most important influences have been MP3 music files and the use of the PC for video editing. Even with the use of CD writing drives for longer-term storage, these applications demand a large amount of hard drive space just for carrying out conversions and editing actions.

Many computers, not just those in the higher price bracket, now come with hard drives of 40 Gbytes, and quite a few feature 80 Gbytes and even larger drives. The key to this increase in drive space is closer packing of data on a single platter, and Maxtor uses a system that allows a single platter to store 40 Gbytes. The early versions of these drives have used the spin rate of 5400 rpm, but it is only a matter of time before large drives with a 7200 rpm capability are announced.

Other manufacturers, of course, are also active in this field and Seagate has several large capacity drives available. IBM has also announced a new technique using a new magnetic material that they whimsically call *pixie dust* to obtain very large data packing figures on a single platter.

You might think that an 80 Gbyte drive is virtually infinite, and in terms of amount of text or even digital still photographs it *is* almost infinite. Digital video, however, is very demanding because uncompressed digital video requires a storage space of around 400 Mbytes per minute of displayed movie. With compression this can be brought down to as low as 650 Mbytes for one hour allowing a one-hour video to be compressed on to an ordinary CD. For the amateur moviemaker, working with camcorder material and recording on video, CD (see later) storage of more than one hour of video material is unlikely. DVD is likely to be in great demand, and with DVD recorders becoming available it will be necessary to have enough hard disk space to store the files that are to be recorded on DVD. You need to remember that when a file is edited you need space for both the source and the destination file on your hard drive.

- In addition, large hard drives can be used in the technology that is replacing the video cassette recorder. A DVD recorder is not necessarily a particularly appropriate solution to the problem of time shifting TV programmes, the major use for video cassette recorders. The use of a large hard drive is a much better solution, enabling many days of programme recordings to be stored, and also allowing much greater control over what is recorded and when and how easily it can be accessed.

The use of MP3 music is also another incentive for the demand for larger hard drives. However, this is not for the storage of MP3 files, which, being compressed, do not require a large amount of space. The problem is that the music may have to be stored in uncompressed format before conversion to MP3, and this, if full CD quality standard is to be maintained, means a storage space of about 650 Mbytes per hour of music. This might not appear much if you are storing the equivalent of one CD, but if you want to keep a few hundred stored that way then the amount of space starts to become quite significant.

By this time, any hard drive should conform in the ATA/100 format, in which the 100 signifies the transfer rate in Mbytes per second. This can be more significant than the rotational speed of the drive, so that if you cannot buy a drive with a 7200 rpm rotational speed, then you can always settle for a slower speed drive but with the faster transfer rate. If you can get the best of both worlds then by all means go for the faster rotational speed and the fastest possible transfer rate, and make sure that DMA is operative.

Are there any limits on hard drive size? There certainly are if you are using an older version of Windows, and even the most recent versions such as Windows *Me* will allow you to use hard drives of up to 32 Gbytes. To be more precise, this is the maximum size of a disk partition. Any hard drive can be partitioned (usually at the time when the drive is first being put into service) so that a separate drive letter is allocated for each partition. For example, a 60 Gbyte drive can be partitioned into two 30 Gbyte portions, which will be allocated the letters C: and D: by the system if this is the first or only hard drive. Because each partition is regarded as a separate drive as far as numbering of sectors is concerned, this drive can then be fully used by Windows *Me*, whereas a single-partition 60 Gbyte drive would be treated as if it had a capacity of 32 Gbytes, the maximum allowed under FAT32.

- Partitioning is normally done when a disk is first put into service, but the utility software Partition Magic allows you to partition a disk even when there is data stored on it, without loss of data. Be careful, however, of old partitioning programs that will scramble a FAT32 disk.

The NTFS system, available on Windows 2000 and Windows XP, has a drive or partition limit of 2 Tbytes, which is 2048 Gbytes. We are not quite ready to worry about that limitation just yet.

The floppy drive

Floppy drives were around long before the hard drive first appeared, and though they use the same principles of magnetic recording they are quite different in many respects. One important difference is speed. The floppy disk is, as the name infers, a piece of floppy plastic, and though it is cased in a hard plastic surround (unlike the earlier types that used a cardboard container) it is vulnerable to dust and smoke.

Because of this, the spin speed is fixed at 300 rpm, and at this speed the rate of reading and writing is not exactly breathtaking. The magnetic recording system is standardized (enabling floppy disks to be interchanged) so that modern improvements in recording systems cannot be used (see later for high-capacity floppies).

The 3½-inch type of floppy (Figure 4.3) is universal for PC machines, and you should not be tempted to omit it because the floppy is still a very convenient way of transferring data in small amounts. In addition, the floppy is a useful backup medium, and if you are concerned about the number of floppies that you need to hold backups you can use *Microsoft Backup*, or the *Zip* utilities to compact the data. Using WinZip, for example, you can compress up to 6 Mbytes of some types of data on to a single floppy that stores 1.4 Mbytes of uncompressed files. The Zip utilities are so well known and universally available that you can exchange floppies with other users in reasonable confidence that both of you can use the Zip files.

- Another way of making use of floppies is the free utility called HJ-split. This allows you to hold a large file split over several floppies, and to reconstitute it on to another hard drive.

Older floppy drives used an interface that worked at 500 Kbits/s, which was fast enough for the floppies of that time. Later types have used higher speeds, typically 1 Mbit/s, but there seem to be a few motherboards still on the market that use the slower speed. This is not something that you are likely to notice unless you connect a device that needs the faster transfer rate, such as a tape backup drive. Nevertheless, if a motherboard uses the older type of floppy interface, how modern is it likely to be in other respects?

If you want to find out the speed of your floppy drive interface, you

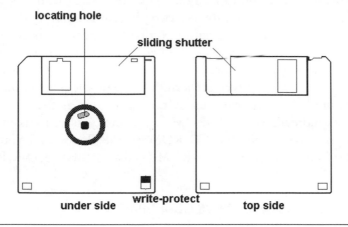

Figure 4.3 The 3½-inch type of floppy disk

can download a small utility called iodetect.exe (about 15 K) from the Iomega site:

$$http://www.iomega.com$$

which runs under DOS and reports the interface speed.

Modern cases come with several 3½-inch bays, but only one is likely to provide for an opening to the front so that a floppy can be inserted or removed. The standard design of floppy drive, available from a number of manufacturers, will fit any of these bays. The other bays, with no access from the front, are intended for hard drives.

One point to watch about a casing design is that some bays are too far away for the cables (particularly the power cable) to reach, and others may not be convenient for other reasons such as internal bracing, though this may be removable. The bay intended for the floppy drive, however, is always conveniently placed.

Some floppy drives use the standard form of power connector that is used also for hard drives and CD-ROM drives. A few makers, however, use a smaller power connector and provide an adapter cable so that this can be used even if your PC power unit does not supply one lead of this type. A few casings have a pair of these leads provided, and since they are only usable for floppy drives one is usually redundant. In theory you should be able to buy an adapter that plugs into the small connector to provide a standard-size power plug, but these are hard to find.

Remember that you can buy a Y-adapter which connects to one standard power plug and provides two plugs at the ends of the cables. This needs some care if it is not to overload the power supply, and the power cable for the floppy is the best one to use for the splitter, because the floppy consumes power mainly when it is working, which is not very often on a modern PC. The problem is to find a unit that is unlikely to be working at the same time as the floppy. An obvious candidate is the CD-ROM drive, since you are unlikely to be transferring data from the CD-ROM to the floppy and you can't transfer from a floppy to a CD-ROM (as distinct from CD-R/RW).

LARGE-CAPACITY FLOPPY VS CD-R DRIVE

The standardized design of floppy drives allows floppies to be used universally, but modern methods of magnetic recording can pack a lot more data on to a floppy, in the region of 100–120 Mbytes. The problem is that unless every PC has an identical drive, you cannot interchange floppies, though as a way of making backups for yourself these high-capacity floppies can be useful.

The snag is that technology has moved on, and you can now buy a CD recorder for much the same price as a high-capacity floppy drive. Even more important, a CD-R disc costs around 50p, compared to the £7–£10 or so for a high-capacity floppy, and the disc can be replayed in any CD drive on another machine. Even if you use the CD-RW type of discs (at £2.50 or less), this works out much cheaper, because you can record up to 650 Mbytes on a CD. We'll look at this later.

CD principles

A CD-ROM, like any other form of digital data store, contains data in digital form, whether this is text, spreadsheet data, a picture file or a piece of music. Each number is in binary form, using only the digits 1 and 0, and it will be possible to have numbers that consist of mainly 1s and mainly 0s, such as 1000000000000000 and 0111111111111111. Now though these numbers cause no problems in the computer's memory, we have to think about how we can record them. This is the same problem as is encountered in the design of a hard (magnetic) drive.

A long string of 1s or 0s is to all intents and purposes a steady signal, and neither magnetic disk nor compact disc is a medium that can record steady levels. Whatever recording method we choose must therefore be able to break up such patterns in a way that changes from 0 to 1 or 1 to 0 take place often enough for either system to respond correctly. In other words, what we are recording and replaying is the change from 0 to 1 or 1 to 0, and if these changes are too infrequent, there's a strong possibility that things will go wrong. Equally, if the changes are too frequent there is a danger that they might be ignored.

The solution to this lies in converting (modulating) binary signals into a form of code that is less likely to cause such problems. This implies that each digital signal byte will be converted into another (longer) string of 1s and 0s with no excessive runs of the same values or rapid changes to and fro.

ERROR CHECKING

Inevitably in any recording system there will be errors. On magnetic tape or disks there will be dropout errors where, because of a tiny fault in the recording material, some signals cannot be recorded. On magnetic media, these dropouts will be caused by missing or poor-quality magnetic coating, and though the incidence of dropouts can be made small it can never be eliminated. The duration of a dropout could result in hundreds of digits being missed, making the problem serious.

Another problem is jitter. Jitter means that the control of speed of the recording medium is imperfect, and this will cause alterations in the rate (frequency) with which signals are recorded or replayed. If the system depends, as all digital systems do, on the maintenance of a set clock frequency, some method will have to be found of keeping this clock frequency in step with any jitter.

Another form of error is more subtle and specific to digital recording methods – it is called intersymbol interference and it concerns recording a pulse, a rapid change in values. However we record a pulse, it is most unlikely that the recorded form will be as brief as the pulse was, whether the recorded form is a magnetic signal or a mark on a disk. This means that adjacent pulses can interfere with each other, and is another reason for the requirement that we need to avoid sequences such as the 101010 type mentioned earlier.

In addition to these errors we have the familiar old enemy of all recording, noise, which adds confusion to signals. It's less of a hazard for digital recording methods than for others, but some care has to be taken to avoid picking up unwanted signals on cables.

One of the problems of any digital number system, irrespective of the system used, is that an error that causes a 1 to change to 0 or 0 to 1 can make a very marked difference to a number. For coded music or a picture, an error in one digit is not necessarily disastrous, nor would it be for text, but the bytes of a program must be perfect if the program is to run correctly. If one letter 'a' in your text changes to 'h' the sense of your message is unlikely to be altered, but if a digit changed in a program and the program fault then caused your hard drive to be altered, it is very serious.

● Curiously enough, some high-street shops insist that you need a 'superior' and more expensive CD-R for recording sound than for recording data. One bit in error on a recorded program could make it crash, but no one is likely to be able to hear a 1-bit error in the sound recording because the CD system is designed to cover up such faults.

Any digital system must therefore make some provision for error checking, and for digital audio checking alone is not enough. There must also be some type of provision made to *correct* any error, because the nature of all recording materials, whether tape or disk, must be that bits of digital numbers will inevitably go missing.

At this stage, we shall not go deeply into error detection and correction, because this is one of the most difficult aspects of digital audio and one that most users never come across because the whole process is controlled as part of the signal processing system. It's useful, however, to know the principles that are involved, and which are used also in magnetic recording. These boil down to digit counting, redundancy and level maintenance.

Digit counting is a method of checking for the presence of one incorrect digit, and the simplest system is the parity system as was once used on serial transmission links between computers and printers. The principle can be useful when a number can be broken down into groups of bits, and where (as in all digital numbers in binary scale) some bits are much more important than others.

Redundancy is another very important method of detection and correction. In its crudest terms it could mean that each and every number was recorded three times, and the receiving circuits arranged so as to take a 'majority vote' on the correct number if the three versions did not agree. A simpler method would be to record each number twice, with parity included, and exclude the number with a parity error. The simplest and most effective redundancy systems, however, are very wasteful of storage space, and we have to think carefully about what we want to correct. Since the higher-order bits in a number convey larger changes in amplitude, it makes sense to employ more redundancy on them than on the lower-order bits.

Like so many aspects of communication by way of digital numbers, redundancy has received close attention from theorists, and is now a very formidable subject in its own right. In this book therefore we shall do no more than skim the surface, particularly as regards the complicated systems that have been evolved for compact disc error detection and correction.

Level maintenance is the backstop of support for error correction for digitally coded music. Music is coded by sampling the sound 40 000 times per second. If an error has been detected but cannot be corrected, then a level maintenance system discards the number that is in error, and retains the number that was present just previously. In other words, we don't expect a musical note to change much in the time between samples.

This can even be made the basis of error detection on the assumption that no amplitude change from one sample to the next can ever exceed a preset amount. Another possibility here is to use the previous signal with a small dither (noise) signal added, and this gives an even better correction for some types of signal. Yet another possibility is *interpolation*, in which the amplitude difference between the two previous signals that were not subject to error is added to the signal previous to the error.

These forms of correction, however, must not be used for computer data, because we do not expect that one signal will be close in value to another. Computer data has not been obtained by sampling musical signals, so the values are less predictable.

The CD system

The CD system is one rare example of international cooperation leading to a standard that has been adopted worldwide, something that was notably lacking in the first generation of video cassette recorders. The CD system did not spring from work that was mainly directed to audio recording but rather from the effort to create video discs that would be an acceptable alternative to video cassettes.

The original CD recording method made use of optical recording, using a beam of light from a miniature semiconductor laser. Such a beam is of low power, a matter of milliwatts, but the focus of the beam can be to a very small point so that low-melting-point materials like plastics can be vaporized by a focused beam. Turning the recording beam on to an area on a plastic disc for a fraction of a microsecond will therefore vaporize the material to leave a tiny crater or pit, about 0.6 millionths of a metre (0.6 µm) in diameter – for comparison, a human hair is around 50 µm in diameter. The depth of the pits is also very small, of the order of 0.1 µm. If no beam strikes the disc, then no pit is formed, so that we have here a system that can digitally code pulses into the form of pit or no-pit. Figure 4.4 illustrates the principles.

These pits on the master disc are converted to dimples of the same scale on the copies. The pits/dimples are of such a small size that the tracks of the CD can be much closer – about 60 CD tracks take up the same width as one LP track. Reading a set of dimples on a disc also makes use of a semiconductor laser, but of much lower power since it need not vaporize material. The reading beam will be reflected from the disc where no dimple exists, but scattered where there is a dimple.

By using an optical system that allows the light to travel in both directions to and from the disc surface, it is possible to focus a reflected beam on to a detector, and pick up a signal when the beam is reflected from the disc, with no signal when the beam falls on to a pit. The output from this detector is the digital signal that will be amplified, and then can be used or processed into an audio signal.

Only light from a laser source can fulfil the requirements of being perfectly monochromatic (one single frequency) and coherent (no breaks in the wave train) so as to permit focusing to such a fine spot. The CD system uses a beam that is focused at quite a large angle, and

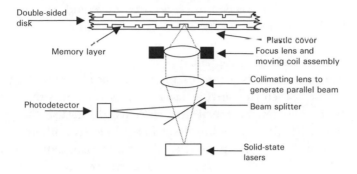

Figure 4.4 CD principles, showing a double-sided disc as used for DVD

with a transparent coating over the disc surface which also focuses the beam as well as protecting the recorded pits.

Though the diameter of the beam at the pit is around 0.5 μm, the diameter at the surface of the disc, the transparent coating, is about 1 mm. This means that dust particles and hairs on the surface of the disc have very little effect on the beam, which passes on each side of them – unless your dust particles are a millimetre across! This is just one way in which the CD system establishes its very considerable immunity to dust and scratching on the disc surface, the other being the remarkable error detection and correction system.

The pits are arranged in a spiral track, like the groove of a conventional record. This track, however, starts at the *inside* of the disc and spirals its way to the outside, with a distance between adjacent tracks of only 1.6 μm. The disc is spun so that the rate of movement of the surface past the laser beam is constant, so that if you can watch the disc you will find it spins faster on the inside tracks (the start of a recording) than at the outer tracks (the end of the recording).

The conventional CD that you find taped to the cover of your computer magazine is of this same type, created by pressing copies of a master disc. This system works by using reflected light; however, there are other ways of creating discs that do not involve vaporizing bits of material or using pressing tools on hot vinyl.

One method is to use a dye that changes colour when it is struck by a laser beam. When a disc that contains dots of different colours is struck by the low-power laser beam of a CD reader, the amount of reflected light will be quite different from the dots of different colour, and this is enough to be used as a way of reading binary signals. A disc of this type can be written once and read as often as you like, but the recorded surface cannot be used again because the dye colour change is permanent. This is the type of system that is used on the CD-R disc, see later.

Another system uses a rare magnetic material whose magnetism affects light. When the writing laser beam strikes this material and changes the magnetism, the ability to reflect light also changes and once again this allows a reading laser beam to detect differences. The difference with this system is that the magnetism can be changed back, allowing the disc to be erased and written again. This is the principle of the CD-RW type of disc.

CD READERS

The CD reader drive uses the laser beam reading system that was developed for music CDs, but the speed of rotation of the disc is usually much higher. When you buy a CD-ROM drive, you will see this speed quoted as a multiple of the normal speed of the music CD, such as ×20, ×32 and so on. This allows the discs to be read at higher speeds, so that information can be read from a CD almost as fast as it could be from old hard drives.

The form of CD-ROM drives (Figure 4.5) is fairly well standardized now as a slim 5¼-inch casing. The front panel holds a drive-on light, a volume control and a headphone jack. This allows the use of the drive for playing ordinary audio compact discs (or you could listen to your data!). The output audio signal is typically 0.6 V rms at 1 kHz.

When a button on the front panel is pressed, a tray slides out so that a CD can be placed in the tray, and pressing the button again will cause the tray to slide back in. The drive motor then spins the disc (taking a second or so to build up to full speed), and from then on the disc can be accessed, usually as drive D:. Windows allows you to specify *Autostart*, so that when a CD is inserted it will run its program(s) automatically. Figure 4.6 illustrates the loading method that is by now universal.

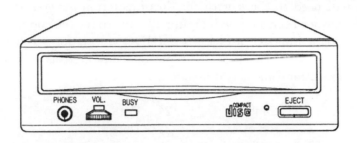

Figure 4.5   A typical CD-ROM drive front panel

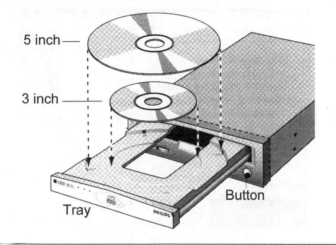

Figure 4.6   Loading in a CD – two sizes are catered for

There are three connectors at the rear of the CD-ROM drive, the power connector feeding +5 V and +12 V DC, an audio output connector for amplifiers and the data interface. The audio interface typically uses a 4-pin connector with connections:

1	Right channel	2	Earth
3	Left channel	4	Earth

or, on other types:

1	Left channel	2	Earth
3	Earth	4	Right channel

You will need to check with the documentation for your drive if a cable has not been supplied. Figure 4.7 illustrates the connectors.

The data interface uses a 40-pin IDC (insulation displacement connector) type. The pins are typically connected as follows (the Panasonic arrangement is illustrated):

1	Earth	21	Earth
2	Reset	22	Data enable
3	Earth	23	Earth
4	Earth	24	Status 2
5	Earth	25	Earth
6	Mode bit 0	26	Status data enable
7	Earth	27	Earth
8	Mode bit 1	28	Status bit 3
9	Earth	29	Earth
10	Write	30	Earth
11	Earth	31	Data bit 7
12	Read	32	Data bit 6
13	Earth	33	Earth
14	Status bit 0	34	Data bit 5
15	Earth	35	Data bit 4
16	N/c	36	Data bit 3
17	Earth	37	Earth
18	N/c	38	Data bit 2
19	Earth	39	Data bit 1
20	Status bit 1	40	Data bit 0

- Note that this interface uses 8-bit data. A different pinout is used for CD-R/RW drives, allowing 16-bit data, though the same cable and connector can be used because the software determines what signals are sent over the lines.

The CD-ROM is also the basis of multimedia work. Multimedia means that a CD can contain program code, digitized images and digital sound, and the computer can use all of these if a suitable sound system board is also added. This allows you to use encyclopaedia CDs that display text and images, and can also play sound. For anyone whose interests include music the use of multimedia promises effects that are unmatched by any other medium, even video tape, because of the extent of the control that the computer program

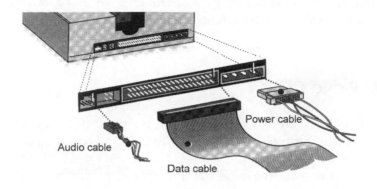

Power cable

Audio cable

Data cable

Figure 4.7   The power, data and audio connectors

exerts over the display. For multimedia work it is desirable to have a fast (16× or more) CD-ROM drive, because the older low-speed units are handicapped when rapidly changing pictures have to be displayed.

Installation of a CD-ROM drive has to be carried out early in the order of commissioning a new machine or one using a new mother-board and hard drive, because Windows will normally be installed from the CD-ROM drive. The drive package should include a floppy that will get the drive working from MS-DOS so that you can install Windows. You might find, however, that the program MSCDEX.EXE is missing, and that the CD-ROM drive cannot be installed until this program is present on the floppy. The MSCDEX.EXE file should be on the Startup floppy or on your MS-DOS floppies if you have them.

When you have the hard drive formatted with the MS-DOS system tracks, the next step is to install the driver for the CD-ROM from its floppy. Once this is done, you can boot the computer so that you see the MS-DOS prompt C: > and you can type D: to change this to D: >, meaning that the CD-ROM drive is detected and logged on. You can now insert a CD into the drive, such as the Windows CD, and run the Set-up program on the CD. Note that the Windows CD will autorun only if you are using it on a machine that already has Windows (an earlier version, for example) installed.

- On some old machines, the CD-drive data has to be connected through the sound board. It is unlikely that an old arrangement like this will be suited to modern uses, so avoid buying any machine that uses this arrangement.

CD-R and CD-RW

The fast CD-ROM drives are read only, but recently both write-once (CD-R) and write-often (CD-RW) drives have become available at comparatively low prices.

These drives use the same size and style of casing, but their read speeds are much slower, typically 4× to 6×, with slower writing speeds, usually ×2. The write-once CD-R drives can use blank discs that are very attractively priced (at around 50p or less) and which like the standard CD will hold about 650–700 Mbytes of data. Compression can increase this to around 1 Gbyte. The CD-RW drives cost more, and the blank discs currently retail at around £2.50. You can expect even this price to drop, and unless you are absolutely certain that you would never want to use the CD-RW type, you can hedge your bets with a drive that can use both types of disc. Currently, a CD-R drive cannot read the discs made by the CD-RW type, and vice versa, so that the all-in-one drive is well worth any extra expense.

The data cable pinout for the Philips CDD3610 is illustrated below – note how different this is from the CD-ROM cable pinout illustrated earlier.

1	Reset	21	DMA request
2	Earth	22	Earth
3	Data bit 7	23	I/O Write
4	Data bit 8	24	Earth
5	Data bit 6	25	I/O Read
6	Data bit 9	26	Earth
7	Data bit 5	27	I/O Ready
8	Data bit 10	28	SPSYNC/CSEL
9	Data bit 1	29	DMACK
10	Data bit 11	30	Earth
11	Data bit 3	31	INTRQ
12	Data bit 12	32	16 BIT I/O
13	Data bit 2	33	DA1

14	Data bit 13	34	PDIAG
15	Data bit 1	35	DA0
16	Data bit 14	36	DA2
17	Data bit 0	37	Chip select 0
18	Data bit 15	38	Chip select 1
19	Earth	39	DASP
20	No pin	40	Earth

The design and availability of these drives changes rapidly, so check out what is available in magazines such as *Computer Shopper* or *Micro Computer Mart* before you make any decisions, and look out for improvements in speed and reductions in price. At current prices, the most attractive offering is the Philips 3610, which will deal with all types of recordable discs. Drives that can use both types of disc will show three sets of speed, such as $12 \times 6 \times 4 \times$, meaning that the read speed is 12×, the write-once speed is 6× and the write-again speed is 4×.

- Windows XP contains a CD writing Wizard, so that you do not need to buy CD writing software if you are using XP.

Modern CD-R/RW drives are often described as burnproof, and this needs explanation. When data is being added to a CD-R or CD-RW, this must be done at a steady rate, otherwise parts of the CD will not be marked and cannot be read, so that the CD cannot be used beyond that point. This steady feed is achieved by storing data in a piece of memory called a *buffer* from which it can be fed at a steady rate to the CD writing hardware. When the computer is being used intensively there is a danger that the buffer might not be kept full enough to ensure that data could be supplied to write the CD. This condition is called *buffer underrun*. A burnproof drive is one that contains hardware that will avoid buffer underrun. Both the drive and the software that controls it must support burnproof operation.

- You may feel that you want to hang on to your present fast CD reader as well as the writer drive because the high speed is useful, and it makes disc-to-disc copying much simpler. You will have to ensure that you have enough power leads. The CD writer can be connected as the slave item in the secondary IDE connector with the CD reader as the master drive.

DVD

DVD (*Digital Versatile Disc*) is a more recent alternative to CD-ROM. DVD is a development of CD that can store much larger amounts of data and transfer it more rapidly. The versatility that forms part of the name arises because the DVD can be used for computer data, music or video. A DVD can be single sided, single layer, storing 4.7 Gbytes as compared to the 650 Mbytes of CD, and the double-sided two-layer version of DVD can store up to 17 Gbytes. Like CDs, DVD can be obtained as read only, write once (DVD-R), or DVD+RW (read/write). In addition, the DVD drive can read all current music or data CDs.

Windows *Me* and XP support the use of several makes of DVD drives, as did Windows 98 version 2. This allows you to use video playback of discs to your TV receiver if you have the DVD decoder card and suitable software for a PAL type of TV display.

At present, DVD players are almost a standard fitting on new computers – they allow replay of either CD or DVD, and can usually offer high-speed replay of data discs. By contrast, DVD recorders are rare and expensive, but, as always, you can expect this to change, along with the cost of rewriteable DVD blanks. A few manufacturers also provide what are known as combi drives, consisting of DVD and CD reader and also CD-R/RW facilities.

For details of fitting any type of drive (hard, floppy, tape, CD or CD/RW) see Chapter 7.

Chapter 5

Adding boards

Though a great deal of the actions that were once handled by cards or boards added to the basic PC are now placed on the motherboard, there are additions that you can expect to have to make on almost any motherboard. Chief among these are the graphics card, modem and sound card. Some motherboards feature graphics built in, others feature sound built in, very few at present have both of these features together. No motherboard currently advertised can boast of a modem built in; and many have none of these actions incorporated into the motherboard.

Graphics boards

The way that all PCs handle graphics, meaning any display other than text, owes a lot more to history than to careful planning, and it's not easy to understand the present methods unless you know how they all arose.

The conventional monitor uses a cathode-ray tube or a set of LCD dots to produce a picture that consists of a set of coloured points, and we can measure the *resolution* (meaning how much detail we can see in a picture) in terms of the number of dots per screen width. Note that a printer achieves much higher resolution than any monitor, measured in terms of dots per inch rather than dots per page width. The equivalent dots per inch for a screen is around 75; the accepted minimum for printers is 300 and many printers achieve 600 dots per inch or more in monochrome (a lower figure for colour).

- LCD displays have fixed resolution, so that if you display a 640 × 480 picture on a screen intended for 800 × 600 the picture will not fill the screen. This is quite different from the behaviour of a CRT monitor which shows a full-screen picture for any setting of resolution.

The type of picture that we can show on a monitor depends greatly on how much control we can achieve over the brightness and colour of each individual dot on the screen, and this is where the graphics card becomes important, because when the PC first appeared it could not display any graphics, only text. This required only minimal control, light or dark for the letters and symbols of the alphabet and digits.

The simplest way of controlling the dot brightness on a monitor is simply to turn the dot on or off, so that *on* means bright and *off* means dark. This scheme was used for monochrome monitors before colour pictures became the universal standard, and it was later extended to colour displays by using on/off control for each of the primary colours of light, red, blue and green.

Signals that use the three colour primaries in this way can produce red, green and blue using the dots for primary light colours and can also show the mixture of red and green, which is yellow, the mixture of red and blue, which is magenta and the mixture of blue and green, which is called cyan. The mixture of all three colours is white. Using a simple on/off scheme like this can therefore produce eight colours (counting black and white as colours).

The simple on/off method can be improved by using a fourth on/off signal, called brightness or *luminance*, whose effect when switched on is to make the colours brighter when this signal is switched on, so that you have black and grey, red and bright red, and so on, a range of 16 colours including black. This 16-colour system has been so common in the past that a lot of software still features 16 colours despite using a graphics system that allows a much greater range of colours.

The alternative to these on/off video signals is to use the *analogue* type of signal that is used for TV monitors, in which each signal for a colour can take any of a range of sizes or amplitudes, not just on or off. This method allows you to create any colour, natural or unnatural, by controlling the brightness of each of the primary colours individually. A monitor like this is much closer to TV monitors in design, and some (but certainly not all) monitors of this type can be used to display TV pictures from sources such as TV camcorders and video recorders.

GRAPHICS CARDS

When the first IBM PC machine appeared in 1982, its provision for display was a simple black-and-white (monochrome) monitor of 12 inches diagonal. Inside the computer, the numbers that are stored in the memory of the machine were turned into signals suitable for the monitor (video signals) by a separate circuit on a card that was inserted into one of the spare slots of the computer.

The design of the machine allowed for adding on all kinds of extra facilities by way of cards which could be plugged into these expansion slots. Since the early machines provided almost nothing in the way of the facilities that we now take for granted (such as connecting printers, floppy disks, extra memory and so on) these slots were a very valuable way of upgrading the machine. Even today, when most PC machines come very fully equipped, a set of four to six vacant slots is still a very valuable part of the specification.

The original type of display was concerned only with text, because the concept of a machine for business use at that time was that only text, along with a limited range of additional symbols, was all that was needed for serious use as distinct from games. The original video card was referred to as the *Monochrome Display Adapter*, a good summary of its intentions and uses, and usually abbreviated to MDA.

MDA produced an excellent display of text, with each character built up on a 14×9 grid. The text was of 80 characters per line and 25 lines per screen, and at a time when many small computers displayed only 40 characters per line using a 9×8 grid; this made text on the IBM monitor look notably crisp and clear. Typical monitors used an 18.4 kHz horizontal scan rate and 1000 lines resolution at the centre of the screen, and they still look good for a text display.

Graphics could not be displayed using the MDA card, however, so that graphs could not be produced from spreadsheets (on screen at least), and applications such as desktop publishing (DTP), painting, digital photographic editing or computer aided design (CAD) were totally out of the question. This latter point was purely academic at the time, however, because DTP and digital photography did not exist at that time, and CAD was at an early stage of development on much larger machines. For a modern machine, however, no one would consider any graphics card that did not supply full graphics capabilities in colour.

As the need for graphics in colour grew, various solutions in the form of different graphics cards appeared. The 16-colour CGA (colour graphics adapter) was used in the mid-1980s, but it was soon replaced, first by the EGA (extended graphics adapter) and then by the VGA (video graphics adapter) cards.

The VGA standard permits full compatibility with earlier types of display, and it adds displays of 640×480 16-colour graphics and 720×400-colour graphics, using a 9×16 grid for characters with colour. The VGA type of card used nowadays is classed as SVGA (S for super), and it permits much higher resolution (such as 1280×1024) and the use of a large number of colours (16 million or more). You should not consider using an older type of graphics card on a modern PC, because some modern programs would not run on an older type of card, and others would provide very disappointing graphics.

The number of colours that you can display depends on the number of digital bits that are used to code the colour. In the first monochrome display, only one digital bit was used for each dot because the dot was either on (1) or off (0). More bits are needed if we want to encode a range of colours, and the formula for the number of colours is 2^N, where N is the number of bits per dot (pixel) on the screen. For example, 8 bits per pixel allows you to display 2^8 colours, which is 256, and 16 bits per pixel allows 2^{16} colours, which is 65 536. For high-quality colour, 24 bits are used (16 777 216 colours), and this is usually referred to as 16 million colours. Photographic images demand the use of 30, 32 or even 36 bits for coding colours.

All this means that a colour picture can use a lot of memory. For example, if you want to print out a picture that is 5 inches by 4 inches at 300 dots per inch, using 24-bit colour, you will need to be able to store $5 \times 300 \times 4 \times 300 \times 24$ bits, which is 43 300 000 bits. With 8 bits in a byte, that's 5 400 000 bytes, around 5.15 Mbytes. Worse still, this picture will need a lot of screen space because your monitor probably works at 100 dots per inch or less, so that the picture appears magnified, and you will not be able to see all of it on the screen. You can opt for a reduced view by zooming out, but the fine detail cannot then be seen because of the limited resolution of the screen.

The more memory your graphics card can use, the more easily it can work with high-resolution and high-colour images, and most graphics cards come with 8 Mbytes or more (figures of 32 Mbytes or 64 Mbytes are fairly common for high-performance cards, see later) of their own memory. Others make do with less, and some will grab memory from the computer's RAM, which is not an ideal situation unless you are using 256 Mbytes or more of RAM.

Another point to consider is that it takes time to transfer the large numbers of bytes that images require, so that the speed of a graphics board is important. Originally, a graphics board would be slotted into the ordinary (ISA) expansion slots of the PC. The abbreviation ISA means industry-standard architecture, and these slots are compatible with the old PCs of the early 1980s. The limiting factor for any ISA slot is its speed of around 4 MHz, 4 million electrical pulses per second, intended to match the normal clock speed of the early processors. This looks woefully slow in comparison with the 800 MHz or more clock speeds of today, but there are still some actions that do not need fast transfer.

To achieve faster rates of transfer of bytes, later graphics cards have used slots connected so that they could operate at higher speeds. During the time of the 286/386/486 machines, several faster systems (such as VLB) came and went, and the current PCI slot, operating at 33 MHz, appeared with the first of the Pentium processors. The PCI slot is still adequate unless your taste in images is towards fast graphics in a large number of colours.

The most recent standard is AGP (advanced graphics port), and this is the current favourite, operating at a standard speed of 66 MHz. At the time of writing, it would be quite difficult to find a graphics card that did not feature AGP connection, very often at a 4× speed. The other change that may come soon is the method of connecting the graphics card to the monitor, with the current 15-pin connector replaced either by USB-2 or by the *Firewire* system, see later.

- See later on how to fit a graphics (or any other type) card into a slot on your motherboard.

CHOOSING A GRAPHICS BOARD

A quick flip through the computing magazines reveals that there is a considerable number of graphics cards at a huge range of prices, and an equally large number of monitors, nowadays mainly in sizes from 15 inches upwards.

I have assumed so far that you are constructing the main part of a PC, and using a monitor, keyboard and mouse that you already have. If, however, you have no monitor, or have an older monitor, you should look at the larger sizes (17 inches and above) because the increased screen area makes it much easier to work with high-resolution graphics, and because prices are falling rapidly.

A graphics card contains three sections of hardware, the graphics processor, the video memory and the RAMDAC. The graphics processor is a chip that prepares graphics data from the instructions that are sent to it by the CPU. The video memory holds the information for a complete screen at a time, and modern graphics cards use a fast type of memory such as SDRAM, SGRAM or DDR-DRAM. The RAMDAC is a chip that converts the digital image information into the type of analogue signals that the monitor can use – the name means random access memory digital to analogue converter. The speed at which the card can work may be limited by the rate at which digital signals can be sent to it, and this is where the AGP connection scores because it is at least twice as fast as the conventional PCI type.

Your choice of graphics card is determined partly by your choice of motherboard, but mainly by your requirements. If you need really fast graphics for 3-D games then your motherboard needs to have one AGP slot, and you need an AGP graphics card. Some motherboards have fast (AGP speed) graphics built in, and this can represent a considerable cash saving – but only if you can be certain that you will not want to change to an even faster system, if one should appear in a few months' time. The advantage of a separate card plugged into a slot is that you can upgrade one item without needing to upgrade everything else. Figure 5.1 illustrates a typical graphics card with space for expanding video memory.

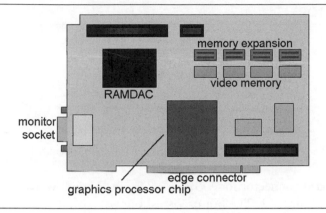

Figure 5.1 A typical graphics card

One item that can help in deciding on a graphics card is the general type of programs that you will use. All Windows programs need a graphics card that is at least of PCI standard, but it is only if you are interested in items such as digital video or advanced games that you will need a graphics board with a really fast response, high resolution and large memory.

- If most of your work is business related, using word processor, database and spreadsheet, a graphics card that has been optimized for 3-D games use is a waste of money and space. For such applications you do not need high speed and you do not need a large amount of memory; a PCI graphics card with a memory of 2 Mbytes is reasonable. By now, however, it is quite difficult to obtain graphics cards of modest performance, and you will probably find that the minimum that you can buy is an AGP card with 8 Mbytes. There is one good reason for installing a modern graphics card – you may find that the most recent version of Windows will not work with older cards.

CONNECTORS

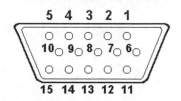

Figure 5.2   The standard 15-pin graphics card connector

The standard connector for VGA is a 15-pin D type, whose shape is shown in Figure 5.2. The pin use is as follows:

1	Red out	2	Green out
3	Blue out	4	NC
5	Earth	6	Red earth
7	Green earth	8	Blue earth
9	no pin	10	Sync earth
11	NC	12	NC
13	Horizontal sync	14	Vertical sync
15	NC		

Note: NC = No connection, pin not used. Pin 9 is removed to act as a key.

In the lifetime of this book, monitors are likely to appear that use USB-2, Firewire or other connectors.

DRIVERS

A driver is a program that is used to control the signal output from the computer to a device such as a monitor, printer, mouse, keyboard, scanner and so on. Windows provides a set of drivers for the most commonly used graphics cards, and also for several that you are not likely to encounter in the UK.

If your chosen graphics card is of more recent vintage than your version of Windows, however, you will have to use one of the drivers that will be supplied along with the card itself. You will usually be offered several sets of drivers, for DOS applications, Windows 98,

Windows *Me*, Windows XP and Windows NT, and you need to use the one that corresponds to the version of Windows that you are using.

- If you want to use DOS, each application (program) that you use must have its own driver. One of the advantages of working with Windows is that once you have installed a Windows driver to suit your monitor and graphics card it is then used for any program that runs under Windows.

The drivers that are supplied along with graphics cards are not always of a high standard, and some will even manage to conflict with Windows. It's always better to go for a graphics card whose drivers are available in your version of Windows, because the Windows drivers are usually more reliable. This means that you should avoid the most recent graphics cards in favour of one that has been around for long enough to have a driver built into your version of Windows. Note that there was a second edition of Windows 98 with an updated set of drivers, released a few months before the release of Windows 2000; a third edition followed later in 1999.

- It is very unusual to have problems if you set a resolution of 640 × 480, and Windows often reverts to this if other drivers are causing problems. Problems are more likely to arise if you are using really high resolutions with a new card that is not recognized by Windows. You may find that an updated driver is available on the Internet.

Remember that you can use the fast AGP type of graphics board *only* if your motherboard supports AGP with an AGP slot. If the graphics capability is built into the motherboard then it is likely to be of the AGP type. A few cases have been reported in the past of the AGP slot working only if USB (Universal Serial Bus) was enabled, so watch out for this if you have problems with an AGP board.

High performance graphics cards

If your PC is intended for use with text and ordinary graphics, as for most business applications, then there is absolutely no point in having a high performance graphics card. Such cards come into use only when you have demanding applications such as fast games and video editing in mind, and one general rule is that the more memory on board the graphics card the better. Beware of graphics cards which claim to have a large memory but which in fact simply use part of the RAM from the computer.

A computer intended for the fastest possible processing rate needs to have considerable attention paid to choosing the processor, the motherboard, the RAM and the graphics card. Of these, the graphics card is often the most limiting factor, particularly any graphics card that fits into the ordinary PCI bus. Such cards are now becoming rare, and it's more usual to find that any graphics card you will be offered will fit the AGP slot that is present on modern motherboards. The more recent motherboards offer an AGP slot that is rated at four times the rate of the original types (identified by the 4× symbol).

Prices of graphics cards can range from around £20 to £300 (including VAT), depending on exactly how much you want from them. At the bottom end of the price scale you can get a card such as the DTI range 128 Ultra 32 Mbyte AGP for around £25 and near the top end MSI make the G3Ti 1500 ProVTG GeForce Ti1500 DDR 64 Mbyte AGP at around £250 inclusive.

● Don't ask me why graphics cards get lumbered with such impossible names.

The cards for higher performance have names that often include the term *GeForce*. This refers to the chipset that is being used, so that cards of this type are available from several suppliers as are also those with the *nVidia* title. At one time the top performing card would be any design using the GeForce2 or GeForce2 Pro, but cards of this type are now be bought for prices ranging between £22 and £60 inclusive. The fastest cards at the time of writing are now using GeForce3, and are considerably more expensive, but you can expect the prices to fall steadily, and then considerably when the next version (GeForce4) appears at a reasonable price.

For any particular design of graphics card you can expect a fair range of one-card memory. The days of cards with 4 Mbytes to 16 Mbytes of memory for fast-moving applications are long gone, though you can still buy these cards at very low prices if your applications are less demanding. Modern fast video cards will use anything from 32 Mbytes upwards and providing that this is fast DDR memory that is actually placed on the video card, these can provide very high performance.

Several types of graphics cards offer rather more than straightforward graphics. Several, for example, offer TV and video signal inputs, providing conversion of analogue to digital for such signals, and TV outputs are yet another option. The ATI All-in-Wonder type of card is a good choice if you want a single card to tackle all these options. See the following section and Chapter 11.

More specialized graphics boards

The normal type of graphics board or card is intended for general purposes, but if you want to specialize you might need to add another card. If, for example, you intend to fit a DVD drive and use the computer to view full-size screen video from DVD, you will certainly need a fast MPEG card. The initials mean *Motion Picture Expert Group*, and they refer to a coding system used to compress video signals so that they can be transmitted and recorded. This board will decode the video at high speed so that you can watch the DVD output.

● Some graphics cards already incorporate MPEG decoding (and these will need an AGP socket). In some cases, however, the use of video may be confined to a small window rather than full screen.

If you want to work with video signals from an older camcorder or from a VCR, then you will require an additional interface card for these purposes, because these devices do not supply digital signals. If you have a modern digital camcorder you can connect to your PC so as to receive video, but only if you have the appropriate connectors (usually Firewire) and software. Viewing video requires a fast PC as well as a fast graphics card and video adapter card.

You can also buy TV cards that require a TV aerial connection and which will allow you to capture TV pictures and, in some cases, teletext. Since teletext is not used in the USA, these cards are less common and may be hard to find. The best known brand of TV and teletext cards for US and UK TV is Hauppage. Remember that the US TV system is not the same as ours, and TV cards made for use in the USA will not work for UK TV signals unless the documentation specifically states that PAL signals can be used. See Chapter 11 for details of converting camcorder video and creating video CDs.

- At the time of writing, there are no cards available for decoding the UK digital TV signals, because this system is not in use in the USA. Suitable cards are likely to appear, but some care will be needed in future because there is no certainty that when the US adopts digital TV it will use the same coding methods. The same applies to digital radio.
- Some video cards also cater for a plug-in camera (a Webcam) so that you can use live video over the Internet for video conferencing. The cameras that are supplied are not intended for high-resolution pictures and they cost remarkably little. For example, you can buy one well-known brand of video card complete with camera for around £110 at the time of writing. Webcams alone can be as little as £40.

Boards that are intended for editing video from digital cameras are now inexpensive and easy to find. Some feature a Firewire (IEEE 1394) connection, and you will have to check, if you are considering this option, that your digital camcorder supports a *full* Firewire connection. Several digital camcorders on sale in the UK have had their Firewire programming changed so that they can be used for output only, and you cannot edit the material on the tape inside the camera.

This is an EEC requirement (it would be, wouldn't it?) that arises because a camcorder that permits editing is classed as a video recorder, and is liable to higher sales tax in some countries. Why it should be imposed on users in the UK is quite another question, and there is information on the Internet about how to reprogram the system to allow two-way transfer. My instincts would be to avoid it all until they get it sorted out, and also to give time for camcorders with a USB-2 connection to become available.

For more modest applications, video editing cards that will work with older (analogue) camcorder and VCR pictures are available at around £50 upwards. These usually allow the edited material to be transferred to VCR or to CD-R.

Modems

The modem is a device that makes use of a serial port to transmit or receive data one bit at a time along a telephone line. Though this action could be built into a motherboard (and is likely to be at some stage), it is at present an item that has to be added. A modem can be external; meaning that it sits outside the computer, has its own mains supply, and is connected to the computer by a serial cable. An internal modem, by contrast, is in the form of an add-on card that is inserted into a slot (ISA or PCI) (Figure 5.3). Either type will need a connection to a telephone point. A modern fast (56K) internal modem will require a PCI slot and a fast processor speed, usually 450 MHz or more.

Figure 5.3   A typical internal modem card. The circular object is a loud-speaker so that you can hear the modem tones

- Some versions of Windows allow only a very limited number of modem types to be used, and you may find that most of them are not available in the UK. The domestic versions of Windows, such as Windows *Me* and XP are much more accommodating. See Chapter 10 for details of how to tell if your hardware is compatible with Windows XP.

The advantage of the external modem is that you can easily transfer it from one computer to another, and you can disable it totally, if you don't want to use it, by switching it off. The internal modem is cheaper because it does not need a casing or an independent power supply, and it avoids the need for a cable connection. At one time, the external modem was recommended on the grounds that you could follow what it was doing by looking at its indicator lights, but now that modem design has improved and communications systems have improved, there is little point in this. The internal modem is therefore the type to go for.

One point about any modem is that it is likely to come with a manual that looks as if it needs Mr Spock to interpret it. This is a hangover from the past, and most modem manuals are written for communications engineers who are writing software for the modem. Nowadays you plug in a modem and let Windows sort it out. It helps, however, if you can understand some of the information you see on screen, and some of the error messages that you might see.

When data is sent one bit at a time, some method has to be used to allow the receiving computer (or other device) to distinguish one group of eight bits (a byte) from its neighbour. This problem does not exist for a parallel system, because in the instant when a character is transmitted, all of its bits exist together as signals on the eight separate lines. For a serial transmission there is just one line for the bits of data, and the eight data bits must be sent in turn and assembled into a byte by storing them at the receiving end. The problem is that since one bit looks like any other, how does the receiving machine recognize the first bit of a byte?

The way round the problem is to precede each transmitted byte of eight bits by a start bit (a zero) and end it by either one or two stop bits (each a 1). Notice that once again there is no standardization of the number of stop bits, though one stop bit is the more common practice. Ten (or 11) bits must therefore be transmitted for each byte of data, and both transmitter and receiver must use the same number of stop bits.

The transmitting computer will send out its bytes of data, and at the receiving computer, the arrival of a start bit will start the machine counting in the bits of data. These are then stored in its memory until there is a set of eight, and then the computer checks that it has the correct number of stop bits after the last data bit. If the pattern of a zero, then eight bits (0 or 1), then a 1, is not found (assuming eight data bits and one stop bit), then the receiving computer can be programmed to register a mistake in the data.

This will start the counting action again, looking back at the stored data and starting with the next 0 bit that could be a start bit.

The recounting is fast, and can be carried out in the time between the arrival of one bit and the next, so that it would be unusual to miss more than one character in this way. All of this is the task of the communications software that you use with each computer and is carried out automatically if, and only if, you have programmed the software to work with the correct settings.

The use of the same number of stop bits and data bits by both computers is not in itself enough to ensure correct transfer, though. In addition to using the same number of data bits and stop bits, both transmitter and receiver must work with the same number of bits per second. In the (rather loose) language of computer communications, they must use the same *baud rate*. Baud rate and bits per second are not necessarily identical, but that's something for the experts to worry about. Quoted figures for the speed of communications often use the phrase *baud rate* to mean the number of bits per second.

- In the past, very slow rates were used, but you should not consider any modem that does not use the fastest rate available, 56 Kbits per second. A modem of this class is labelled V90, and is capable of automatically switching to a lower speed (such as 33 Kbits per second) if the telephone lines cannot support the higher speed.

Good software can make use of methods of adding data so as to provide for better checking and can even provide for the correction of errors to some extent. The checking methods can range from the simple checksum system to the very complicated Reed–Solomon system (also used in compact discs), but they all have one factor in common, redundancy. All checking involves sending more bits or bytes than the bytes of the data, with the extra bits or bytes carrying checking and error-correcting signals. Some of these can work on individual bytes, even on individual bits; others are intended to work on complete blocks of 128 bytes or more.

Because these checking methods all involve the transmission of extra bytes, they slow down the rate of communication of useful data. For text transmissions, the use of elaborate checking is often unnecessary because an occasional mistyped character in text is often not important compared to the need for a high speed of transmission.

For sending program files, however, one false byte is usually enough to ensure that the program does not run correctly, so that much better checking methods must be used even if this means taking longer to transmit the data. You often have to select, by way of your communications software, different methods for transmitting different types of data. If you use communications for purely business purposes you are likely to be concerned mainly with exchanging text rather than program files, but you might need to use exchange methods that employed checking if you transmitted, for example, your Lotus 1-2-3 data files from one office to another.

PROTOCOLS

The individual items of number of data bits, number of stop bits and the use of even, odd or no parity, make up what we call the modem serial *protocols*. You can't get very far in communications without knowing something about protocols, because unless both the transmitter and the receiver are using identical protocols there will be no communication, and only gibberish will be received.

There is no single protocol that is used by everyone, so you need to be able to set your communications software to the protocol that is being used by the machine to which you want to be linked. Modern software makes this considerably easier than it used to be, but you still need to know what protocols are being used by the computer with which you are trying to communicate. Communications is just about the last part of computing in which you cannot bridge a gap in technical knowledge with clever software, though as we shall see, it is possible to use software that requires only an initial effort from you.

- If you use e-mail and the Internet only, you do not need to worry about protocols, because these are fixed. Protocols become important only if you want to connect directly to other users, particularly to bulletin boards.

Given that the transmitter and the receiver are set up to the correct protocols, meaning that the baud rate, the number of stop bits and the use of parity will be identical, we still need some method to ensure that signals are transferred only when both transmitter and receiver are ready. This is called *handshaking*.

You might, for example, be recording data on your disks as it arrived, so that there would have to be a pause in the reception of signals while the disk system got into action. Another possibility is that you are printing out the data as it is transmitted, and your printer operates at a speed slower than the baud rate of the transmission. Whatever the reason, just to have transmitter and receiver working at the same rate is not enough, because you also have to ensure that the bits are in step at all times, and you have to make it possible to pause now and again without any loss of data.

A serial link to a printer can make use of 'hardware handshaking' meaning that the handshaking can be implemented by using electrical signals over another set of lines, but this option is not open to most communications applications because we can't use extra telephone lines.

The handshaking is therefore implemented in software by using the XON/XOFF system. This uses the ASCII code numbers 17 and 19, which are not used for printed characters, sent between one computer and the other. Data can be sent out from a computer following the ASCII 17 code, and disabled following the ASCII 19 code. Since these codes are sent over the normal data lines, no additional electrical connections are needed. The rate of data transfer is slower because of the time that is needed to send the XON/XOFF signals, so that if you organize your system in such a way that the least use of handshaking occurs, you will transmit or receive faster. The use of XON/XOFF is by far the most common method of software handshaking that is used in communications (another older system is called EIA).

- The normal scheme on a PC is to use hardware handshaking between the computer and the modem (at the fastest allowable rate of 115 Kbits/s) and XON/XOFF software handshaking over the telephone line.

Beware, incidentally, of modems that are not BT approved. They may be cheap, but if BT cuts off your line because it has discovered that you are using a non-approved modem you will be charged again for reconnection. An even nastier prospect is the refusal of an insurance company to pay out after a fire if non-approved equipment has been in use.

Nowadays, you should not contemplate using any modem that was slower than 56 Kbit/s, and preferably you would go for one that was a fax modem and a voice modem. A fax modem allows you to send and receive fax (there are still places that do not use e-mail). A voice modem allows you to pass voice messages (converted to digital signals) over the Internet, allowing you to telephone anyone with suitable equipment anywhere in the world at the price of a local call. That does not mean, incidentally that you can dial anyone up as you would with a conventional phone – the other user needs to be running the voice-modem program, and you will have to find some way of synchronizing things so that you are both online at the same time.

Even if the modem is internal you still have a serial link between the computer and the modem, and you need to know at what rates this can be used. Your software will refer to serial 'ports', meaning the connections through which serial data can be transmitted and received. These are distinguished by using COM1 and COM2 to refer to the port connectors at the back of the PC, and (usually) COM3 to refer to the internal port that is part of an internal modem. If you use an external modem, you need to use COM1 or COM2. Problems that used to arise when more than two serial ports are used have now been resolved for anyone using an up-to-date motherboard and using a Windows version that is 95 or later.

A faster rate of data exchange can be obtained by using an ISDN (Integrated Signals Digital Network) connection. This requires a special line that is expensive to install and rent, and it needs a different form of modem in the computer. The benefit is that it allows faster communication and is particularly suitable if you want to leave the computer running on communications 24 hours a day, or if you want to send sound and video data from one place to another. Other fast access schemes, such as ADSL (available over ordinary telephone lines) are available, but until recently the cost was, as usual in the UK, prohibitive except for business users. Recent changes have made ADSL more affordable, and for a comparatively light user of the Internet such as myself it still looks much too expensive.

Internet use of a modem can run up large telephone bills, even with a provider that uses a local-call number which is placed on your BT *Family and Friends* list. Cable TV providers can often offer both telephone and Internet facilities at lower prices, and to my mind this service is a lot more appealing than the TV programs on offer. You may, however, have to take a package of TV channels in order to get the useful stuff. Many of the uses that are promised for the Internet will be possible only when we can all get high-speed, low-cost connections, otherwise the Net becomes too cumbersome and costly to use.

OTHER MODEM FEATURES

What other modem features should you be aware of? One facility that is provided on practically every modern modem at any price range is auto answer, meaning that the modem will accept calls automatically. In other words, while you have your computer switched on and your communications software working, an incoming call will be put through to the computer without the need for you to lift a telephone receiver. This allows your computer to act rather like an answering machine, but without your voice being heard by the caller, and it is handy if you expect data to be sent to you while you are out. The auto answer modem will provide the correct signal to the remote transmitter that you are connected, using the same type of signal as would be sent by lifting a handset.

Remember, however, that there is no point in receiving messages while you are out unless your software provides for passing such software to a disk file as 'voice mail'. In addition, if messages can be sent to you while you are out, it may also be possible for a caller to read what is on some files in your disks. The more elaborate communications software will allow only a limited number of files to be read unless a special password is used to gain access to disks' commands (commands that are often termed 'shell' commands because they are carried out by the operating system or shell, usually MS-DOS).

Another feature which appears on many, but not all, modern modems is auto dial. As the name suggests, this allows you to carry out dialling without the use of a separate handset, and it's a very useful facility even if you are only going to use a voice transmission. To be able to dial numbers automatically requires that the modem can issue either pulses (for the old UK system) or tones (almost universal now).

Any modern modem can be configured for either pulse or tone dialling, selected either manually or automatically, but if your telephone system uses pulse dialling it is unlikely to allow the use of a fast modem. If the auto dial system is described as 'Hayes' then it conforms to the standards laid down by the Hayes Corporation, the (US) leader in modem design. Using an auto dial modem opens the door to the use of software that stores and selects telephone numbers. You can, for example, store up to 100 telephone numbers with some types of software and dial up any number simply by requesting a name. In addition, most suitable software will provide for redialling an engaged number (currently frowned on by BT) and for providing your password(s) when the other machine answers.

The third common and very useful facility is auto detect, also called *auto scan*. A modem fitted with this facility can detect what baud rate is being used by the remote machine, and set itself accordingly, so that you never have to bother about setting a baud rate for yourself. This is particularly useful if you use an auto dial system with many different numbers that use different baud rates. It does not, however, automatically set the number of data bits or stop bits for you, so that there is still something to do for yourself. Suitable software will allow you to keep a file of contacts that includes all of this data so that you never have to key it in more than once.

Other features are of more interest for specialized applications. Some modems allow a set of very fast baud rates for the few users who have access to ISDN data transmission lines. A few types feature built-in error detection and correction systems, but this is just as easily provided by software. Unless your needs are rather specialized, then a comparatively simple modem will be sufficient for both business and leisure communications, but simple doesn't mean crude, and modems at bargain prices can provide all the facilities we have looked at here.

Modems are now available (as external units only) that will accept incoming fax messages and voice calls and store them independently of the computer. You can then retrieve these when you next boot up the computer. This type of modem is the perfect answer to a modern problem – the remote fax machine that has been programmed to ring your number (whether you have a fax machine or not) at odd times of day or night (usually selling double-glazing). This type of modem allows you to find who is sending the junk fax so that you can contact BT to have the nuisance ended.

Sound capture and editing

The arrival of low-cost CD rewriters and their matching software makes it very much easier now to create audio CDs as well as data

CDs, and in another part of this book we take a look at video CD as well. A sound card is normal provision for any modern PC, but it is usually capable of considerably more than just supplying noises that go along with games or with Windows actions. One important use is in digitizing audio signals so that they can be recorded in the form of an audio CD.

Before you embark on this, you need to know what sort of quality you will be aiming at. The usual requirement is to replay some cassette tapes and digitize the sound to store on CD. This assumes, of course, that you are not breaking the copyright agreements and, as I read it, you would not be in breach of copyright if you had paid for the cassette tapes in the first place and if you destroyed them after copying on to CD. The legal situation is exactly the same as it was in the days when people copied the contents of the vinyl disc on to cassette tape so that they could play the tapes in the car.

Unless you have used a cassette recorder of very high quality with a noise-reduction system such as Dolby C (or higher) or dbx, then it is most unlikely that you need to digitize at a quality that would match a commercial CD. For such purposes you can use an ordinary sound card such as the SB128 from Creative Laboratories. If your requirements are to maintain the highest possible quality, then you need to look out for a sound card that is specified to convert analogue sound signals to digital while maintaining CD quality. Such a card will be quite expensive, because fast and accurate analogue to digital conversion is, even now, not a cheap and simple operation. For the purposes of this book, I'll assume that your interests are in the conversion of what are now usually known as bog standard tapes.

One common feature of many sound cards is that they have low sensitivity on the line input. This means that if you try to convert analogue to digital using your cassette equipment connected to the line input on the sound card, you will find that nothing appears as an output, because the amplitude of the sound signal is simply not enough to operate the analogue to digital conversion. The obvious way round this is the use the microphone input, but this is usually so sensitive that the signals from a cassette recorder will overload the circuits and cause severe distortion.

The only way out of this is to make an attenuator, a circuit gadget that will reduce the amplitude of the sound signal from the cassette recorder so that it can be used at the microphone input. It is possible to buy such things, and if you are seriously interested in doing a lot of this work then it might be worth it. On the other hand, if you are handy with a soldering iron and you know what you are doing it is very easy to make your own.

Figure 5.4(a) shows the circuit of a simple attenuator which uses nothing more elaborate than a dual channel potentiometer bought from Maplin. The photograph (Figure 5.4(b)) shows what this looks like in real life. The potentiometer is initially set to reduce the signals very considerably and you need to make a few trial and error recordings using software such as Microsoft Sound Recorder. This will allow you to make a short digitized recording and observe the amplitude of the signal as you do so. You can then check on playback to see if the quality is acceptable, and if the amplitude is too low you can increase the potentiometer setting or if the amplitude is too high you can reduce it. Once you have achieved the correct setting you can simply leave the potentiometer untouched for all your transcribing work.

For serious recording work you can use specialized software or you can make use of the sound editor software that comes with the creative SB 128 card. The version that I have is CTWAVE32.EXE, and it allows you to digitize input signals from any source and then edit the result. This makes it possible to cut out unwanted portions, and even (with a considerable amount of effort) to cut out unwanted clicks, scratches and other noises. You can replay the digitized signal as often as you want to check that it is of the quality you require, and if it is not, you can specify the quality in terms of sampling rate and number of bits for each sample.

If you want to record these digitized signals on a CD-R disc that will play in an ordinary CD player, you must record them at full CD quality. This means a sampling rate of 44 kHz and using 16-bit samples. If you simply want to record discs that you can play back using Windows Media Player, you need not go to this quality, and you can record in compressed form such as the popular MP3 files. Note that MP3 files can be replayed on many makes of DVD player, though not generally on ordinary CD players. The use of MP3 allows you to place very much more music on to a CD than you could possibly get using normal CD recording.

If you are coding your audio signals in compressed form or with reduced sampling, you can simply record them onto CD as if they were ordinary data files. If you want to record in MP3 format that can be replayed on a DVD player, you will need CD-R software that

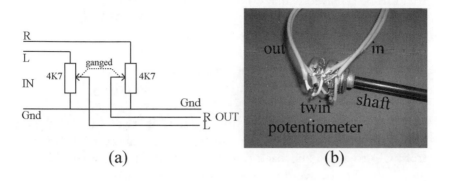

(a) (b)

Figure 5.4 (a) Circuit for an attenuating potentiometer (stereo version illustrated), (b) the appearance of the circuit

provides for correctly formatting these files. If you want to make a CD that will play in ordinary CD players, then you need to specify to your CD-R software that you are creating an audio CD. This is because the layout of the CD must correspond exactly with that of an ordinary commercial CD. You cannot record your files as data files and expect a CD player to make anything of them. For all these types of applications, I have found the Click'N Burn software particularly useful.

CD rippers

Another form of audio recording is the conversion of CD tracks to MP3 files, enabling you to make a single CD of MP3 files that covers many hours of music. This music can be replayed using your computer, or by using a suitable DVD player. Many modern DVD players will allow the use of CD, CD-R, or CD-RW discs with MP3 files, and will provide outputs that can be taken to a hi-fi system rather than being played through the TV receiver.

If you have a CD writer drive, even one of fairly ancient vintage, then you can make use of the software described as *CD rippers*. These will extract the files from a CD in digital form and convert directly into MP3, avoiding any intermediate audio stage. You can then use your CD writer software, such as Click'N Burn, to write a CD-R disc that can be replayed using Windows media player or a suitable DVD player. Two well-known (freeware) rippers are CDEX and FreeRIP whose websites can be found at:

http://www.cdex.n3.net and
http://www.mgshareware.com, respectively.

The advantage of this reading system is twofold. As already mentioned, there is no need to go through the sound card and convert from CD to audio and back to MP3, so that there is a considerable gain in quality by avoiding these conversions. The other point is that the ripping can be carried out much faster than would be possible if you were playing the CD at a normal rate to feed the sound card. If you have a fast CD ROM drive, then the conversion to MP3 files can take less time than would be needed to play the CD. The gain is *not* enormous (you cannot expect a gain of 32 times by using a 32-speed drive) because the rate is limited by the speed of conversion to MP3, but it is rather better than you could get from going through the sound card.

The slowest method of conversion is to read this CD in as a set of WAV files and then convert these to MP3 and save them. This is also a method that requires a fair bit of space on your hard drive, typically around 700 Mbytes, for the WAV files. Some rippers can convert direct to MP3, but if your computer is not fast this may leave a set of irritating clicks on the MP3 files. In this case most ripper software provides for saving to WAV files and then converting and deleting the WAV files, so that the space that is ultimately used on your hard drive is only that required for the MP3 files. Note, however, that you must still have sufficient space available on your hard drive. This is not usually a problem on a modern computer with hard drives of 20 Gbytes or more.

Not all software rippers are identical and there are curious differences between CDEX hand and FreeRIP. I find FreeRIP much easier to use, with a simple interface, but the files that it creates are larger (for the same audio track) than those created by CDEX. For example, one track that CDEX created in MP3 form as 894 Kbytes was rendered by FreeRIP as 1.52 Mbytes, indicating that CDEX uses the more modern MPEG-2 version of MP3 compression. FreeRIP uses a more intuitive display of the progress of the operation, with one display showing extraction from the CD and another showing the coding. CDEX uses one display showing the total progress of the operation, with an indication of volume levels.

In addition software rippers will allow you to specify the bit rate used by the MP3 files. CDEX allows you to specify a normal rate of up to 160 Kbits/s, with a higher rate for best quality, and two lower rates labelled as low frequency (top limit 16 kHz) and voice. FreeRIP allows you to select from nine rates ranging from as low as 16 Kbits/s up to 256 Kbits/s. For extracting from CDs you would normally use the highest rate unless you particularly wanted a high compression for a long playing time.

You have to make up your own mind on this, because a lot depends on the equipment you use for listening and the judgement of your own ears. For example, the test track referred to above can be ripped by FreeRIP using 16 Kbits/s to give a file of only 223 Kbits, using 96 Kbits/s to give a 1.3 Mbyte file, and at 256 Kbits/s to give a 3.5 Mbyte file. The perceived differences on small loudspeakers attached to the PC are quite small, and the only give-away is that the 16 Kbit/s file sounds rather muffled. The differences are much more apparent on a good hi-fi system. The WAV file for this test track, incidentally, amounts to some 19.2 Mbytes.

CDEX also allows several quality settings, but you have to be careful how you apply them, otherwise you end up with the same size of file for any setting. You can also opt for advanced settings of variable bit rates. CDEX is more suited to the audio enthusiast who is prepared to juggle with settings to achieve the conversion he/she wants, whereas FreeRIP is more suited to the less dedicated who simply want to make MP3 versions of some CD tracks without the need to go into details of coding methods or settings.

Fitting sound and other cards

If you need sound, particularly for multimedia uses, there is no great problem about installing the soundboard on the modern type of PC machine. You can install a sound board/card in an ISA slot or a PCI slot, and the trend nowadays is to use a sound card that is PCI fitting, because modern motherboards fit as few ISA slots as possible, often none.

- The main decision then is whether to try to use an assortment of bits and pieces that you already have or have seen advertised, or to use a complete add-on sound package.

A typical soundboard package will consist of the board or card itself, two, sometimes three, loudspeakers (not always of high quality) and (sometimes) a microphone. There is usually a MIDI interface either built into the board or available as an add-on, and additional software such as the Creative (SoundBlaster) programs which can be used to replace or supplement the software supplied in Windows 98 or Windows *Me*. The stereo amplifier that is needed for a reasonable sound output is almost always contained in one of the loudspeakers (the right-hand one). The board is plugged into a slot inside the PC, and will need to be connected to the CD-ROM drive if you have one (or are installing one at the same time).

In selecting an add-on sound system, you should consider the quality of sound from the loudspeakers before anything else, because you may find it difficult to live with poor-quality sound. The lower-cost packages are certain to omit a microphone, and, more important, may omit any software that allows sound files to be compressed so as to take up less disk space. A microphone can be useful because it allows you to use dictation software and voice-command software, in addition to adding your own comments to the CDs that you make for yourself, or additional soundtrack for videos that you record on to CD.

- If you want CD quality in all your sound capture, you will need to specify a sound card that can perform A–D conversion at high speed, and such a card will not be cheap.

The software is the next important item, and should be suitable for your requirements. One standard item should allow you to add narration to documents or images, and another piece of software that is often included is a voice synthesizer which will read text from a spreadsheet or a word-processed document (usually contained in the Windows clipboard). This latter application can often be, on its own, justification for adding a sound board because it has indisputable business uses – it can be very useful, for example, for proof-reading letters or other text if you don't want to be watching a screen at the time. Some boards come only with software suitable for games, and should be avoided if you have serious applications in mind.

INSTALLING A BOARD

Add-on devices are fitted to a PC machine by using the plug-in slots on the motherboard inside the casing. This description covers the installation of any type of card, but the details concern the sound card.

Looking at the back of your computer you will see the existing set of connectors along with some metal blanking plates that cover the vacant slots (Figure 5.5).

hole for
retaining screw

notch to hold
lower end

Figure 5.5   The blanker plate that covers the slot

Turn the power off, and wait for a minute. Remove the power-input cable from the computer, and then remove the cover so that you can see inside. When you open the casing you will see the other side of the blanking plates, and for each blanking plate there will be a 'slot', a set of electrical connections in the form of a long thin socket.

The metal blanking plate is unscrewed from the rear of the casing so that connections can be made to whatever board you plug in, and the same fixing screw is used to hold the new board in place.

- At one time, sound cards had to be configured, and contained sets of jumpers that needed to be adjusted. If you are installing a modern plug'n'play card on a modern Pentium computer, there will be no jumpers and no need for adjustments.

Your sound card will have a set of connectors (audio connectors) that connect with the CD-ROM drive. A special cable is needed, and this is another good reason for buying a combination package rather than piecemeal. The usual connectors are labelled as Mitsumi, Sony and Panasonic, and one of these will be suitable for the type of CD-ROM drive you are using. If this connection is not made, you cannot play audio CDs through your sound system, except by way of the front socket on the CD-ROM drive.

Now take a look at where you will insert the sound card, remembering that this must be either one of the long ISA slots or a spare PCI slot. Place the card temporarily over the slot (do not push it into the slot yet) and check that the little audio cable from the CD-ROM drive will reach.

Now remove the metal blanking strip at the end of the slot where you will install the sound card. Place the sound card over the slot, and check that the tongue on the card is correctly lined up with the aperture of the slot. Push the audio cable connector into its socket at this stage, because it will not be so easy to reach later – the connector fits only one way round. Gently push the card down, rocking it slightly to help open the spring contacts, until the card slips into its holder. You can now clamp the card into place with the screw that was used to hold the blanking strip – do not force the card into position or overtighten the screw because the purpose is only to ensure that the card does not pop out of place.

You can now replace the cover of the computer and turn the machine so that you can see the connectors on the rear of the sound card – Figure 5.6 shows a typical set.

If all is well, this can be a simple and quick operation. Problems arise, however, if you find that you have difficulty in setting the screw that holds the card into place. This is usually because the motherboard is not quite close enough to the rear of the casing, and though you can sometimes overcome this by loosening the motherboard pillars and then gently screwing them up again with the motherboard pressed towards the back of the case, this does not always work. If you simply cannot fasten the extension board down without severely straining it and the motherboard, then it's better to take the drastic step of filing the slot that fastens the card in place. Remove

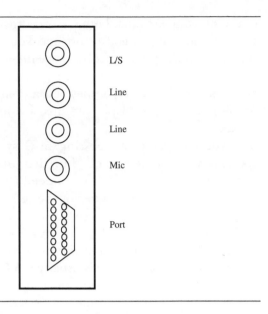

L/S

Line

Line

Mic

Port

Figure 5.6   The rear of a typical sound card, showing connectors

the card, put it into the plastic bag that it came in with the slot
fitting protruding from the top. Now use a small Swiss file to elon-
gate the fastening hole and at intervals wipe this clear of metal filings
and try the card in place again. Eventually you should be able to
fasten it down without problems.

You can now plug in connectors to the rear of the sound card from
the outside of the computer. The main connector is for the loudspeakers and this connection is made by way of a jack plug pushed
into the appropriate socket (Figure 5.7).

Figure 5.7   A stereo jack connector as used for a sound card

Check with your sound card manual before you make this connection, because there are usually several connection points all of which
are jack sockets (more correctly, jill sockets). The loudspeaker jack is

of the stereo type so that both speakers are connected by inserting one jack. If you don't intend to use speakers you can plug stereo headphones into the same jack, but remember that the jack fitted to the Sound Blaster is the 3.5 mm size, and your headphones, unless they are of the Walkman type, may use a ¼-inch jack. Suppliers such as Maplins can supply adapters to link a ¼-inch jack plug to a 3.5-mm socket.

If you connect to an existing hi-fi system rather than to loudspeakers which were part of a bundled kit, you will have to sort out connections for yourself. You will need an adapter which has a stereo jack plug (or whatever connector the sound card uses) at one end and a DIN plug or phono plugs (whatever your hi-fi needs) at the other.

The other connectors for the sound card may not be needed at present. These are for sound inputs, games and MIDI connections. The microphone connector is usually a 3.5-mm jack, and is normally a mono jack rather than a stereo one. If you have a microphone (take a look at the low-cost dynamic microphones in the Maplin catalogue) then it can be plugged in now – this does not interfere with other inputs because the software allows you to control which input is being used.

The *Line* connector allows you to connect to devices such as a cassette recorder, an external CD player, a synthesizer or the output of a radio. If you connect to the output from the pre-amplifier stage of a hi-fi you can select the sound source with the pre-amplifier.

● Remember that you cannot control with software an external CD player that is connected through the line input.

The large connector is a 15-pin D-type which serves for both games (a joystick connection) and MIDI interface. On the Sound Blaster card a single joystick can be plugged in, and dual joysticks can be connected by way of a splitter cable. The MIDI interface needs additional hardware on some Sound Blaster cards and this is packaged with suitable software for managing MIDI files. Sound Blaster also provides for upgrades by way of an add-on Wave Blaster board, a MIDI synthesizer, and the Advanced Signal Processor (ASP) chip which can allow the system to carry out speech recognition. These advanced features are not covered in this book. Speech recognition programs, such as *Dragon Naturally Speaking*, do not require this extra hardware.

Once the sound card is installed you can adjust the position of the cables so as to ensure that none of them are likely to be trapped when the lid is closed. If you have already installed the CD-ROM drive then all the hardware work is now completed and you can shut the lid.

The use of sound from DOS is rather more complicated than from Windows, and is not covered in this book because multimedia users will work exclusively from Windows.

Unwanted noise

This, particularly in the form of hiss, is a common complaint with inexperienced users of any sound system when you try to make recordings for yourself. Any recording system works well only when the volume of sound input is high enough. This is because all electronic circuits generate some noise, which is heard as a hiss when a recording is played back with the volume control set to a high level. Whatever you are recording should be at a high enough level to drown the hiss, so that the most obvious way to avoid hiss on playback is to make the recording at as high a level as is possible. Distortion will be caused if the recording level is too high, so you have to find a suitable level for yourself. Software which controls inputs will always provide an AGC action – this sets the volume control automatically so that the recording level is kept high enough to avoid hiss but low enough to avoid distortion.

Another source of unwanted noise is the use of unwanted inputs. If all the inputs to the sound board are connected, there may be interfering signals from the other inputs, and even if no connections are made there can be noise signals at these inputs. Use the *Mixer* software to ensure that only the wanted inputs are used. If your encounter hiss on sound that you have not recorded for yourself, use the *Treble Cut* control of your hardware to reduce this. On some games, sound was recorded using 8 bits only, and this sound will inevitably cause hiss which can only be reduced, not eliminated.

Noise will also be a problem if you are using too high a volume level on playback. This is particularly likely if you have several sets of volume controls. For example, if you have the master volume control on the mixer, the CD volume control on the mixer and the hardware volume control(s) on your sound card or active speakers all set to maximum, noise in the form of hiss is almost inevitable, and when you play sound it will be much too loud.

Chapter 6

Connections

Ports

Ports are used to carry out the interfacing actions that are needed to connect a PC to peripheral devices such as printers, scanners and cameras. At one time, ports were supplied as cards that were plugged into ISA slots, but all modern computers feature ports that are built into the main motherboard, sometimes attached through short lengths of cable to the connectors on the back of the computer casing. You need to add a card only if you want additional ports, and this is seldom necessary, though an additional parallel port can often be useful. The normal provision on a motherboard is one parallel port, two serial ports and two USB ports, and this is enough for many purposes unless you want to use devices (some scanners and removable hard drives) that require an additional parallel port.

● The current system of separate ports for different purposes is now being superseded by the use of USB (Universal Serial Bus) that uses the same connections for all, but currently motherboards still carry the traditional serial and parallel ports as well as providing for USB. In the UK, provision of USB devices is patchy, and if you want to use a printer or other device that you already possess, it makes more sense to use the well-established port system as well. I prefer to use USB only for devices that must use USB rather than for devices that have another form of connection available.

• Just to be clear about this, a port is not just a connector. It is the combination of connector, electronic circuits, memory and driver software that allows data to be transferred between the computer and other devices outside the casing. For example, the speed of transferring data is never as high as the speed of data on the bus, and the port has the task of controlling the rate of flow.

The parallel port

The older style of parallel port is often termed a *Centronics* port because its standardized format was due to the printer manufacturers Centronics who devised this form of port in the 1970s. The PC uses a 25-pin D-type female connector at the PC end of the cable and 36-pin Amphenol type at the printer end. This can be confusing, because the older serial port (COM1) connector on the PC is the 25-pin D-type male connector.

The original form of Centronics parallel port was intended for passing signals in one direction only, from a computer to a printer. Several designers made use of the unmodified system for bi-directional (two-way) signals by using the four signal lines that communicated in the reverse direction along with four data lines so as to get 4-bit bi-directional signalling. This in turn gave rise to a standardized system for allowing the use of the parallel port for 8-bit bi-directional signalling. This is the standard IEEE Std.1284-1994 system, and is otherwise known as the EPP (extended parallel port) system. A version of this, ECP (extended capability port) is now a standard fitting for PC machines.

The ECP system is used for modern printers to allow for better software control so that, for example, an inkjet printer can signal that it is running low on ink, or a laser printer can signal that it is running low on toner. The EPP system has been used for industrial applications as an interface between the computer and machines connected to the computer and controlled by it. Printers of recent manufacture also feature a USB connection (see later for details) as an alternative to the use of a parallel port.

The IEEE 1284 standard provides for high-speed signal transfer in both directions between the PC and an external peripheral. The speed of data can be 50 to 100 times faster than was possible using the older Centronics port, but the ECP connection on your PC is still fully compatible with older printers and other peripherals that use the parallel port. You can also use an ECP port (on the motherboard) along with an older Centronics port (on an ISA card) on the same PC.

The type of port is normally set up by using a (default) option in the CMOS ROM. The system offers five modes of operation, four of which maintain compatibility with older methods:

Mode 1	Data in forward direction only (out from computer), used for a normal Centronics printer connection.
Mode 2	Bi-directional action using four status lines for data in reverse direction along with four data lines in forward direction. This is also known as *Nibble* mode, and has also been used in cables for connecting two or three computers together in a simple network.
Mode 3	Hewlett-Packard *Bitronics* bi-directional mode, using data lines.
Mode 4	ECP (extended capability port) mode for printer and scanner use.
Mode 5	Fully bi-directional EPP (enhanced parallel port) mode used by some printers and also for computer peripherals such as external CD-ROM, hard drive, etc. The usual options in CMOS-RAM allow for an EPP/ECP setting which will cover both requirements.

The older bi-directional systems require software to implement each transfer, and this limits the transfer rate to, typically, 50 to 100 Kbytes per second. Modern PC machines have a port that can be used for ECP and EPP modes, and the I/O controller chip firmware allows for direct control of the port action with a greatly reduced external software overhead. A good comparison is the difference between a DMA transfer and one made by using the processor to read data and write to memory.

The 1284 standard also provides supporting methods (protocols) that allow the PC and its peripheral to agree on which mode to use. The standard also defines the cable and connector formats, with electrical signal specifications.

Having EPP/ECP capability on a computer does not guarantee that it will be used when you connect a printer to the port. The printer itself must be capable of operating (usually) in ECP mode, and the operating system must also be capable of using the ECP mode. Though an ECP port can operate in Centronics mode faster than the older type of parallel port, full ECP speed with a printer that can work in this mode requires the ECP port to be set up in the CMOS RAM, and an operating system that can use it. Windows 98, Windows *Me* and Windows XP can all make use of ECP, but older operating systems cannot.

If you are using ECP hardware under a modern version of Windows, you should check the Control Panel – System tab and locate the *Hardware Driver* panel. In the *Communication Ports* section, select *LPT1*, and click the *Properties* button. This should show the device as *ECP Printer Port (LPT1)*. If it appears simply as *Printer Port*, then it is not set up for ECP. The remedy is to remove this port, shut down and restart into CMOS RAM to ensure that the ECP mode is selected. This done, allow Windows plug and play to find the port and set it up with suitable software. Once the port is shown as an ECP port, all is well. If you have a second (LPT2) ordinary printer port you may have to remove it as well and reinstall as *non-plug & play hardware*.

● If you need to use EPP connections also, make sure that the CMOS RAM is set up for ECP+EPP, not just for ECP or EPP alone.

Connectors

The 1284 standard also defines the mechanical and electrical properties of a suitable connector. Though the DB25 female connector has become a *de facto* standard for the PC by way of Centronics use, there has been in the past no standardization of drivers, resistors, capacitors, etc. The IEEE 1284 system defines and standardizes these in a way that ensures compatibility with older equipment, allows for maximum data transfer rates with new equipment, and also allows the use of longer parallel data cables, up to 10 metres.

Three types of connectors can be used. One, type A, is the existing DB25 type updated to 1284 electrical standards. Type B and C are

36-pin connectors, of which the type C is the standard that is recommended for new designs. Type C is smaller than older 36-pin types, uses a simple clip as anchor, and permits the use of additional signals, *peripheral logic high* and *host logic high*. These additional signals are used to find if the devices at each end of the cable are switched on.

Figure 6.1 shows these connectors; the types A and B are the familiar DB25 and Centronics types that are currently used, but the type C connector is likely to appear on new equipment.

Figure 6.1   The connectors recommended for use with ECP/EPP ports. The type C connector is not yet established in the UK

Fitting an extra parallel port card

A parallel port, usually to IEEE 1284 standards, is normally part of the motherboard, and it will be automatically detected and set up when you first switch on the computer running Windows. You can, however, add other parallel ports on a card, but because modern parallel port cards are thin on the ground, you may find that the added port is of the older type.

The use of a modern port card plugging into a PCI slot is desirable because it will allow the computer to perform the setting-up actions (by plug and play), whereas an older type of parallel port card will almost certainly have a set of jumpers that requires you to make settings of quantities called *Address* and *Interrupt*.

The computer software refers to the parallel ports as LPT1, LPT2 and so on, and also to PRN, which normally means LPT1. When only one printer is fitted, it will use the LPT1 settings, which are:

Address   0378   Interrupt   IRQ7

When two printer ports are in use, these are referred to as LPT1 and LPT2, and the LPT2 port uses the settings of:

Address   0278   Interrupt   IRQ5

In the unlikely event of using three printer ports, the third port, LPT3, will use the address of 03BC and Interrupt IRQ5, with the LPT1 and LPT2 ports sharing IRQ7.

A typical conflict symptom is that a printer connected to LPT1 suddenly responds only to LPT2 when a second port is added, even if the ports have been set to the correct addresses. These conflicts can arise even with only two printer ports and diagnostic programs can be very helpful in pinpointing problems. You will also get a screen report on the port addresses and interrupts when you boot up the computer. The use of modern plug and play methods avoids all the problems that used to plague us when we added cards, but they will all return to haunt you if you use older cards or if you use MS-DOS or LINUX (or other non-Windows systems) in place of Windows.

Add-on units that make use of a parallel port are usually of the 'feed-through' variety, which means that the plug that engages with the printer socket carries a socket on its back. The printer can be plugged into this socket and used normally because the operating system can control the port so as to distinguish its dual uses. You should not attempt to stack several such add-ons, however.

Note that add-on EPP/ECP ports can be bought in card form and are available from suppliers such as *Global Direct*. You can specify ISA or PCI slot connections and prices range from around £15 for a single port suitable for a printer to around £60 for a high-speed parallel port intended for such purposes as external hard drives.

Serial ports

Serial ports are used for external modems and for linking PC computers together into simple networks. These ports send or receive one bit at a time, and at their simplest they need only a single connection (and earth return) between the devices that are connected. Serial ports are seldom quite so simple, however.

- The keyboard and mouse use serial ports, but these are dedicated types, meaning that you cannot use them for other devices. The serial ports we are dealing with here are the COM types used for connecting other peripherals.

The serial transfer of data makes use of only one line (plus a ground return) for data, with the data being transmitted one bit at a time at a strictly controlled rate. The standard system is known as RS-232, and it has been in use for a considerable time with machines such as teleprinters, so that a lot of features of RS-232 seem pointless when you are working with modern equipment.

When RS-232 was originally standardized, two types of device were used and were classed as Data Terminal Equipment (DTE) and as Data Communications Equipment (DCE). A DTE device can send out or receive serial signals, and is a terminal in the sense that the signals are not routed anywhere else. A DCE device is a halfway house for signals, like a modem (see later, this chapter) which converts serial data signals into tones for communication over telephone lines or converts received tones into digital signals.

The original concept of RS-232, long before computers became available, was that a DTE device would always be connected to a DCE device, but with the development of microcomputers and their associated printers it is now just as common to require to connect two DTE devices to each other, such as one computer to another computer. This means that the connections in the cable must be changed, as we shall see.

The original specification also stipulated that DTE equipment would use a male connector (plug) and the DCE equipment would use a female (socket), but you are likely to find either gender of connector on either type of device nowadays. The problem of how connectors are wired up is one that we'll come back to several times in this chapter. What started as a simple and standardized system has now grown into total confusion, and this sort of problem occurs all the way along the communications trail, not least in the use of words.

The original cable specification of RS-232 was for a connecting cable of 25 leads, as shown in the illustration of Figure 6.2. Many of these connections reflect the use of old-fashioned telephone equipment and teleprinters, and very few applications of RS-232 now make use of more than eight lines.

Figure 6.2   The old type of 25-pin RS-232 connector

The standard connector for PC machines is now the D-type 9 pin, illustrated in Figure 6.3, but even in this respect standards are widely ignored and some manufacturers use quite different connectors. Worse still, some equipment makes use of the full 25-pin system, but uses the 'spare' pins to carry other signals or even DC supply lines.

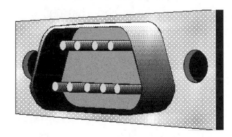

Figure 6.3   The standard 9-pin serial connector, now almost universal

If any cables that you need along with serial equipment are supplied along with the equipment you have a better chance of getting things working than if you try to marry up a new piece of equipment with a cable that has been taken from something else. The important point is that you cannot go into a shop and ask for an RS-232 cable, because like the canned foods, RS-232 cables exist in 57 varieties. When you need a cable, you must specify precisely what you want to connect with it.

The advantages of using serial connections, however, outweigh the problems, because when a modem is connected by the RS-232 cable to your computer you can use a simple single line (telephone or radio link), and distance is no problem – wherever you can telephone or send radio messages you can transfer computer data providing that both transmitter and receiver operated to the same standards. A huge variety of adapters (such as gender-changers) can be bought to ensure that your cable can be fitted to a socket that may not be of the correct variety, but this does not guarantee that the connections will be right.

- RS-232 serial links can be used up to their maximum speed of 115 000 bits per second, but no faster. If some day you are offered an Internet connection at a higher speed than this it will require a different form of serial interface. The proposed Internet connections through mobile phones will also need special connection arrangements (plus a healthy bank account).

All of this information may look academic, but the conclusion is practical enough. If you are going to join two computers that are in the same room or the same building and pass data between them, you need a serial cable which is described as non-modem, or DTE to DTE. If you are going to transfer data over telephone lines or radio links then you need a modem and a modem cable, or DTE to DCE cable. The good news is that if you use for your telephone line transfers the type of device that is referred to as an 'internal modem' you don't have to worry at all about this problem of using the correct cable. The differences are that the modem or DTE to DCE cable has corresponding pins connected, and the non-modem or null-modem type has several reversed connections.

- Nowadays, linking computers is usually done using dedicated network cables and ports, so that the standard type of serial ports are used only for an external modem or for a serial mouse, perhaps not at all. The expanding use of USB may eventually make the older types of serial port obsolete.

SETTING UP THE SERIAL PORT

Whatever you intend to connect to the serial port, you need to have at least one port available, and the usual provision on a modern motherboard is to have two serial ports, one using the 25-pin connector and the other using the 9-pin connector. Note that the 25-pin serial connector at the computer is a male type to distinguish it from the 25-pin female connector used for the parallel port of the PC.

- If, like many users, you have an internal modem with its own serial port (COM3), you are likely to use only one of the external ports for a serial mouse. If your mouse is of the PS/2 type, then you probably do not use the external serial ports for anything. Modern motherboards are usually provided with a PS/2 mouse port.

The serial ports are referred to as COM1, COM2 and so on, but the use of more than two serial ports on older motherboards was fraught with problems because a COM3 port, for example, had to share the IRQ4 interrupt signal with the COM1 port. This is not a problem for modern motherboards, and it's quite normal for an internal modem to use its own COM3 port without interfering with the actions of the COM1 and COM2 ports.

The Universal Serial Bus (USB)

The essential simplicity of serial connections for linking a computer to a peripheral has spurred designers into looking for something better than the old telecommunications serial ports that belong to the pre-computer age. What we need is a type of serial port that can be used for all the normal computer connections, and which can be connected in a 'daisy-chain' type of network with each device connected to another with only one of them needing to be connected directly to the computer.

The answer to this is called the Universal Serial Bus (USB). It has been designed to be *hot-plugged*, meaning that devices can be connected and disconnected with the computer switched on and working. This is possible only if the system is supported by the computer, the peripheral device and the operating system. At the time of writing, USB 1.1 is fitted to motherboards, but is being superseded by USB-2.

USB 1.1 permits communications between devices that are equipped with suitable interfaces at serial data rates ranging from 1.5 Mbits/s to 1.5 Mbytes/s. This is very much faster than the old-style serial port system. The interconnecting cable can have a maximum length of 5 metres and consists of two twisted pair cables, one pair for power and the other for signalling. The distance can be extended to about 30 metres by using a *hub* terminal device as a line repeater.

Terminal devices, such as keyboard, mouse and printer, are added to the basic PC in a daisy-chain fashion and each is identified by using a 7-bit address code. This allows up to 127 devices, in theory at least, to be connected. In practice, not all devices allow daisy-chain connection (picture a mouse with two tails!), and so the computer needs more than one USB connector (Figure 6.4).

● Other terminal devices can include scanners, fax machines, telephone and ISDN lines, multimedia display and recording systems and even industrial data acquisition devices.

New computers generally provide for at least two USB sockets, and many machines provide four or more. Few of the peripherals that are at present fitted with USB sockets have additional sockets that allow another device to be daisy-chained on. The exception to this is that most new keyboards for USB have a mouse connector available. Add-on USB hubs are being used to allow the connection of more peripherals. Figure 6.4 shows the two main types of USB connector, one used on the computer and the other used on the peripherals.

Figure 6.4   The two main types of USB connectors

You should ensure that your motherboard has USB provision, but do not be in any hurry to make too much use of the system. For one thing, your printer, keyboard and mouse probably use the older type of connections, and if you don't need to change them, why do so? The other point is that until USB is part of everything that can be connected you cannot be sure that everything will work together well. When you are building for yourself it's not a good idea to be a pioneer. Problems reported to date include conflicts that can lead, for example, to a USB Webcam switching on and taking pictures whenever a document was sent to the USB printer. Other users have reported that the order of switching on devices that use USB can be critical.

USB-2

USB-2 is a comparatively new standard that represents a considerable enhancement of the older USB 1.1. The original USB 1.1 allowed for transmission at 12 Mbits/s, whereas USB-2 will run up to a maximum of 480 Mbits/s, some 40 times faster. USB-2 uses the same connectors as the older standard, and for many applications can use the same cables. This very much higher speed allows USB-2 to be used for the same type of data transfer applications as Firewire, and the first set of applications seem likely to be video cameras, scanners, external hard drives and external CD-ROM drives including CD-R/RW.

Quite a lot of thought has gone into maintaining compatibility with the older standard, so that if you have any equipment that runs using USB 1.1, it will continue to be fully operative when you change over to USB-2. The big difference is that you can also plug in the new faster USB-2 devices as well. As for USB 1.1, you can insert or remove the USB-2 plugs with the machine switched on (*hot plugging*), and you can (in theory at least) connect up to 127 devices to the computer.

At the time of writing, motherboards with USB-2 built in were rather thin on the ground, but add-in cards to link the PCI bus to USB-2 ports are readily available. There is a UK source for such cards, it is:

> Belkin Components Ltd
> Round Spinney
> Northampton NN3 8RX
> Tel: (01604) 678300

but by the time this book is in print, such cards should also be available from all the usual sources of computer components.

- Chapter 11 illustrates the use of USB connections for a digital camera.

Mouse and keyboard ports

A mouse port is more specialized type of serial port that is used only for the mouse or its equivalent trackball or graphics digitizer, and when you construct your own machine you can opt for a motherboard with a PS/2 mouse port, or one that can use the serial port for the mouse. What you choose depends very much on whether you have a mouse at present, because it makes sense to use the type of connection that your mouse already uses.

- You can buy converter cables, PS/2 to serial or serial to PS/2, if you want to change the mouse connections. If you have to buy a new mouse to fit more than one computer, then it's better to opt for a serial mouse because most computers have at least one serial port available, but you cannot be certain that a PS/2 port will be available on an older machine.
- The keyboard port is permanently fitted to the motherboard and is not available as a separate card. If a USB keyboard is used then any USB mouse can be plugged to it.

A games port is often included as part of a sound card. There is no standard for such games ports, and no two seem to be identical in pinout. The connections to the port refer to buttons and positions for connection to a joystick. Since a PC machine is intended for serious computing uses rather than games, the games port can be disabled.

Firewire (IEEE 1394-1995)

Firewire is a trademark of Apple Computers Inc. who, during 1988, originally designed and established this type of serial signalling system as the basis for a very fast, low cost and easy to use network for digital audio signals. The system has been developed and standardized by the Institution of Electrical and Electronics Engineers (IEEE) in the USA and is now well suited to be used as an interface for fast computer systems. Since 1995 the network has become an established IEEE standard which is supported by a worldwide trade organization of more than ninety manufacturers and constructors.

Firewire allows any device equipped with a suitable interface to be simply coupled to the computer to form a fast communication system. This flexibility now allows, for example, the home PC, the television receiver and telephone systems to be connected. Because Firewire allows hot plugging (you can add or remove connections with the computer switched on) it makes interconnections very quick and simple for the non-technical user.

Any devices that are fitted with the appropriate interface can be coupled together through any one of a number of ports using a simple cable without any consideration for the order in which the devices appear on the network. The services currently available to this network include home video editing, security monitoring, photo-CD handling, image enhancement, video- and teleconferencing, plus professional broadcast and industrial applications. Note that these are the applications that need faster transfer of bytes than can be achieved using USB 1.1, but it is possible that USB-2 will replace Firewire for these applications.

Firewire terminal devices may be fitted with single input and multiple output port interfaces which can be coupled together through a special cable unit. Any new device can be added to the network by simply plugging into a spare port anywhere on the network. The devices may be coupled in a mix of clusters or stars or the daisy-chain format, the only restrictions being that there should be no more than 16 hops between any two nodes and without any loops being formed. The maximum length with no repeaters is about 10 metres, but 4.5 metre lengths are more common.

The most important feature of Firewire is its simplicity, at least as far as the domestic user is concerned. Any new device may be plugged into a spare port without switching the power off and the system then dynamically reconfigures itself to suit the new situation without the need to reset any switches or jumpers.

The most significant feature of Firewire, as far as computer users are concerned, is its ability to move data that is in packet form at very high speed. This makes it very suitable for working with MPEG TV signals. Until the introduction of digital television, the Firewire system was virtually unknown to domestic users. Now, however, Firewire connectable digital video cameras, television receivers and the later versions of CD and DVD players are appearing in the domestic entertainment market place.

At the time of writing, computer motherboard designers appear to be ignoring Firewire in favour of new and faster USB systems.

Firewire add-on boards are now available at very much lower prices than they were a few years ago. Digital camcorders with Firewire sockets sold in Europe have the input function disabled so that editing cannot be carried out on the camera tape. Still pictures can, however, be downloaded and edited for printing. Details of how to restore the two-way action of such systems can be found on the Internet, but carrying out such changes may invalidate a warranty.

SCSI boards

The Small-Computer Systems Interface (SCSI) is a connecting system that has been around for a considerable time, certainly for as long as hard drives have existed. SCSI is fast, and it allows a large number of devices to be connected together. In that respect it resembles Firewire, but with the difference that a SCSI cable uses a large number of strands, and that hot plugging is not permitted. Each device that is connected in a SCSI chain has an identification number that is used to ensure that the data is correctly routed.

Unless you just happen to have a number (more than four) of large and fast SCSI hard drives that you want to use, SCSI is not a system that you should attempt to fit into a machine you are building for yourself. The interface card can be expensive to start with, and you need a thorough understanding of the system if you are to avoid problems.

You cannot connect EIDE hard drives to a SCSI interface, and SCSI hard drives are always more expensive than their EIDE counterparts. Now that the EIDE cards can be obtained plugged into a PCI slot, providing additional hard drive cables, there seems very little reason for the home computer user to have a SCSI interface.

Chapter 7

Connecting it all up

The essential bits

The essential main bits of a working PC are the casing (with its power supply), the motherboard, graphics card and the disk drives. To check that a machine is working you also need a monitor, keyboard and mouse, but since these are bought ready-made and can outlast several computers we do not count them or the printer as part of a DIY project. If you have followed everything up to this stage you will have decided on what suits you best, and invested in the case, motherboard, processor, memory, graphics card and drives.

- Heed the warning, earlier, and do not attempt to convert a TV receiver into a monitor, or convert an old monitor into something suited to a modern PC, unless you have considerable experience of working on TV equipment, along with information in the form of circuit diagrams, advice, etc.
- Even with all the hardware present, the computer is unusable until the software of an operating system has been installed. This cannot be done from CDs described as *upgrades* unless you already have an operating system on your hard drive or can install one. For example, you cannot use the Windows *Me* Upgrade CD unless

you currently have Windows 95, Windows 98 or Windows 3.1 on your computer. You cannot upgrade from Windows 3.1 directly to Windows XP.

With all the essential bits in hand you can connect up a working PC machine in under an hour, though it will not necessarily do everything that you want. From that stage, however, you can add other facilities by plugging in expansion boards or cards to extend the capabilities of the machine. You can also plug in additional DIMM memory units, because whatever you do with a machine is likely to require more memory sooner or later unless you start with as much memory as the motherboard can take. At the time of writing, memory is not expensive but don't buy until you really need to.

- Start by making a checklist, so that you do not forget minor items such as fasteners and cables. Fasteners are easily lost and overlooked, and you cannot simply pop down to the local DIY shop to replace them because they are not a stock item.

Motherboard preparation

Before you can consider starting assembly, the motherboard needs to be inspected carefully, and you also need to read the manual or other documents that accompany it. Apart from anything else, you need to be absolutely certain that your motherboard will accept the type and speed of processor you intend to place into it. If there is no form of documentation, contact the suppliers of the motherboard because you *cannot* assume that you will be able to find the correct connections or to make the correct settings by instinct or by comparing it with an older motherboard. Some motherboards need no adjustments – they can sense the processor you are using and make the settings using software. Nevertheless, the more information you have on everything, the better placed you are to detect something that is not quite right. Manufacturers' websites are useful, but only if you have access to them while you are building the computer, and that means using a spare computer.

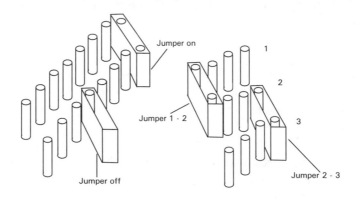

Figure 7.1   Typical jumpers

Jumpers (Figure 7.1) are used on many motherboards and, particularly the older types, to switch actions in or out, or to allow for options. Each jumper unit normally consists of a row of three small pins with a bridging clip, the jumper itself, which can be placed over two pins to provide two settings (sometimes three settings if the design provides for the jumper to be removed altogether). Jumper settings should be correct if you have bought a bare-bones system with the motherboard already installed in its case, and very often there is little chance of altering jumpers once the machine is fully assembled. Many types of motherboard designs now are self-adjusting or set by software, so that no jumpers are provided.

When you have read all the information on the motherboard and made notes about anything you need to watch out for, unpack the motherboard. The final wrapping will be of a material that is slightly electrically conducting, and when you take the motherboard out of this material you should lay the board down on this sheet of material to make an inspection. Touch the motherboard only at the edges at this stage, and try to keep your hands away from the metallic connections as far as possible at all times.

You will need to check any jumper settings very carefully again before you place the new motherboard into the case. The small (and usually anonymous) manual or leaflet that comes with the motherboard will list the jumper settings, and these are often preset correctly, particularly if you have specified the type of processor chip you will be using. If they are not, it is not always clear what settings you ought to use, and you may need to enquire from the supplier of the board.

● Make a sketch for yourself on a larger scale of the way the jumpers are set. This makes it easier to check before, during and after installation.

Another problem is that manuals usually show the pins numbered, but this numbering is not necessarily printed on the motherboard or, if it is printed, it is obscured by chips or other resident obstacles. The description that follows is of jumpers on a recent Socket-A board. This is fairly typical of modern practice on older Socket-A boards, and most boards that you are likely to come across will provide for a similar list of jumpers. Many motherboards, however, are jumperless.

TYPICAL JUMPERS

● If you have to alter jumpers on a board that is already in place, you must always switch off the computer and allow a few minutes for voltages to decay to zero before you attempt to change jumpers. Always check jumper settings after you have made a change.

One jumper is used to control CMOS RAM, and its default position keeps the CMOS RAM cleared of any data. This will have to be reset to the working position before the motherboard is installed. Another jumper sets the voltage supply for DIMM memory, usually to 3.3 V, with the alternative, seldom needed, of 5 V.

Some boards have a jumper termed the Function jumper, and if this is used its settings are important. Typically these will allow three options labelled Normal, Configure and Recovery. In the *Normal* configuration, the BIOS uses the current CMOS-RAM settings (see later) for booting. In the *Configure* setting, the BIOS set-up will run and the screen will display a maintenance menu (this corresponds to the use of keys to activate the CMOS-RAM display). The *Recovery* option can be used only if you have inserted a floppy containing BIOS information and this data will be read and used.

A very important set of jumpers deals with CPU type and voltage. One jumper setting is for Pentium type, either P54C (dual voltage) or P55C (single voltage) types. Another set of jumpers will set the

CPU (core) voltage to the required voltage within the set 2.5 V, 2.8 V, 2.9 V, 3.2 V, 3.3 V or 3.5 V. You need to set the jumpers for the type of chip and the exact voltage that your CPU chip needs.

That's easier said than done. Motherboard manuals are not always up to date, and a chip is often supplied with little or no data. A good rule is that the faster chips use lower voltages, so that if you are going to use a chip that runs at 800 MHz or more it is likely to use the lower range of voltage settings. In particular, if the chip is of the old MMX type it is likely to run at 2.8 volts, though some motherboards insist on using 3.2 volts. The sure sign of using too high a voltage is that Windows will not run correctly and even some DOS commands (like DIR) will not run correctly. If reducing the core voltage restores normal operation, you can be certain that the higher voltage setting is incorrect, whatever the documentation states.

The next important settings are the internal clock speed jumpers which are set for the type of processor you are using. The settings are usually graded as 1.5×/3.5×, 2.0×, 2.5× and 3.0, and the usual default is 2.0×. You will need to check the manual for the motherboard and any leaflets that come with the processor to know how to set this. Several modern motherboards can make this setting automatically by sensing the type of CPU that is inserted, and some jumper settings work differently with different processors. These internal speed jumpers allow you to overclock the CPU, and some CPUs (such as the later Celerons) will totally ignore the settings.

The other clock setting is labelled *External clock* and typically allows for bus speeds of 60 MHz, 66 MHz, 75 MHz, 83 MHz and 100 MHz, often higher speeds also. The 66 MHz speed is the usual default for the slower old-style chips, and 100 MHz is used for the newer, faster chips, including AMD Duron, with 133 MHz or 266 MHz used for the faster Athlon and Pentium types. You will, once again, need to check carefully to find if you need to use a different speed.

- Remember that if you are using a 100 MHz (or faster) bus speed that your memory chips need to be of the faster type. This setting is sometimes referred to as the FSB (front-side bus) speed. Motherboards for the faster Athlon and Pentium chips will need to provide a 133 MHz (or more) bus speed, and must use memory that is capable of operating at this speed. This speed capability extends to the other supporting chips, but if the motherboard can use 133 MHz it's almost certain that the chips that come on the motherboard can also.

- Note that the motherboard design fixes the maximum speed of CPU that you can use. If your present requirements are for a comparatively slow chip it makes a lot of sense to spend a few pounds more on the motherboard that can be used with a chip running at double the speed you actually require. This makes it very much easier to upgrade your system when you need more speed.
- Raising the *External clock* speed is one way of making a chip work faster than the maker has intended, but you must not experiment unless you are prepared to lose your CPU. Some users have reported that this *overclocking* can be done safely on some chips, but it's on your own head if you do so and burn out the CPU. You also have to be certain that other chips on the motherboard will accept the higher rate. Check Internet sites such as:

http://arstechnika.com/paedia/celeron_oc_faq.html

http://www.sysopt.com/howtooc.html

http://www.speedguide.net/overclocking/overclocking.htm

before you make any attempts to overclock a chip.

Take your time, enquire if necessary, and do not install the motherboard into the case until you are totally satisfied that the jumper settings are correct. A familiar problem is that the documentation may tell you that the setting you want is to jumper pins 1 and 2, but there is no pin numbering on the motherboard. If you come across this problem, you will often find that you can deduce pin numbers by looking at other settings which you are fairly sure have been correctly preset. You may find, for example, that pin 1 is the pin closest to the end of the motherboard that contains the expansion slots.

Once the jumper settings have been dealt with and double-checked, you can install the CPU, unless this has already been done by the supplier. Normally, if you buy a board and a CPU by mail order, the CPU will have been inserted and the jumpers set, except for the CMOS-RAM jumper. If you buy the motherboard and processor separately (at a computer fair, for example), you will have to insert the CPU for yourself and also check that the jumper settings are correct.

● See later for details of setting up a chip using a jumperless motherboard. This has to be done after the chip has been installed on the motherboard.

SOCKET INSERTION

The procedure for inserting a CPU into a socket is much the same for the main types of sockets (Socket-A, Socket-370, Socket-478) and the following description is for a Socket-A CPU. Before inserting the CPU check that it is the type you ordered. Note which corner has a pin missing, a notch and a white dot, because this locates which way round the chip will fit in the socket. Take a close look also at the heatsink. This usually comes with a paper cover over the flat surface that is clamped against the top of the chip. Do not peel this paper away until you are going to place the heatsink over the chip, because it covers the heatsink compound that helps transfer heat from the chip to the heatsink. If this is exposed to the air for some time it will no longer transfer heat so efficiently.

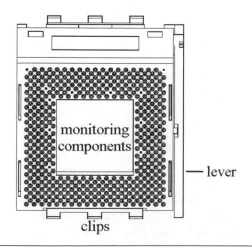

Figure 7.2   The view over an empty Socket-A holder

Pull the lever away from the body of the Socket-A on the motherboard and then pull it upwards (Figure 7.2). A CPU for Socket-A has a pair of notched corners where there is no hole for a pin (Figure 7.3) and you have to insert the chip so that it drops the socket into place with the corresponding positions aligned. In this way, the CPU should easily drop into place – any resistance probably indicates that it is the wrong way round. Once the CPU chip has been dropped in you can replace the lever so that the chip is then locked in place.

You can then fit the heatsink and cooling fan (Figure 7.4). This item clips over the top of the chip, and the clips are very strong because they have to keep the fan in very close contact with the chip. You will need to support the motherboard to avoid excessive flexing when you press down the clips on the fan, and the best way to do this is to lay the motherboard down flat on the conductive plastic that was used in transport, and press the heatsink and fan unit down until the clips can be homed.

Figure 7.3   The socket and the chip (pins up) showing the corresponding points. Photo courtesy of AMD, Inc.

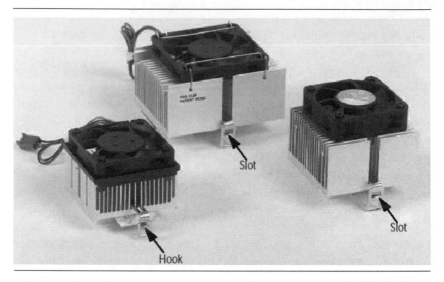

Figure 7.4   Typical heatsink and fan assemblies for Socket-A use, photo courtesy of AMD Inc.

MEMORY

Following these settings of jumpers, if applicable, and CPU insertion you will need to install memory, and on all modern motherboards this is usually done using DIMMs. A DIMM uses 168 pins, and is inserted directly into its slot and clipped in place – the older SIMMs had to be inserted and then turned to lock them in place.

- By this time you will have sorted out which of the many varieties of memory chips your motherboard can use and bought the appropriate type.

Connections are made to the DIMM just as they are to expansion cards, using an edge connector, and a set of tiny metal tongues on the card which engage in springs on the holder (Figure 7.5). The DIMM is clipped in by spring-loaded holders at each end. Nowadays DIMMs come in sizes from 32 Mbytes to 256 Mbytes, and you currently can use a DIMM singly, so that you could use a single 128 Mbyte DIMM for this amount of memory, allowing you to expand your memory later as required.

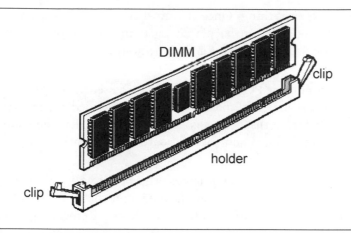

Figure 7.5   Fitting a DIMM memory board into its holder. The clips at each end are pushed inwards to complete the insertion

Currently you should not put more than 512 Mbytes total into the motherboard (which usually takes 128 Mbytes or more) unless you are certain that your operating system will cope with a memory of more than 512 Mbytes. For Windows 95 or earlier, the limit is 64 Mbytes, but if you are using Windows 98, Windows *Me* or Windows XP you can use (and are likely to need) up to 512 Mbytes. A RAM size of 256 Mbytes has become almost standard for the more expensive machines now on offer.

DIMM units come in several types, and there are two notches in each DIMM board that must match with the socket to ensure that only the correct type of DIMM will fit. One notch determines voltage supply (3.3 V, 5.0 V or reserved); the other is marked *Unbuffered*, *Buffered* or *Reserved*. The reserved positions are likely to be used if or when new varieties of DIMM boards are manufactured.

MOTHERBOARD INSERTION

Once the CPU and memory units have been inserted, the mother-board can be mounted into the casing, but don't rush into this task. Take a close look at how the motherboard will be mounted into the base of the casing. Many modern case designs allow a complete 'pan', a metal base sheet, to be removed. The motherboard is then mounted on this pan, so that you do not need to fumble your way past other units to reach everything. Once the motherboard has been mounted on the pan, the pan can be placed back into the case. If you can remove the motherboard pan for fitting, do so.

● Metal cases for the PC have their locating fasteners located in standardized positions, and motherboards are provided with matching location holes, so that it is very unusual to find that there are any problems in fitting a new motherboard into a new case.

Do *not* expect, however, that a new motherboard will have exactly as many mounting holes as there are fasteners on the casing, or that all of the mounting holes will be in the same places. Remember, though, that a motherboard should *never* be drilled because the connecting tracks on the surface are not necessarily the only tracks that exist; most boards are laminated with tracks between layers. Drilling through any of these tracks would be a very expensive mistake. It is possible that you cannot make use of all the pillars that come with the casing, but you should certainly be able to use as many as the motherboard provides holes for. Remember that at least one pillar must be a metal one that makes good electrical contact to both the casing and the motherboard.

The fitting methods vary, but the most popular systems use either a brass pillar at each fixing position or a single brass pillar with plastic clips at other positions (Figure 7.6). The brass connectors are screwed into threaded holes in the case and the motherboard is bolted in turn to the pillars; the plastic clips that fit into slots in the case are pushed into the holes in the motherboard and then slotted in place.

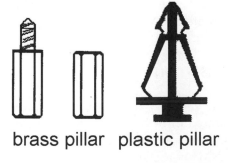

brass pillar plastic pillar

Figure 7.6   The shape of brass and plastic motherboard fastenings

There must be at least one brass pillar fixing that is used to earth the motherboard electrically to the casing. Quite often, only two screwed fittings are used, with the rest being either clips or simply resting points. The motherboard must be well supported under the slots, because this is where pressure is exerted on it when cards are plugged in. If there are no supporting pillars in this region you may be able to get hold of polypropylene pillars of the correct size and glue them to the floor of the casing – do not under any circumstances glue anything to the motherboard itself.

When you have the motherboard in place, check everything again. You may find, for example, that you have put pillars upside down, resulting in the motherboard being too high to match up with the holes in the back of the case, or that some expansion slots do not line up correctly. It is much easier to make changes at this stage than after you have thoroughly fastened the motherboard into place. In particular, some of the plastic pillars can be quite difficult to remove once they have been put in.

- Before you tighten up the fastenings on the motherboard, check that you can insert an expansion card and fasten it to the top of the casing. A surprising number of motherboards and casings do not fit particularly well, and make it very difficult to fit and clamp expansion cards. If there are going to be difficulties, it's better to file out the fastenings for the expansion cards rather than alter the mountings of the motherboard.

If jumpers have been set on the motherboard, remember that it is remarkably easy to plug in jumpers with only one pin making contact, for example, and when you come to make other plug and socket connections this is also a hazard to look out for. If the paperwork that came with the motherboard did not have a sketch of the motherboard, this is the time to make one for yourself that shows where the board is mounted and where the jumpers are. Remember that it is often very difficult to alter jumpers once a motherboard has been fitted in place, particularly if the jumpers are underneath the power supply box.

Once the motherboard has been fastened into place, you can fit the PSU cable connectors (Figure 7.7) supporting the motherboard with a finger underneath if necessary because you may have to use a fair bit of force to insert the plug. The thick and stiff set of cables from the

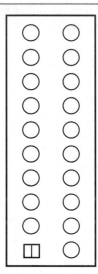

Figure 7.7   The 20-pin connector type used for the power socket on an ATX board

PSU makes this task of fitting more difficult than you might expect. The pin connections for the PSU connector are listed below.

Pin	Use	Pin	Use
1	3.3 V DC	11	3.3 V DC
2	3.3 V DC	12	−12 V DC
3	Earth	13	Earth
4	+5 V DC	14	Power on
5	Earth	15	Earth
6	+5 V DC	16	Earth
7	Earth	17	Earth
8	Power OK	18	−5 V DC
9	5 VSB	19	+5 V DC
10	+12 V DC	20	+5 V DC

Note: The 5 VSB line is a standby supply which should be capable of operating with a 10-mA load.

SWITCHES AND INDICATORS

With the motherboard now in place inside the case, the next step is
to fasten the set of leads for switches and indicators that come from
the front end of the case and are plugged into two rows of pins on the
motherboard. This set includes connections for the small loudspeaker
that is fastened inside the casing.

The leads are colour-coded and also usually labelled, though you
may need to use some intuition to match the name on a cable with
the name that is used on the motherboard description. Figure 7.8
shows a typical arrangement of two lines of pins at the front end of
the motherboard, with the names that are used on the motherboard
documentation. Some of these connectors might not be used, but
others are essential.

Looking at the example in order, the *Suspend* leads must be
connected, otherwise the computer cannot be switched on. These
leads come from the on/off switch, and their connection to the motherboard allows the computer to be put into standby mode and
switched on by the main switch, or by selected events like pressing a
key, moving the mouse, or getting an e-mail (if you have a permanent
Internet connection).

The *Hard drive LED* connections are needed to ensure that the LED
indicator on the front panel will light when the main hard drive (the
boot drive) is working. The *Power LED* similarly indicates that the
computer is fully operative, not on standby.

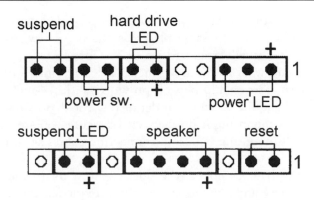

Figure 7.8   Switch and indicator connections to the motherboard

The *Suspend LED* indicates when the computer is on standby, and this LED may not be provided on some cases, so that there will be no leads to connect. The loudspeaker leads should always be used so that you can hear the welcome beep that indicates the machine is booting up correctly. Finally, the *Reset* pins allow the Reset pushbutton on the front panel to act.

The thin strands of cable from the case connect to these pins using tiny clips, and you might find it easier to use tweezers to hold the clips and insert them. Note from your documentation of the motherboard where the connections need to be correctly led to a pin marked +; in general, switch connections can be either way round, but LED connections must be correctly oriented, and it isn't always clear which strand of a cable pair is + and which is –.

ADDING DRIVES

We need to look at the installation of a hard drive first, because on a flip-lid casing it is normal to keep the hard drive in the lowest of the drive bays of a set, making it inaccessible once the floppy drive has been fitted. The tower type of casing sometimes provides a bay at the back of the case for the main (or only) hard drive, making this easier to get to without removing anything else. Modern tower casings often group all the 3½-inch bays together, with one set up for a floppy drive (Figure 7.9). It's difficult to make any hard and fast rules here, because casing designs can vary quite amazingly from one example to another.

Do not assume that a drive will be provided with mounting brackets at exactly the same places as the drive bay, though these positions are usually standard on PC clones. An adapter will be needed if you want to put a 3½-inch hard drive into a 5¼-inch bay, but modern cases should be well provided with 3½-inch drive bays. You should enquire when you order or buy the drive what provisions are made for mounting it on the style of casing you are using. Make sure that all mounting bolts and connecting cables are supplied with the drive.

The drive bay has slots at the sides to allow for to and fro adjustment of a drive and two sets are usually provided at different heights in the bay. These should fit the hard drive in a 3½-inch bay without any problems and also fit a 5¼-inch bay using an adapter plate. Hard

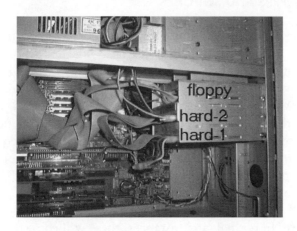

Figure 7.9   Typical drive bays in a casing

drives must be mounted to the bay or the adapter plate by way of small bolts fitting into their threaded mounting pads. This is important because these pads act to cushion the drive against shock. Any drive that has external access should be adjusted so that its front panel is flush with the front panel of the casing.

Under no circumstances should you ever consider drilling the casing of a hard drive in order to mount it in any other way. You should also handle a hard drive by its casing, not holding its weight on any other points. In particular, avoid handling the connector strips at the rear of the drive or any of the exposed electronic circuits. Read any documents that come with the hard drive to find if there are any prohibitions on the use of mounting holes – sometimes you are instructed to use only the outer set of holes.

The 3½-inch drives use underside mountings as well as side mountings, which makes it easier to attach them if the side fastenings are difficult to reach. If you have problems, which is nowadays unusual, Meccano brackets and strips can usually ensure that you get the drive unit firmly fastened. In a desperate situation, there is nothing wrong with fastening the drive to a metal plate and sticking this to the casing with self-adhesive foam pads. Maplin supply very useful side plates for fitting a 3½-inch drive into a 5¼-inch bay.

DRIVE JUMPERS AND SWITCHES

The simplest possible installation of a hard drive is fitting the first hard drive in a machine which has only one floppy drive; or the replacement of an existing hard drive with an identical type. You will, however, encounter more difficulties when software has to be installed. Mechanical complications arise only when a second (or further) hard drive is being installed, or when there are uncertainties about the compatibility of parts. The methods that are required vary according to the type of drive that is being fitted, and in this book we shall concentrate on the modern type of EIDE/ATA UDMA drive which is standard on modern PC machines.

An EIDE hard drive can be installed as a first (master) or a second (slave) drive. In normal circumstances, these will correspond to drive letters C and D respectively. The complication here is that these letters, known as logic drive letters, are assigned by the computer automatically, with both A and B reserved for use with the floppy drive(s), whether you have one or two floppy drives. The first hard disk will be assigned with the letter C, and other drives, such as CD-ROM, with letters D onwards. If you have two hard drives, these will be assigned as C and D, and your CD-ROM will then be drive E. This assignment is carried out when you first switch on after installing the drives.

- This automatic allocation system also works for partitioned drives. For example, you can install a 40 Gbyte drive and partition it, using FDISK or other suitable software (see later) into two 20 Gbyte sections. One of these will be assigned as C and the other as D. This partitioning is essential if the operating system cannot deal with partitions of more than 32 Mbytes.

Rather than talking about drive numbers or letters, it is preferable at this stage to talk about first and second hard drives. Some manuals will refer to these as hard drives 0 and 1, or 1 and 2. When you install a single EIDE drive on a machine, it should be configured as the *master* or *only* hard drive. This means that jumper or switch settings have to be made to ensure that the hard disk signals are taken from the correct point in the computer, so that the operating system can make use of the disk.

In technical terms, this is done by selecting the correct BIOS address number and the correct port address range on the controller board. The settings are made by way of jumpers or DIP-switches. For a first hard drive, these settings are almost always ready-made for you, and you need only check them. For a second hard drive, alterations will have to be made unless the suppliers have done them for you. On a modern drive, this usually amounts to a single switch setting.

The main complication can arise if you are fitting a second hard drive in a machine which has previously used a single hard drive. You will need to alter jumper settings so as to configure the second drive as a *slave* of a pair of drives. On *older* drives, you will also need to take out the first hard drive (if it is already fitted) and configure this as the *master* drive of two. You will also need a data cable that has two hard drive connectors and which is long enough to reach drives that may be some distance apart. The documentation accompanying an EIDE drive is often very sparse, no more than a sheet of paper. Using modern drives, you do not normally have to alter jumpers on the master drive, only on the slave (Figure 7.10).

• Using more than one hard drive can be very useful. For example, my operating system is on the C: drive, and everything else is on the D: drive. If I am trying out a new operating system and have serious problems, I can reformat the C: drive and start again without losing the contents of the other drives. Certain files, like e-mail contacts and favourites lists, need to be backed up on the D: drive.

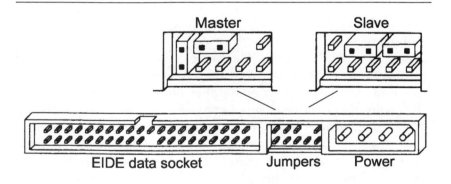

Figure 7.10   Typical hard drive jumper settings

If you are installing a second EIDE drive in an existing computer, try to use a drive from the same manufacturer as the first drive, and cables to match. This will help to avoid any problems of incompatibility. If this is not possible, enquire of the suppliers to check that the new drive you intend to fit will be compatible with the first type. This is normally not a problem with modern drive types, but some makes of drive in the past have been notoriously temperamental in this respect.

- Using modern drives, you have less to worry about, as long as the drive is set correctly as master or slave.
- If you want to use more than two hard drives you can add another drive on the Secondary IDE connector, with the CD-ROM as master and the added drive as slave. For a larger number of hard drives, your options are either to add another EIDE card fitting into a PCI slot, or to fit external drives that are connected either to the parallel port or by USB.

Drive installation

Before you start, check the drive package to make sure you have all of the mounting bolts, any adapter that is needed, cables (if not already on the computer) and instructions. Check that you have the necessary tools – a Phillips screwdriver (possibly a plain-head type) and a pair of tweezers are usually needed.

The bolts are usually either 6-32 UNC $\times$ 0.31 (5/16″) or metric M4 $\times$ 0.7-6H, but some drives use M3 $\times$ 0.5. UK suppliers use millimetre sizing for the length so that the size will show 5 rather than 0.5 or 6 in place of 0.6. The frame of the drive may be stamped with M for metric or S for UNC. If you need spare UNC bolts you will need to contact a specialist supplier, but the M4 metric types can be bought from electronics suppliers such as the well-known Maplin or RS Components.

At this stage, check that any jumpers or switches are correctly set. Once the drive is in place these will be impossible to reach. Use tweezers to manipulate these devices. It is not always obvious from the accompanying instruction what settings are needed, and though drives are often set ready for use in a standard type of machine you cannot rely on this. Jumpers will quite certainly need to be set if you intend to use more than one hard drive.

Unpack the drive carefully and read any accompanying manual carefully, particularly to check any prohibitions on drive fastening or mounting positions. Make a careful noted of any settings that are printed on to the disk casing, because these will be needed in the event of the settings not being automatically recognized. No drive should ever be mounted with its front panel facing down, but most drives can be placed flat, or on either side. Check that any adapter plate fits into the mounting bay on the casing and that all bolts and cable adapters (see later) are provided.

The hard drive is usually placed as the lowest in a set of drives on a desktop casing, and in a position nearest to the motherboard in a tower casing. Check also that the drive data cable will reach from the EIDE connector on the motherboard to the drive – you may need to put the IDE board in a different slot if the cable is short (as they often are).

- You may need to juggle with positions of hard drives if you are using more than one, because your first hard drive (C:) will have to be connected using the plug at the end of the IDE cable, and your second hard drive on the plug that is a few inches further down the cable. If the cable is rather short, as they often are, you may need to place the hard drives so as to suit the cable, rather than placing them where you would most like to have them. It's a lot easier to check out these positions before you secure the drives into place than after.

Fasten the 3½-inch drive to its bay or adapter, using the small bolts that are provided to bolt into the mounting pads. Tighten these up evenly and not excessively. If an adapter is used, bolt this into its bay. Check that you can still place a floppy drive above the hard drive unit, if this is where it will be put. This latter point is important, because some floppy drives have an exposed flywheel on the underside, and the slightest contact against this flywheel will prevent the floppy drive motor from spinning. There should be no such problems if the 3½-inch floppy drive is being mounted sideways in a bay specially provided for this purpose, because such a bay is usually well clear of any others.

Installation is not a particularly skilled operation, though experience with a Meccano set as a child is helpful. Problems arise only if the mounting pads on the drive do not correspond with openings in the bay, or you have no adapter for a 3½-inch drive, or an unsuitable adapter, or you manage to lose a mounting bolt. A mounting bolt that falls inside the drive casing or the computer casing can usually be shaken out or picked out with tweezers. Do *not* use a magnet to retrieve a bolt from a disk drive casing. Do *not* attempt to make use of other bolts, particularly longer bolts or bolts which need a lot of effort to tighten (because they are ruining the threads in the drive). It is better to mount a drive with only three bolts rather than to add one bolt of the wrong type.

EIDE/ATA INTERFACE

Now connect up the cables to the drive(s). There are two sets of cables required for any hard drive, the power cable and the data cable. The power cable is a simple four-strand type with a four-way connector (some drives use only two connections of the four). This connector (Figure 7.11) is made so that it can be plugged in only one way round.

The same power cable is used for floppy drives and for hard drives, and modern AT machines usually provide four or five plugs on the cable. The plug is a tight fit into the socket and usually locks into place. The socket for the power plug is obvious but some disk drives need an adapter which should be supplied.

The data cable (Figure 7.12) that connects to the IDE drive is of the flat 40-strand type. This plugs into the matching connector on the motherboard at one end and into the drive at the other, with no complications. Look for one strand of the cable being marked, often with a black, striped or red line to indicate pin 1 connection. This makes it easier to locate the connector the correct way round. Do not assume that one particular way round (such as cable-entry down) will always be correct, or that a second hard drive will have its pin 1 position the same way round as your first hard drive.

- The conventional system is to use the IDE plug at the end of the cable for the master drive and the other (mid-cable) connector for a slave drive.
- If you make a mistake and get the hard drive data cable the wrong way round this does not, in my experience, cause any damage, but the hard drive will not appear in the CMOS-RAM screen display.

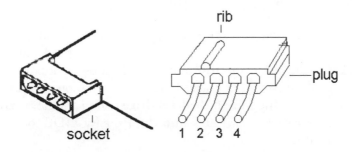

Figure 7.11 The standard form of power connector for drives

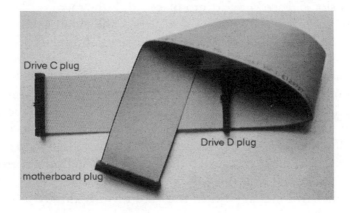

Figure 7.12 The standard form of IDE cable, showing drive connectors

When you have the hard drive running satisfactorily, see later, it is desirable to mark the cable connectors so that you can replace them correctly in the event of having to remove the drives for servicing. Use *Tippex* or other white marker on the top side of each connector and write on the use (DATA 1, DATA 2, POWER1, POWER2 and so on). Mark also the pin 1 position on the cable and on the drive.

CHECKING OUT

When a hard drive, whatever the type, has been installed so that all the relevant steps described above have been carried out, you can check that the disk is mechanically capable of use. Check first that all connectors are firmly in place. It is quite common to find that all your efforts in plugging in the hard drive end of the cable have loosened the other end that plugs into the Primary EIDE socket on the motherboard.

You need to make the machine ready for use. Plug the keyboard connector into its socket on the motherboard – this is usually a DIN-type socket located at the back of the machine close to the PSU. Insert the video graphics card that you intend to use, easing the card into its slot and screwing it into place. Plug the monitor data cable into the socket on the graphics card. Insert the monitor mains plug – if this is a Euroconnector it can be plugged into the socket on the PC main case, otherwise use a standard mains plug for the moment.

With all cables plugged into their correct places and the lid shut, switch on the power. If the monitor is separately powered make sure that it is plugged in and switched on. You should hear the high-pitched whine of the hard disk drive motor start and settle to its final speed. If absolutely nothing happens, check that the Suspend cable is connected from the front panel to the correct pins on the motherboard.

If you hear a lot of disk activity and the machine boots (possibly with some error messages) then the hard drive is already formatted, and the formatting steps noted in the following chapter can be ignored. Congratulate yourself – you have avoided several tricky steps. This, however, is most unusual unless you have transferred a hard drive from another machine. It is much more likely that the drives are formatted, so that it cannot be used, but can be recognized by the machine. There will be more on this point later.

This is as far as you can go for an unformatted hard disk, because you cannot use the drive until it has been formatted. If this is a second drive you have added, you can check that the machine is still booting up correctly from the first drive, and that the second drive is recognized. You should always check that the new hard drive is recognized in the CMOS-RAM settings, see later.

- Normally, a hard drive is supplied with no formatting, and you have to use both the FDISK utility and the *Format* command, see later. When you try switching on the machine you will get a message to tell you that you need to insert a *System disk*. At this point you can insert a System floppy to check that the machine will boot and run MS-DOS.

- Some hard drives feature SMART, meaning self-monitoring and reporting technology. If your new hard drive has this feature you might need to look for a CMOS-RAM entry to ensure that it can be used. Once SMART is installed, disk problems will be notified.

At this stage, unless the machine has booted from the new drive, you do not really know whether you have any major problems, because all you can tell is whether the hard drive motor is running or not. If there is no sound from the drive, particularly when you are using a single hard drive, then the drive motor is not running. Check the power cable if the drive has just been installed or replaced. This requires you to switch off, disconnect the mains lead, remove the monitor and open the lid.

It is most unusual to have this problem, because the power supply cable can be inserted only one way round. It is possible, however, that if an adapter has been used it is incorrectly wired or that a wire is broken. Check also for any signs of a break in the power cable, particularly at the connector.

- If the hard drive is not recognized in the CMOS-ROM (see later) this is almost certainly due to the data cable being incorrectly inserted. Check to see which end of the connector is the wrong way round.

Floppy drive installation

So much of the installation of a floppy drive follows the same pattern as fitting a hard drive that very little needs to be said here. Fitting a 3½-inch drive into a 5¼-inch bay is done by way of an adapter kit, but this is most unlikely to be needed if you are using a modern casing with more 3½-inch than 5¼-inch bays. As before, take great care never to lose the fixing screws for these conversion holders and for drive bays, because they are types that are not easy to replace unless you have access to a computer shop with a good selection of hardware.

Never assume that because a bay is provided this means that the cables supplied with the machine will be able to reach a drive added to that bay. Cables are often supplied that are so short as to restrict your layout seriously, and you may have to alter the positions of drives in the bays so that the drive with the shortest cable is closest to the motherboard.

- If the case layout is such that some cables cannot possibly reach a drive then you will have to look for cable extenders for power cables. Longer data cables can be bought, and this is a better solution than any kind of extender for a data cable.

Check before you tighten a drive into place that there is clearance between the underside of the floppy drive and any drive that is fitted beneath it. This is not a problem when the floppy drive is fixed on its side in a bay intended for this purpose, but when you need to fit a hard drive and a floppy drive into adjacent bays you may encounter problems. The problem is that the flywheel of a floppy drive is on its underside and can easily be fouled by any slight projection from the drive above it. The amount of leeway in the mountings usually allows you to separate the drives enough to avoid the problem.

That apart, the main points to note are that the floppy drive has its jumpers set for use as Drive A or 0, and that the power cable is correctly used. Power cables nowadays are fitted with two types of plug, one of the standard size for hard drives and a smaller type for some makes of 3½-inch drives. The plugs are easy enough to insert, but it is not always easy to ensure that they are inserted correctly with all pins engaged. It is remarkably easy to insert a power plug with each of its pins against a piece of insulation rather than against the metal of a socket.

On the older versions of power units, all the power plugs are of the larger type, and an adapter is needed to fit to some makes of 3½-inch units. This is straightforward, but if you do not have the adapter then you cannot proceed until you lay your hands on one. A good computer shop will often have some in stock. Remember to ensure that the connector to the 3½-inch drive is correctly inserted. The data connector should be plugged in the right way round, using the pin-1 marking on the data cable as a guide. Do not assume that the plug goes in with the cable facing down – this can vary from one cable to another. Inserting the data plug the wrong way round has not caused any damage when I have tried it, but the disk system does not work.

Testing a floppy drive is easy enough. With the machine set up with monitor and keyboard (see above), place an MS-DOS boot disk (see later) into the drive that is to be the A drive. Switch on, and wait to see evidence of activity from the drive. The machine should boot up if all is well.

If you are assembling from scratch, you should have a floppy that has been formatted as a System or Startup disk, with the MS-DOS tracks. This is essential if the hard drive is not formatted, because it allows you to format the hard drive and transfer the system tracks to the hard drive, allowing you to boot from then on directly from the hard drive. When you install Windows (see later) you should always take the option of creating a new system disk.

CD-ROM and DVD drive(s)

Because most CD-ROM or DVD drives for internal fitting (meaning that they fit inside a computer in the same way as a conventional disk drive) are so similar, a typical description will serve to show how to go about this task. The software that accompanies the drive will usually be on a floppy, and will have running instructions on its label.

- Note that the speed ratings of CD-ROM and DVD are not the same – a DVD drive rated at 5× speed for a DVD disc is roughly equivalent to 32× for CD-ROM use.

In order to add an internal CD-ROM or DVD drive, you need to have a 5¼-inch drive bay free. If you want to use multimedia you also need to have a sound board installed, but if you are not interested in sound you need not fit this board. Remember that you can hear CD sound through earphones by using the jack point at the front panel of a CD-ROM drive. If you are using a DVD drive for video you will need a decoder card or software.

On some machines the hard drive will be fitted in the lowest of the drive bays, but many modern cases locate the hard drive elsewhere in the casing. Unless you have specified a machine with other drives (such as a tape drive), there will probably be no other 5¼-inch units, so that all the bays of this size will be free for use.

- Do not assume that a CD-ROM drive will be provided with mounting brackets at exactly the same places as the drive bay, though these positions are usually standard on PC clones. You should enquire when you order the drive what provisions are made for mounting it on the style of casing you are using. You must never drill the casing of a CD-ROM or DVD drive.
- Modern CD-ROM drives use a 40-strand IDE type of connector such as is provided on the hard drive cable. On a modern motherboard you would normally use the Primary IDE connector for a hard drive and the Secondary IDE for the CD-ROM. Check when you order a drive that it uses this type of connection because a few use the SCSI system which is suitable only if your computer uses this type of interface. Check also that your computer uses the EIDE system that allows more than one type of drive to be connected to the hard drive cable.

The drives are provided with mounting holes at the side, rather than the sprung pads that are used for magnetic disk drives. This makes it easy to fasten them into the standard type of bay which has slots cut in the sides for the mounting bolts. The drive bay normally has slots at the sides to allow for to-and-fro adjustment of a drive, and two sets are usually provided at different heights in the bay. These should fit the mounting positions of the CD-ROM drive without any problems.

The fastening is by way of small bolts fitting into the threaded holes. Under no circumstances should you consider drilling the casing of a CD-ROM drive in order to mount it in any other way. You should also handle the drive by its casing, not holding its weight on any other points. In particular, avoid handling the connector pins at the rear of the drive. Be careful also not to lose the bolts, because they are not easy to replace.

Installation work

Before you start, check the drive package to make sure you have all of the mounting bolts, any adapter that is needed, cables (which may be packed with the sound board, but are more usually with the CD drive) and instructions. The power cable for the CD-ROM drive will be one of the existing set that is used for the hard drive and floppy drive. The power supply is usually fitted with five or more connectors so that one should certainly be spare, but check that it will reach the CD-ROM drive. You may need to cut one of the plastic cable ties in order to pull the cable connector over so that it reaches the drive.

Check also that you have the necessary tools. A Phillips screwdriver (possibly also a plain-head type) and a pair of tweezers are usually needed. The bolts are either 6-32 UNC × 0.31 (5/16″) or metric M4 × 0.7-6H. If you need spare UNC bolts you will need to contact a specialist supplier, but the M4 metric types can be bought from electronics suppliers such as the well-known Maplin Electronics or RS Components.

At this stage, check with your manual for the CD-ROM drive if any jumpers or switches need to be set. The modern plug'n'play (PNP) system usually ensures that no such settings are necessary, and if you see jumpers or switches this might indicate an old model of drive. Remember that once the drive is in place, any adjustment points will be impossible to reach. Use tweezers to manipulate these devices.

Switch off the computer if it has been running, wait for a minute, and remove the main cable. Open the cover – some hinge out of the way, others need to be removed completely. You can now install the CD-ROM drive. Handling the drive by its casing, place it into the mounting bay and check that the slots in the mounting bay match with the fixing positions in the drive.

Place the bolts by hand and tighten evenly. Check as you tighten the bolts that the drive is positioned correctly. The CD-ROM drive will need to have its front panel flush with the computer front. Once again, this installation calls for patience rather than skill.

Problems arise only if the mounting pads on the drive do not correspond with openings in the bay, or if you manage to lose a mounting bolt. A mounting bolt that falls inside the drive casing or the computer casing can usually be shaken out, or you can use the flexible grabs that are sold in tool shops. Do not use a magnet to retrieve a bolt from a disk drive casing (don't bring a magnet anywhere near a computer at any time).

Do not attempt to make use of other bolts, particularly longer bolts or bolts which need a lot of effort to tighten (because they are ruining the threads in the drive). It is better to mount a drive with only three bolts rather than to add one bolt of the wrong type. There is no great amount of strain on these fastenings because the CD-ROM drive is much lighter than a hard drive.

There are two essential sets of cables for any CD-ROM drive, the power cable and the data cable set. The power cable is a simple four-strand (thick wire) type with a four-way connector (some drives use only two connections of the four). This connector is made so that it can be plugged in only one way round. The same power cable is used for floppy drives and for hard drives, and modern PC machines usually provide four or five plugs on the cable. The plug is a tight fit into the socket and usually locks into place. The socket for the power plug is obvious.

- The small data cable is for audio signals and will connect to a corresponding socket on the soundboard. You must use the data cable that was packaged along with your CD-ROM drive – do not try to use the cable from another type.

The main data cable that connects from the IDE controller board to the CD-ROM drive is of the flat type, usually ending in a 40-pin plug at the CD-ROM drive end. This plugs into the matching connector on the controller board at one end and into the drive at the other, with no complications. Look for one strand of the cable being marked, often with a coloured or speckled line, to indicate pin-1 connection position. This makes it easier to locate the connector the correct way round.

As before, do not assume that one particular way round (such as cable-entry down) will always be correct, or that a board connector will have its pin-1 position the same way round as it is on another board. Check carefully with illustrations in the leaflets that come with the units. If you are fitting a CD-ROM writer as well as a fast CD-ROM reader, use the (primary) connector at the end of the cable for the reader and the secondary connector for the writer.

- Remember that if you have bought different units in different places there will be no guarantee that the connectors will match – this is why you are strongly recommended to buy a package from one source.

Now tighten up any mounting screws that you may have had to loosen so as to slide the CD-ROM drive into place. Check everything again – it's always easier to check now rather than later. Replace the cover of the computer, push in the power cable connector, and get ready to install the software.

CD-R/RW drives

If your interests include sound recording, or if you need to store large amounts of text, graphics files or even video files, a CD writing drive is a very useful accessory. At the time of writing, there are many types available at very attractive prices (under £100), and all of them offer the three options of reading, preparing write-only disks (CD-R) or preparing rewriteable disks (CD-RW). Though this type of drive can be used as your only CD drive, it is preferable to install it along with a (much cheaper) fast CD reader drive. The CD-R/RW drive is then connected as the slave drive to the CD reader drive, using the connector that is placed midway along the data cable.

- Combi drives are also available, which combine the actions of a CD-ROM drive, a CD-R/RW writing drive and DVD reading drive. These are very often supplied with new computers, but my preference is always to have the writing drive separate.

The installation of a typical CD-R/RW drive follows the same procedure as for the main CD reader drive, and though there is an audio connection provided it will not be needed unless the CD-R/RW drive is your only CD drive. Look in the manual to see if any jumpers need to be altered – this is usually necessary if you are installing the CD-R/RW drive as the only CD drive, or if you are installing it as the second drive on the hard drive data cable.

The CD-R/RW drive will need added software (the reader drive is operated from software that is built into Windows), and this software can be installed once Windows is up and running. Currently, drives are usually packaged with software from Adobe or with the Nero software, making the creation of CD-ROM disks simpler, if anything, than the creation of floppies. If your drive, unusually, comes with no software, you should consider buying the excellent Click'N'Burn software from Starland of Plymouth.

If you want to use the CD-R/RW drive for recording sound from sources such as old cassette tapes or LP recordings (see Chapter 5) you will need to have a sound board connected so that the audio input can be converted to digital form in a file that is then transferred to CD. This is not always straightforward because the recorder must be fed with data at a steady rate with no gaps. A fast hard drive system and processor is needed.

Chapter 8

Preparations

Positioning the boxes

Once you have installed all the cards on the motherboard on a machine that you have constructed from scratch, you should check again that all connections are sound. Then, and only then, you can close the lid or put the covers back on.

You should now turn your attention to the set-up of the whole computer system. This is something that is often neglected, and by spending just a little more time at this stage you can make it all much easier for yourself later. The first point to consider is how you intend to locate all the separate sections that make up a PC. When you are first testing your handiwork, the sections should all be accessible, and the monitor is best placed temporarily on one side of the main casing.

The conventional format for a flip-lid desktop case (Figure 8.1) is to place the monitor on top of the main casing, with the keyboard in front and the mouse to one side. This places the weight of the monitor on top of the lid of the case. If the monitor is a heavy one, as all colour monitors using cathode-ray tubes are, you should spread the weight with a square of plywood or chipboard placed between monitor and case, so that the edges of the case are taking the weight

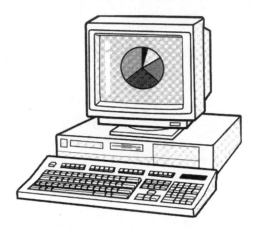

Figure 8.1 The conventional desktop arrangement with monitor on top of the main unit

rather than the more vulnerable lid. This scheme is really not suited to the larger sizes of colour monitor (17 inches upwards), though it will come into its own again when thin, flat, LCD screens become more affordable.

This arrangement, though very popular, does not allow you to flip open the lid without first moving the monitor, and a much better method is to place the main casing on a separate shelf, preferably under the desk or table. An old coffee table of the low variety can be used, and if there is enough clearance above the main case this allows you to remove the cover without the need to shift anything. This is a much more suitable set-up if you are likely to be making frequent changes to cards and other aspects of the interior of the machine. You may, however, need cables between the monitor and the main unit that are rather longer than are usually supplied.

- Some mice of anonymous (or anonymouse?) manufacture have very short connecting leads, preventing you from placing the main unit under a desk. Since you cannot tell from the packaging what length of connecting cable is supplied, this makes mouse replacement rather a haphazard operation. The Microsoft mice all seem to come with a good length of cable. Extension cables for the mouse can be bought, though you have to search for suppliers.

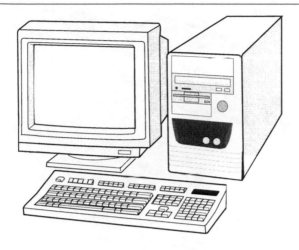

Figure 8.2   Typical tower case arrangement

The popularity of the tower form of construction, particularly the mini or midi tower, is due to the small *footprint* it makes on a desk (Figure 8.2). A tower can sit on the edge of a desk, allowing the monitor and keyboard to be arranged more centrally. An alternative is to place the main tower under the desk – this is essential for a full-size tower which would be too large on a desktop. Another advantage is that using a tower for the PC box allows space for a larger monitor now that such units are reasonably priced. It also makes more space for other items such as a printer and a scanner.

You can place the mouse to the left or to the right, and software will allow you to interchange the functions of the mouse switches to allow for left-hand or right-hand use. Both mouse and keyboard should come with leads that are long enough to give you considerable choice about where you place them relative to the main casing, but see the note on short mouse leads, above.

POWER CABLE CONNECTIONS

The standard form of power supply that is used in the PC has a Eurosocket connector that is intended for the power to the monitor or the printer; sometimes both can be connected. This supply may be separately fused inside the power supply unit, or it may share the

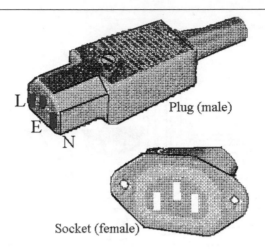

Figure 8.3   The Euroconnectors

mains fuse in the 3-pin mains plug of the computer. Some monitors
are provided with a Euroconnector, but if none is provided, you can
connect your own.

Euroconnectors (Figure 8.3) are available from the main electronics
supply firms such as Maplin and RS Components (Electro-
Components). Remember that the Euroconnector you use for a
monitor power lead should be the cable-end pin type to match the
socket type used on the computer. The exposed pins of the connector
must *never* be connected to a mains plug. The Euroconnector can be
obtained as cable fitting (plug) or as chassis fitting (socket), and
either form can be male or female.

If you have several auxiliary units such as powered loudspeakers, a
scanner, a low-consumption printer, etc., you may want all of these to
be switched on and off with the computer. This is particularly important now that so many items come without a separate mains switch,
and it avoids the usual scenario that you switch off the computer and
go away, leaving a printer or monitor on standby. You can solve this
by buying one socket strip that is connected to the mains and which
feeds the computer and the monitor, along with other switched
socket strips that can be used to supply items such as printer, scanner,
loudspeakers, digital camera and other items.

The power cable to the main casing will use another Euroconnector, and you will normally have a mains plug ready fitted. If

you need to fit a mains plug for yourself this must be a standard UK 3-pin plug, and the fuse *must* be a 3 A type. Do not on any account fit a 13 A fuse, because the internal cabling of the machine is not rated to take such a current without serious damage. If a plug has been supplied, check the fuse rating for yourself, even if you have been assured that it is a 3 A type. At this stage, do not insert the mains plug.

To connect up the units, you need complete access to the rear of the main case – do not try to insert connectors by feel. The keyboard connector should be inserted first. If you have decided to go for the older system and avoid using USB, the connector is usually a rather small and fragile PS/2 type of plug, and its socket is directly mounted on the motherboard.

Locate the keyway for the plug, and try to use the minimum of force when inserting it, because the socket on the motherboard is not particularly rugged. If the plug does not slide easily into the socket, stop and try to find out why – you may be trying to put the plug in with the pins turned to the wrong angle. The keyboard cable is usually coiled, and if it does not stretch far enough in its coiled form, pull it out a bit. You can buy cable extenders if needed.

• A keyboard can be easily replaced in the course of an upgrade, though there is seldom any need to do so unless you have been working on a very old machine with the 83-key arrangement. Do not worry about having a keyboard whose plug does not match the motherboard socket, because you can buy DIN-to-PS/2 and PS/2-to-DIN adapters. Some keyboards, such as those of the old Amstrad PC 1512, are non-standard and cannot be used with a new PC.

The mouse can now be connected, either to its PS/2 mouse port if it is the bus type of mouse, or to a serial port. If you are using the USB type of keyboard and mouse, the mouse will fit into the USB outlet of the keyboard. If you have a 9-pin connector on the COM1 port, use this for a serial mouse. The connectors that are used for this port can normally be screwed into place but do not screw them down when you are first testing. Drape the mouse cable to one side of the keyboard, leaving enough slack to allow you to move the mouse easily.

Now connect the monitor, inserting the Euroconnector into the PC (female) socket, or plugging in to a mains power point if you have opted to keep the monitor separate from the PC supply. The monitor data plug then has to be inserted. The standard type of 15-pin monitor D-plug will fit only one way round, and even for testing purposes it is advisable to fasten the plug into the socket using the screws at the side. The data cable for a monitor is usually thick, because it uses several sets of twisted leads, and it is also stiff because of metal shielding, so that the connector is likely to be pulled out if you move the monitor unless the plug is fastened in.

- Note that the conventional monitor data plug uses three rows of pins, unlike the 15-pin games port plug. The USB type is slimmer and easier to work with.

Once all the essential parts are connected you can start setting up and testing. Items like printers and scanners should not be connected until you have thoroughly checked out the computer using Windows. Before the operating system can be used, however, you need to check the settings in the CMOS RAM.

CMOS-RAM set-up

When you switch on a PC without any operating system installed, you can make use of small fragments of programs stored in the ROM memory. These allow very limited control (no use of the mouse and only a few keys recognized) over the machine so that you can prepare it for use and installation of the OS.

The PC keeps some data stored in CMOS-RAM memory backed up by a small battery that is located on the motherboard. This data includes the vital statistics for the hard drive(s), so that the computer can find how to make use of the hard drive each time the machine is switched on. At this point, you should be certain that you switched the jumpers on the motherboard so that the CMOS-RAM was active.

Some motherboards provide for an external battery to be used either together with or in place of this internal one, and if you encounter problems such as a request to alter the CMOS-RAM set-up each time you boot the machine, battery failure is the most likely cause. For a machine you have constructed with a new hard drive you are likely to get a message when you boot to the effect that an unrecognized hard drive is being used. Along with this you will be asked to press a key to start the CMOS set-up. This type of message is delivered when the machine senses that there is a discrepancy between what is stored in the CMOS-RAM and what is physically present, but minor changes such as adding ports will not necessarily affect the CMOS-RAM.

- Some motherboards are set up so that a hard drive will be automatically recognized, and even if you change a hard drive there is still no message from the CMOS-RAM.

Older machines used a nickel cadmium rechargeable battery on the motherboard, but this has now changed in favour of a single lithium cell, which is more compact and has a longer life. Do not attempt to measure the voltage of this cell (nominally 3 V) using an old-fashioned voltmeter because a conventional voltmeter will take more current from the cell than the CMOS-RAM does, and will shorten its life. If you must check the lithium cell, use a digital voltmeter.

If you do not get a CMOS-RAM set-up notice when you boot, you may see a notice on the screen notifying you that you can press a key in order to get into the CMOS set-up. The way this is used to make the machine run its *Set-up* depends on the make of chips that it uses (the chipset). One common method, used with AMI BIOS machines, is to offer you a short interval in which pressing the Del key on the keypad (at the right-hand side of the keyboard) will enter Set-up. Some AWARD chipset machines require you to press a set of keys, Ctrl-Alt-Esc in this interval.

Note that if your motherboard is of the type, as most of them now are, that uses soft set-up, the first screen you'll see on the CMOS-RAM is for setting up the processor. Normally, the processor that you have fitted on the motherboard will be recognized and its speed and other settings will be correct. You will need to use this screen if you change your processor, or if you want to overclock the processor to obtain more speed (so invalidating any warranty). A portion of a typical soft set-up screen is illustrated (this is a simulation rather then a screenshot) in Figure 8.4, showing an AMD Duron 850 installed, with the settings that have been made for it through this software. When you opt to fill in values for yourself, the items that are shown in the illustration starting with a letter 'x' are shown with

	CPU Name is	AMD DURON TM
	CPU Operating speed	850
x	Multiplier Factor	×8.5
x	CPU FSB/PCI Clock	100/33 MHz
x	CPU FSB Plus (MHz)	0
x	Speed Error Hold	Disabled
	CPU Power Supply	CPU Default
x	Core Voltage	1.6V
x	I/O Voltage	3.40V
	Fast CPU Command Decode	Normal
	CPU Drive Strength	2
	Enhance Chip Performance	Enable
	Force 4-Way Interleave	Enabled
	Enable DRAM 4K-Page Mode	Enable
	DRAM Clock	HCLK+PCICLK

Figure 8.4   A soft set-up page of the CMOS-RAM for an AWARD BIOS

a hyphen to indicate that you have to supply a value. You would supply values only if you were experimenting with overdriving the chip, or if you needed to set values for a chip that was not automatically recognized by the system.

Whatever key or key combination is to be used to get to the CMOS-RAM screen, it should be noted in the documentation for the motherboard, and also on the screen when you start up the computer. Note that pressing the *Delete* key (in the set of six above the cursor keys) as distinct from the Del key will have no effect – this is because the machine is at this stage being controlled by a very small program in the ROM which allows only very limited capabilities.

The snag is that if, as recommended, you have wired your monitor to the Euroconnector so that it is switched on by the computer, the monitor may not have warmed up in time to display the message. Colour CRT monitors in particular tend to miss the message because they warm up slowly. The remedy is to boot up in the usual way, and when the monitor is fully active, press the Ctrl-Alt-Del key combination. Use the Ctrl and Alt keys to the left of the spacebar and the Del key on the keypad at the right. This key combination causes what is called a *warm boot*, meaning that the computer restarts (clearing its memory on the way), but omits some self-test routines so that the restart is faster. During this restart you should see a message such as:

WAIT...
Hit <DEL> If you want to run Set-up

– the AMI BIOS message is illustrated here.

Whichever method is used, when you move from the soft set-up screen to the first of the options screens, it should be possible to see a display such as that illustrated in Figure 8.5. This is a simplified example of a modern AWARD BIOS and chipset display and those for other machines will differ in detail.

The important point is that you are offered a set of optional menus to choose from, of which the first (already selected) is by far the most important at this stage. Until you are thoroughly familiar with the system, do not attempt to use any menus other than the *Standard CMOS Set-up*. The only exception is that if you find the system misbehaving after a change in the CMOS set-up you can recover by entering the Set-up again and selecting the *Set-up Defaults*. The BIOS set-up reminds you of this when you opt to use either of the main Set-up menus.

This main menu contains the Password options to allow you to create a password for either *Supervisor* or *User* or both. Passwording can be useful when a machine is available to a large number of people, but unless you have security problems it is best to avoid passwording. For one thing, you need to remember your own password(s). If a password is easy to remember, it is usually easy for someone else to guess.

CMOS • SETUP • UTILITY	
STANDARD CMOS SETUP	SUPERVISOR PASSWORD
BIOS FEATURES SETUP	USER PASSWORD
CHIPSET FEATURES SETUP	IDE HDD AUTO DETECTION
POWER MANAGEMENT SETUP	SAVE AND EXIT SETUP
PNP AND PCI SETUP	EXIT WITHOUT SAVING
LOAD BIOS DEFAULTS	
LOAD SETUP DEFAULTS	
ESC : QUIT	⯅⯆⯇⯈ : Select Item
F10 : Save and Exit Setup	(Shift) F2 : Change Colour

Figure 8.5   A typical CMOS-RAM menu display

If you forget a password you will be locked out of your own machine and there is no simple way then of disabling the pass-wording, though it can be done by an expert. If you are desperate, some varieties of AMI BIOS provide for the password changing to *AMI* when the backup battery is discharged or momentarily discon-nected. Another option on other boards is to change over a jumper to clear the CMOS-RAM by disconnecting the battery. Find out for yourself how to reset a forgotten password if you decide to use this form of protection. Note that you may have to re-enter CMOS-RAM information after this action.

When you opt for the Standard set-up, you will see a display that is, typically, as illustrated here in Figure 8.6.

The important point is that the information on the drive types should be present. Any alteration in the installed drives has to be notified, otherwise the CMOS-RAM Set-up table is likely to be presented to you each time you boot. If you have constructed a machine from scratch, or altered the drives of an older machine, you will certainly need to alter the particulars shown here.

Altering a line of information is, typically, done by using the arrow keys (cursor keys) to move the cursor to the item(s) you want to change, and pressing either the *Page Up* or *Page Down* keys to change the item. Note that you cannot type in numbers or day names, only cycle through the options that are provided. What is less clear is how to find and enter the information about the hard drive that you need to supply to the system. At this stage in its action, the computer cannot make use of the mouse, and only a few keys, such as the cursor and Esc keys, are recognized.

STANDARD CMOS SETUP

Date (mm:dd:yy) Thu. Apr 23 1998
Time (hh:mm:ss) 11:15:22

HARD DISKS	TYPE	SIZE	CYLS	HEAD	PRECOMP	LANDZ	SECTOR	MODE
Primary Master	User	2568	622	128	0	4981	63	LBA
Primary Slave	None	0	0	0	0	0	0	----
Secondary Master	Auto	0	0	0	0	0	0	AUTO
Secondary Slave	None	0	0	0	0	0	0	----

Drive A : 1.44M 3.5 in.
Drive B None

Floppy 3 Mode Support : Disabled
Video : EGA/VGA
Halt On : All Errors

Base Memory	:	640K
Extended Memory	:	64512K
Other Memory	:	384K
Total Memory	:	65536K

Figure 8.6   A typical CMOS standard set-up panel

The important section is headed HARD DISKS, and there are columns labelled TYPE, SIZE, CYLS, HEAD, PRECOMP, LANDZ, SECTOR and MODE. The list under the HARD DISKS column contains Primary Master, Primary Slave, Secondary Master and Secondary Slave, and each line that is filled in corresponds to a device. Normally, you will use the *Primary Master* line for a hard drive and *Secondary Master* for a CD-ROM drive. The information in the other columns either will be read automatically from a new drive, or can be filled in from the information supplied with the hard drive. You should have copied this information from the casing of a hard drive or from documentation that came with the hard drive, in case the automatic recognition system fails.

- The *Primary Slave* can be used for a second hard drive, and the *Secondary Slave* for a CD-R/RW drive.

The usual method of forcing the computer to recognize the hard drive is to select *Auto* as the TYPE, so that the drive will be recognized the next time you boot the computer. Another method is to use the option in the main menu of IDE HDD AUTO DETECTION. If you need to use manual entry for any reason (an older hard drive, usually) then moving the cursor to the *Primary Master* line allows you to use the *Page Up* and *Page Down* keys to alter the setting to USER. You can then fill in figures for your own hard drive.

If you cannot find any useful information for a second hard drive, and you can boot Windows from the first drive, you can generally set up the second drive by using Windows. If the drive is to PNP (plug and play) standard then the *Add New Hardware* option of Control Panel will allow Windows to detect the drive and set up the CMOS-RAM correctly for it. There would be little point in buying a drive that is not to PNP standard, because it would be too old and of inadequate size. If you have settled on the use of SCSI drives, none of this applies.

- Unless your ATA hard drive is recognized correctly in the CMOS-RAM settings it will probably not operate correctly – you might find that at best its capacity was incorrectly recorded; at worst that it did not retain data. There is no point in proceeding further until you are sure that the main hard drive is being recognized.

FLOPPY AND DISPLAY DETAILS

Once the hard drive details have been entered you must fill in the portion of the *Setup* form that deals with the floppy drives. Place the cursor on the line for Drive A and use the *Page Up* and *Page Down* keys until you see the type of drive you have installed, usually a 3½-inch 1.44 Mbyte type – note that this counts 1 Mbyte = 1000 Kbytes rather than 1024 Kbytes.

There is a *Not Installed* option which is used for machines that are part of a network and which do not need disk drives. It is also a simple way of preventing a casual user of the computer from inserting a floppy and loading in software that contains a virus. A knowledgeable user would know how to change the CMOS-RAM setting (though you can protect this using a password, see later). The *Drive B* option is seldom needed.

The display line is selected in the same way. The normal option is *VGA/EGA*, whether you use a colour or a monochrome VGA monitor. There may be a *Not Installed* option that would be used for server machines on a network, and, as before, if you are refurbishing such a machine or using its motherboard you might find this option set. In this type of BIOS you have options for *Halt On*, specifying the kind of errors that will prevent the boot action from proceeding, and the usual option is *All Errors*. Other options are *No Errors*, *All but Keyboard*, *All but Diskette* and *All but Disk/Key*. The *All Errors* option is the default and you should not change this unless you know what you are doing.

You can then go back to the start of the list to correct the calendar and clock details if necessary. The calendar details are usually correct unless the board was not set up correctly initially, or the battery has failed, but the clock may be a few minutes out. The clock and calendar will probably need to be set from scratch if you are using a new motherboard and the CMOS-RAM has been cleared. You are not obliged to set the calendar and clock at this stage, but it is useful to do so. If you want to correct the time later it can be done using the Windows *Date and Time* controls rather than by using the CMOS-RAM option.

You are now ready to start installing the essential operating system into the computer, and you need some way of doing this. The Windows system comes on a CD-ROM, but this is of little use until the PC has enough software stored to allow it to read a CD. What you need is described as a bootable floppy, one that contains the essential parts of the MS-DOS operating system, particularly the driver software for the CD-ROM drive.

FLASH BIOS

Many motherboards now use a *flash BIOS*. This is a BIOS chip that can be reprogrammed, so that you can download an up-to-date version of the BIOS and use it to replace the existing one. Normal operating voltages have no programming effect, but when a higher voltage is applied, data can be fed into the chip and will be retained.

- It sounds a risky business and my own personal view is that I would rather replace a complete motherboard than risk the damage that a faulty reprogramming of the BIOS could cause. The process is deliberately made difficult to avoid the possibility of your BIOS being corrupted by signals from a hacker over the Internet.

Reprogramming is definitely *not* for anyone who has not worked with MS-DOS, because the actions cannot be carried out with Windows running. Full instructions for reprogramming the flash BIOS should be included in your motherboard manual. If you don't understand the terms used or the procedure, don't do it!

For the sake of illustration, this is an outline of how the reprogramming is carried out on one well-known motherboard. You need to know the model name and version number of your motherboard, which is printed on a sticker on the board (typically on a slot).

1. Check the existing BIOS ID number which appears when you boot (while the *Press DEL to enter SETUP* notice is on screen). The last two digits of the string of numbers under this notice provide the BIOS ID number.
2. Download the new BIOS file from the motherboard manufacturer's website.
3. Extract from the downloaded file a BIN file, and copy this to a bootable floppy disk along with the flash utility (EXE) program.
4. Set your computer to boot from a floppy, and use the disk you have just loaded with the BIN file.

5. Run the computer in DOS (no Windows) and execute the flash program from the floppy. Your motherboard manual should indicate the precise form of DOS command to carry out the reprogramming.

Booting up

Booting up means starting up the operating system of the computer, and if you have built a machine from scratch there will be no operating system ready. If you now leave the CMOS set-up program, taking the option to *Write to CMOS and Exit*, the machine will try to boot, and will usually recognize the hard drive and try to find the operating system on the hard drive.

With a completely new main hard drive, there will be no operating system, and you should get a message asking you to insert a floppy with the MS-DOS operating system in place. The message is:

Error loading operating system

OR

Non-system disk or disk error

and this is a signal to you that you need to insert the MS-DOS (system) floppy into its drive and press the Enter key on the keyboard. Once the floppy has completed its work you will see the screen display:

A: >

meaning that the A (floppy) drive is in use, and that MS-DOS is running. You can now start to format the hard drive so that it can accept the main operating system which for 99 per cent of users will be Windows.

- Note that Windows is supplied in two forms. If your computer already contains an older version of Windows you can use the (cheaper) upgrade CD-ROM. If, as is most likely, you are starting from scratch then you need the full version, sometimes referred to as the OEM version. When you insert an upgrade CD-ROM, you will usually be asked to insert the previous full version as a check that you have bought a complete version of Windows at some stage.

USING FDISK

FDISK is an old type of program that at one time seemed obsolete because hard drives were once supplied with the FDISK action (disk partitioning) already carried out. Nowadays a new large-capacity hard drive is normally supplied without partitioning so that you *must* use FDISK, even if you do not want to create extra partitions. Every hard drive has at least one partition, and though Windows 2000 allows you to dispense with FDISK, earlier versions do not. You will need a modern version of FDISK such as is included with Windows *Me*, or use software supplied by the manufacturer or retailer of the hard drive. FDISK is usually provided on the MS-DOS boot disk that you have used in the A: drive to boot up the computer.

Start the computer with the MS-DOS system disk in the floppy drive, and wait until the prompt A:> appears. Now type the command:

FDISK

– and press the ENTER or RETURN key. You will see a display that includes the lines:

```
Current fixed disk drive: 1
Choose one of the following:
1   Create DOS partition or Logical DOS Drive
2   Set active partition
3   Delete partition or Logical DOS drive
4   Display partition information
5   Change current fixed disk drive
    Enter choice : [5]
    Press ESC to exit FDISK
```

If you are setting up the one and only hard drive, use option 1, but if you are setting up a second hard drive use option 5 (as illustrated) to select your slave drive. This option 5 will show the drive details for both drives so that you can select which one to partition. Once the drive is selected, the display returns and you can choose option 1. You will be asked if you want to set the whole drive as a single partition, and for a drive smaller than 32 Gbyte you should answer Y to this question. The partitioning action will be carried out, and you can press the ESC key until the system reboots.

You may, however, want to partition a large hard drive into two or more (the limit is four), and this is done using option 1, following which you have to use option 2 to set the active partition, meaning the one that contains the operating system. FDISK is a very old program that runs only under MS-DOS, and which must never be used on a hard drive that contains data or programs. FDISK will *always* delete any existing data on a drive. If you need to alter partitions on a drive that is already in use, or if you just want a more user-friendly partitioning program, look for a copy of Partition Magic (from PowerQuest), which is an excellent modern solution to the problem of partitioning.

- If there is no response to typing FDISK (ENTER), or you see a message that no such filename exists, this means that your boot disk does not contain the FDISK software, and you will have to find a copy on a floppy.

Once FDISK has been used (a very fast operation) you can then use the MS-DOS system disk in Drive A to format the hard drive. For a single master drive, the command is:

FORMAT C:

– and press the ENTER or RETURN key. For a second hard drive, you will probably use D: as the drive letter, so that your command becomes FORMAT D:. If you are formatting a slave drive be very careful that you do not reformat your main (master) drive instead.

A new hard drive is not usually provided with Windows pre-installed unless you have specifically asked for this and paid for it, so that once you have MS-DOS working you can proceed to install Windows, see Chapter 9. You should now test that you can boot from the (master) hard drive by taking out the floppy system disk and rebooting. If your CMOS-RAM set-up allows you the option of booting from the hard drive directly without checking the floppy drive, take this option.

CMOS-RAM fine tuning

When you first fire up the computer, the only part of the CMOS-RAM that you need to use is concerned with the correct settings for the hard drive(s), and most other settings can be left at their default factory settings. Once you can boot from the hard drive, however, it is useful to check what other settings exist. Some of these can be left, a few can be changed, and any that you do not understand or have inadequate information about can be left severely alone.

• As before, the illustration is of a typical CMOS RAM, and there will invariably be some differences between this and the one fitted on your own motherboard.

The CMOS BIOS Set-up section contains no standard set of actions, and the examples here are taken from an AWARD BIOS. Others are likely to differ, though several important options will be the same. Some of these options can be used without the need for deeper understanding of the computer, but those which deal with memory allocations, particularly with ROM shadowing (see later) should be left strictly alone until you know what is involved on your machine. A typical set of items is illustrated in Figure 8.7.

The first item here is *Virus Warning*. This protects the parts of a hard drive (boot sector and FAT) that can be damaged by a virus, and the default setting is *Disabled*. This is because you cannot load an operating system (DOS or Windows) without modifying these parts of the hard drive. You can set this to *Enabled* after Windows has been installed, but you will need to disable it again if you upgrade your Windows software.

The following two items deal with *Internal* and *External* cache, meaning memory that is used as a temporary store for the microprocessor. These should both be set to *Enabled*, because the speed of the machine will be noticeably lower if you disable either of these. The *Quick Power On Self Test* should be enabled to make booting faster

BIOS FEATURES SETUP

Virus Warning	:Disabled	Video ROM BIOS	Shadow	:Enabled
CPU Internal Cache	:Enabled	C8000 – CBFFF	Shadow	:Disabled
External Cache	:Enabled	CC000 – CFFFF	Shadow	:Disabled
Quick Power ON Self Test	:Enabled	D0000 – D3FFF	Shadow	:Disabled
HDD Sequence SCSI/IDE First	:IDE	D4000 – D7FFF	Shadow	:Disabled
Boot Sequence	:C;A	D8000 – DBFFF	Shadow	:Disabled
Boot Up Floppy Seek	:Disabled	DC000 – DFFFF	Shadow	:Disabled
Floppy Disk Access Control	:R/W			
IDE HDD Block Mode Sectors	:HDD Max	Boot up Numlock Status		:On
Security Option	:System	Boot Up System Speed		:High
PS/2 Mouse Function Control	:Disabled	Typematic Rate Setting		:Disabled
PCI/VGA Palette Snoop	:Disabled	Typematic Rate (Chars/Sec)		:6
PS/2 Onboard Memory > 64M	:Disabled	Typematic Delay (Msec)		:250

Esc: Quit   ↑↓←→   : Select Item

F1 : Help   PU/PD/+/– : Modify

F5 : Old Values   (Shift)F2 : Colour

F6 : Load BIOS Defaults

F7 : Load Setup Defaults

Figure 8.7   Typical CMOS-RAM BIOS settings

by eliminating excessive testing. This testing is a hangover from the time when memory was considered unreliable.

The *HDD Sequence* option is a feature of the AWARD BIOS, and it allows you to choose whether to use the IDE hard drive to boot from or to use a SCSI drive.

The *Boot Sequence* line has the default of C;A and this will cause the machine to boot from the hard drive, using a floppy only if the hard drive cannot be used. This is a useful default, and you can change it to A;C if you want to test the machine without using the hard drive. Along with this, you can disable the action of seeking the floppy drive so that the machine does not activate the drive needlessly at each boot. Another floppy option is to allow the floppy to be used for reading only (the default is read/write).

The *IDE HDD Block Mode Sectors* option is set by default at *HDD*

MAX for modern hard drives, and this provides optimum performance. Other settings can be used for older drives.

Security Option decides when you need to enter a password if you have opted for this. The default is *System*, prompting for the password on each boot. The alternative is *Set-up*, when a password is needed only when the CMOS Set-up is used. These settings are used only if you have opted to use passwording.

The *PS/2 Mouse Function Control* is normally set to *Auto*, allowing the system to detect the use of a PS/2 mouse automatically at boot time. This can be disabled if you use a serial mouse. The *PCI/VGA Palette Snoop* is usually disabled, but can be enabled if a non-standard graphics or video card shows colours incorrectly. The *OS/2 Onboard Memory >64M* item is also disabled by default. You can enable it if you are using the OS/2 operating system with more than 64 Mbytes of memory. The OS/2 operating system is only a memory now, and all recent motherboards can cope with 512 Mbytes of memory when using Windows 98, Windows *Me* or Windows XP, more if you use Windows 2000 or the NTFS file option of Windows XP.

BIOS shadowing means that the data in the BIOS ROM will be copied to RAM at boot time, because RAM is faster than ROM. The default is to enable this for the *Video ROM*, but you should not enable the other shadow options unless you know that you are using cards that contain ROM addresses in the six other ranges illustrated. This is unlikely unless you are networked.

The *System Boot Up Num Lock Status* option should be enabled, so that the number keypad on the right-hand side of the keyboard is set for numbers rather than its optional cursor keys. This avoids the need to have to press the *Num Lock* key after booting. The *Boot Up System Speed* setting is *High* by default and should not be altered.

Another set of BIOS options deals with the *Typematic rate*. This is the rate at which a key action will repeat when a key is held down, and there are two factors, the time delay between pressing a key and starting the repeat action, and the rate at which the key action repeats once it has started. The Set-up options are to enable or disable the *Typematic* action, to set the delay and to set the repeat rate. Typical default values are to have the action disabled, the delay set to a long 500 milliseconds (0.5 second) and the rate to a fast 150 characters per second. The time and rate settings have no effect if the Typematic action is disabled. Since Windows will override these settings and impose its own, there is no point in making the settings unless you plan to type data into MS-DOS programs.

DANGER AREAS

The *Chipset Features* set of the AWARD BIOS, and comparable section of other BIOS settings, should be left at default settings unless you know what you are doing and have the necessary information such as the response time of DRAM. You should also be careful about using the *Power Management* options, and keep the default settings if you are in doubt. Just because an option appears in one of these sets does not mean that your motherboard can cope with it. It is reasonable to use the action that shuts down the hard drive after a period of inactivity, but only if you are using a modern version of Windows that supports power management features of this type. Be wary of shutting down the fan unless your are certain that the control system will protect against overheating.

- Power management use can have unexpected consequences. For example, if you opt for your hard drive(s) to shut down after some specified time you may find that when you are trying to log on to a website you are refused on the grounds that your *cookie* files are disabled. This is because the hard drive is not spinning and though you will awake it when you carry out any keyboard or mouse action (like clicking on a program or on a textfile) that needs the drive, requests for a file that are made by a remote Internet site will not start up your hard drive unless you have opted to have this type of action enabled. The point is that you might not connect the problem with its cause, and this is common with power management problems.

BUS MASTERING

Modern computers feature bus mastering, meaning that data can be transferred to and from hard drives and CD-ROM drives at a high speed without the need to make use of the main processor. This system is also called DMA, direct memory access, and its use can be detected in Windows Control Panel. Modern hard drives use a version referred to as Ultra DMA.

Not all motherboards (particularly older motherboards) see to this automatically, and you may have to use a floppy disk containing bus-mastering software. For some motherboards, this can be run only after Windows has been installed, and you will have to check with the documentation that you have. It is very important to use bus mastering, because in its absence the computer will run at a much slower rate than you would expect after upgrading.

- If your motherboard needs a floppy to install bus mastering, this can be a hint that this is a fairly old motherboard model. Modern motherboards should not require additional software for bus mastering.

Chapter 9

Upgrading

This short chapter is intended particularly for the reader who has taken or wants to take the simple and cost-effective route to a fast, modern PC starting with an older machine. The essence of this, however, is what we mean by an older machine. Machines such as the 80386 or 80486 type and even the early Pentium type are simply not upgradable to modern standards. If you really want to work on a machine of such a description, refer to Chapter 12 of this book to see what amount of upgrading is possible on such a machine.

- The point is that all these older machines used the AT casing and AT motherboard which are now obsolete, and many of the items such as disk drives are also obsolete so that it is almost impossible to get anything working properly to modern standards unless you can get hold of these older items in good condition. At the time of writing (2002) such items are becoming quite difficult to obtain and there seems no point in spending as much money on a machine that is out of date as you would spend on one that is totally to modern standards.

If you intend to use Windows XP Home Edition as part of your upgrading, you should carry out all the hardware upgrades before you install Windows XP. If your machine uses XP already, be aware that hardware changes may require you to reactivate Windows XP, see Chapter 10.

A machine suitable for upgrading may be one that you have had for some time, but which was the fastest thing on the block at the time when you bought it. It may be one that has been bought at a very low price at auction or in a car-boot sale (where machines recovered from skips outside hospitals or offices often end up). Another route for the upgrader is to buy a new machine which is at a rock-bottom price because it contains the essentials of a case, power supply and motherboard only. There are few suppliers of such machines nowadays, but the prices for such machines are lower than you would have to pay if you bought the parts and assembled them for yourself. The important point, however, is that it must use a casing of the ATX type so that it can accept a modern motherboard even if the motherboard that it currently contains is out of date.

● The methods used in upgrading are essentially the same as for building from scratch, so this chapter is concerned more with choices and decisions rather than with the assembly methods and software installation methods that are covered in other chapters.

Machines bought at auctions, particularly from bankrupt office firms, can present you with an interesting gamble. Some of these are likely to be very powerful machines, particularly if a network has been in use and you can lay your hands on the server machine. You can also find fast and efficient machines that have been used as network terminals, with no disk drives but with a fast processor and a lot of memory. You have to be able to look inside the cases for yourself and determine, from the processor type number and the number of DIMMs or SIMMs you can see, whether a machine is likely to be a bargain or not. Do not depend on an auctioneer's description, because they are not computer experts and have to rely in turn on whatever description they can find. Goods bought at auction are usually bought 'as seen' with no form of warranty as to content or origin.

In general, if a machine has the Pentium-3 or Athlon chip on its motherboard and 32 Mbytes or more of DIMM memory, it will be snapped up by a dealer who can refurbish it and resell. You are not likely to get the chance to buy it cheaply for yourself. That said, a small local auction may not attract any dealers who know what to look for, and you can be very fortunate. The usual 'bargains' at the larger auctions are the 80486DX and the older Pentium-1 machines, and these are simply not capable of being upgraded to modern standards. An old machine with a large hard drive will almost certainly use SCSI, and you should ask yourself if you want to be tied to this system for other drives. Another point to consider is that the memory is unlikely to be of the modern, fast EDO type, and the local bus on a pre-Pentium machine will be VLB, assuming that there is any local bus. The big worry with an old machine is that you might have to upgrade practically everything, and it will end up costing you far more than if you had started from scratch, or had bought a *bare-bones* package.

Some modern machines, usually the ones bearing famous names, are difficult (to the point of being almost *impossible*) to upgrade, which is why they found their way to the auction in the first place. Read all of this chapter before you consider this path to a new PC, because trying to upgrade some machines could be considerably more expensive than starting from scratch. Avoid in particular machines with plastic, or very slim metal, cases. Avoid any whose disk drives are stamped with the same name as that on the case – a standard drive might not fit in the same space. Some famous-name machines came from manufacturers who made their own motherboards and cases and ensured that the standard types could not be fitted.

If the name on the case is unfamiliar you are more likely to be in luck. Machines which use unfamiliar layouts should be avoided – they are likely to be good machines for their age, but they will be costly and difficult to upgrade. It helps if you keep a note of the dimensions and a layout sketch, like Figure 9.1, of a modern ATX motherboard so that you can check that this is much the same as the board inside a computer that looks like a bargain. Don't worry too much about the positions of the mounting holes on the motherboard, because you can always drill holes into the case (**NEVER** into the motherboard) to suit. The golden rule is that if an ATX motherboard will not fit inside then the machine is not a bargain at any price.

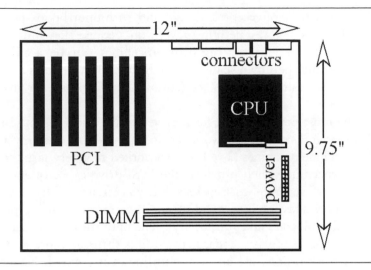

Figure 9.1 The outline and overall size of a standard ATX motherboard

Drive change

One common upgrade route starts with the machine that has no hard drive, and sometimes no floppy drive, because it has been used as a workstation on a network. Another is the machine which uses a totally inadequate hard drive. In theory, you can use a hard drive of as little as 120 Mbytes to run Windows 98 or *Me* in minimal form, but then there really is not enough room to install much else. You might, depending on how modern the motherboard is, be able to install a second hard drive, but don't take this for granted. Remember that you have to avoid machines that use old 5¼-inch floppy drives, and old hard drives (other than SCSI types) are most unlikely to be useful. They will be too small to start with, and they are also likely to have just too many miles on the clock for comfort. Unlike electronic parts, hard drives are mechanical devices that will wear out in the course of time.

The comments in Chapter 4 apply to drive installation in general, and what follows is aimed particularly at the user who is stripping out an old drive or adding a drive to an older casing, rather than installing a new drive into a new case. Obviously, the methods of installing and using a drive are the same. What you need to beware of are machines of eccentric design and with unorthodox fastenings. Nameless clones are a delight to work on, because they follow a well-worn standard pattern. Big-name machines can be a nightmare, because only their own spare parts will fit, and these parts are usually three times as expensive as the (almost identical) part for the nameless clone.

The most pressing need for a drive occurs when the machine is a diskless workstation, or a workstation machine that has only a floppy drive. These machines have been networked to a very fast and larger server machine which provided the hard drive capacity and printer port for the separate workstations, but you often find that each workstation has a fast processor and plenty of memory (allowing programs to be downloaded and run locally). The only thing to watch out for is that the casing is standard, providing three or more drive bays. Some workstations use an ultra-slimline casing which has no space for drives of any description, and this would not be a good buy even at a very low price unless you fancy starting from scratch with a new ATX case. Another likely problem is that the motherboard has no hard drive interface. If you have to buy a new case and motherboard, think what else you need to buy and ask yourself how this compares with a new machine of the same specification.

- Remember the adage about horses for courses. If your aim is to make a spare or second computer, then you need not be so fussy about keeping up to modern standards or how future-proof you are going to make it. Chapter 12 will guide you to what needs to be (and can be) done. The main thing is not to pay silly prices even for quite respectable machinery. Take a look at a current issue of *Micro Mart* to see just how cheap and completely assembled a modern computer can be.

On a diskless machine, check that the power supply unit has connectors for power leads to disk drives. These are usually provided because the power units are of a standard design, but if the supply has no connectors for drives you cannot proceed unless you buy a new power supply or add a set of drive cables to the existing one. In the absence of a circuit diagram and layout diagram for the power supply unit this would not be advisable. If you are familiar with the type of switch-mode supply that is used you can make up your own cables – always provide at least four drive connectors so as to provide for future expansion. If you are not familiar with switch-mode power supplies, don't take the lid off the PSU.

Now check the drive bays. You may need to loosen off the front panel to gain access to the lowest bay so that you can secure a drive to its sides; the bolt holes are usually inaccessible when the front panel is in place and the drive bays fastened down. Make sure that you have fastening bolts of the correct type for your drivels. If the drive bay container is of the type that allows several 3½-inch drives to be mounted you are in luck, because this makes the installation of the hard drive much easier. If you have one 3½-inch bay and several 5¼-inch bays you can install new drives using adapter plates.

Always install the hard drive first; in the lowest bay or in a sideways position if this is available. If no sideways fasteners are provided, you will need to bolt the drive into the lowest bay and then bolt the set of bays into the case – after checking that the drive is firmly in place. Replace the front panel if you have had to remove it. Connect the power cable connector to the power connector on the drive, making sure that the two are correctly engaged. The point about using the lowest bay is that this one has a permanent front cover – the bays above will have removable front covers so that floppy drives can be installed.

If you need also to install a floppy drive, do so now, or replace whatever floppy drive was on the machine if it lacked only the hard drive. Remember that a 3½-inch drive will often require an adapter for its power supply, and these are not always easy to find in local shops. If the machine has come with a 3½-inch floppy drive included, check that this is not the older 720 Kbyte drive, because you will need the 1.4 Mbyte variety for modern software packages. The cost of a new floppy drive of either type is under £10 at the time of writing.

At this stage, you might want to consider drives other than straightforward magnetic drives. The best options currently are tape streamers, and CD-R/RW drives. The prices of CD-R/RW drives have fallen considerably since they were first introduced, and they are much more economical than the high-capacity floppy systems that are still available. For backup purposes (meaning that you will not necessarily need to read the files back very often), a tape streamer can be much more cost effective than other methods.

Currently, conventional tape streamers, other than the DAT type, of 2 Gbytes (upwards) are inexpensive, and the tape cartridges that they use are also reasonably inexpensive. If you need the peace of mind that backups provide (or you feel that your bargain hard drive might not be such a bargain for long) then a streamer of this type can be a good buy. It is installed in much the same way as a conventional 5¼-inch floppy drive, and usually connects to the floppy interface (though a few use the hard drive/CD drive connectors). Avoid parallel port devices unless you have no bays available – remember that you will probably need to install an additional parallel port for such a device.

- Tape streamers that are connected into the floppy drive cable may cause problems if the motherboard runs the tape interface at a low speed. As noted earlier, you can check the speed of the tape interface before you buy a tape streamer by downloading and running diagnostic software from the site:

http://www.iomega.com

Remember that when you have made changes to floppy or hard drives you will have to notify these changes to the CMOS-RAM of the machine as detailed in Chapter 7. The tape streamers that make use of the floppy data cable do not need to be notified in the CMOS-RAM.

- Note that your tape streamer may not be recognised by Windows 2000, making it useless if you have upgraded to this system. Windows *Me* and XP will recognise the usual makes of tape streamers.

Graphics card

The need to upgrade the graphics card is usually less immediate than the need to upgrade memory and disk drives, because the VGA type of card has been a standard for some considerable time. Machines that used a CGA card are likely to be thoroughly obsolete by now, and not worth the trouble and expense of upgrading. You might, however, want to upgrade the existing VGA graphics card so as to speed up the use of Windows or to be able to use the higher SVGA modes such as 800×600 graphics in 256 or more colours.

Your choice of graphics card is important if you want to perform such an upgrade. If you are retaining an existing motherboard your choice is limited to the slower cards because no AGP slot will be available. If you are also upgrading a motherboard and going for a Socket-A type, the new motherboard will use mainly PCI local bus slots, which operate at a much higher speed than the older ISA slots. If you want to take advantage of this extra speed, you will need to buy a graphics card that is designed for use with a PCI bus. You can expect to pay around £25 for a competent graphics card, much more for one that will cope with ultra-fast 3D graphics (but would the rest of the system cope?). Though you can pay £150 or more for a graphics card, the lower cost PCI cards are very effective, and faster than any card on an ISA bus. If you want ultra-fast 3-D graphics and video, you will have to pay more, use the AGP slot, and ensure that the rest of your computer is as fast as it can be made. By the time you read this, graphics cards that fit the PCI bus may be quite difficult to find, and you will need to ensure that you use a motherboard that has an AGP slot.

PORTS

If you need more than the standard allocation of ports, upgrading is simple enough in mechanical terms by inserting a card, but you may need to give thought to setting jumpers or DIP switches before doing this. The main problem is that you probably have one parallel port and two serial ports on the existing motherboard. This means that any port card you add is likely to cause some conflict with the existing ones unless you are careful to select the correct address and interrupt settings. A modern motherboard has PCI slots so that you can add PNP cards that need no setting-up actions (though the price is likely to be higher than for the older ISA cards).

Updating the motherboard

The complete updating of an old computer using a new motherboard involves stripping the PC down to an empty case, which must be of ATX type if the job is to be worthwhile. Remove all cables from the old motherboard, including the power cable. You then need to remove the earthing and retaining supports from the old mother-board, and open any spring clips that retain the board. You can then ease the old board out of its place without disturbing anything else.

You can then install another motherboard in the way described in Chapter 7. Do not be tempted by offers of a upgraded add-on processor chip, usually by way of an accelerator board which replaces the old chip, because this is often more costly than the motherboard, and leaves you with a motherboard whose performance may not be up to that of the upgraded chip. Upgrading by removing the existing chip and substituting a later type is an option only if you have a motherboard which can be set to take a faster type of chip. This is why a new motherboard is often the only feasible way of upgrading, because an older board will probably not allow the use of faster processors.

Chapter 7 also deals with choosing a motherboard so that you can upgrade further in future. The main concern is not to get boxed in so that future upgrades can be achieved only by buying very expensive chips or by yet another motherboard replacement. You will quite certainly need a new motherboard if you change from an AMD to an Intel processor or the other way round.

The memory of a modern machine will be held in DIMM form. All modern motherboards will provide several DIMM sockets. You should not use more than 512 Mbytes of main memory unless you are certain that your software will cope with the extra amount. If you are using Windows *Me* or any other consumer version of Windows, you should stay below the 512 Mbyte limit.

You should not add memory to an existing motherboard unless you have the documentation for the motherboard, which is not always easy to achieve when you are refurbishing a machine. Old mother-boards were constructed so that jumpers or switches had to be set before adding memory, and incorrect settings could cause damage to the memory chips. More modern motherboards are designed so that, provided the memory is added in the correct way, no jumper or switch settings are needed. If a machine is so old that it will not accept DIMM then a motherboard upgrade is indicated, and if the motherboard is as old as that it is probably not suitable for an ATX case.

Chapter 10

The operating system

The operating system, as far as most constructors are concerned, will be Windows, and it might as well be the latest version you can get your hands on. This, for business and networked users, is currently Windows XP Professional, but home users should go for the Home Edition which is more tolerant of older software and hardware. If you feel that you do not want to use XP, then Windows *Me* will probably still be available for some time to come, though Microsoft does not usually support a Windows version for more than three years. You should not consider earlier versions, though a very cheap (or free) full (not upgrade) copy of Windows 98 SE is not to be sneezed at, not least because you can upgrade from it to later versions at a comparatively low price using the *Upgrade* version of Windows.

New machines will come with a working copy of Windows XP Home Edition, and this is a new version of Windows that looks nothing like Windows *Me*, or any earlier version, together with many additions that greatly improve stability and security and which provide more actions that previously were performed by other software (such as CD-writing). The snag with putting Windows XP on to a machine that you are building is that this version of Windows will not work for more than 30 days until it has been *activated* by Microsoft. This is an anti-piracy move, and the activation can be carried out over the Internet (automatically), or by telephone. Windows XP is set up to detect changes in your hardware, so that it will resist being copied to another computer, but a side-effect of this is that changes to your hard drive, memory, or other internal hardware may trigger a request for reactivation. This is not such a problem as you may think, and some users have reported that reactivation has not been needed even for a hard drive change. The reactivation procedure following a change of hardware (as distinct from a change of computer) seems to be reasonably flexible.

- If you buy or construct a new computer using XP, you can transfer settings and files from an older machine to your new one, using network connections, CD-R, or floppies. Windows XP Home Edition features a file transfer wizard that selects the files and settings for you and makes the task much easier.

My preference is to use XP, because it is so much better than anything that has been available for the home user before, but you might want to buy a full version of Windows *Me* and use that initially, because it is likely to be usable for several years to come, and you can switch to XP later.

- If there is no existing version of Windows on your hard drive (and for a new drive this is quite certain), you will need the CD-ROM for the OEM version of Windows, not the (cheaper) upgrade version. This comes with a floppy that will install MS-DOS, allow you to partition and format a hard drive, and make use of the CD-ROM drive. If you have an earlier full version of Windows 95 or 98, you can install this on the new hard drive and then use the upgrade version of Windows *Me* or XP Home.
- The setting up processes should ensure that you can boot the computer from its hard drive, and that the CD-ROM drive will be recognized, allowing you to install whatever version of Windows you want to use.

Windows is a complete operating system that allows you to run both Windows and DOS programs, though a few (very old) DOS programs can be run only by baling out of Windows completely. You should think about whether you really want to continue using DOS programs at all. Installing Windows does not erase MS-DOS from your hard drive but it reduces the number of DOS files and ensures that MS-DOS does not load in automatically when you start up the computer.

The more RAM memory your computer contains the better Windows *Me* or XP can use it, certainly as far as 512 Mbytes. A large amount of RAM greatly improves the ability of Windows to run several large programs simultaneously without reducing speed. For most machines, adding extended memory means buying DIMM, or other memory modules, and you must take care to install modules that are compatible with your computer.

The installation of a hard drive of adequate size is assumed – Windows is simply not intended for machines with small (less than 5 Gbyte) hard drives. Even a moderate selection of Windows *Me* files will require about 720 Mbytes. A hard drive of several Gbytes is necessary if you are to be able to use modern programs along with Windows *Me*. Currently, 40 Gbytes is quite common on package-deal computers, partitioned into two 20 Gbyte sections.

In the course of installation, Windows will create *folders*, meaning portions of hard drive space that are reserved for storing files. The advantage of using folders is that files that belong together can be viewed together rather than in alphabetical order of all files or in the order in which they were installed. A list of all the files on a drive would be difficult to work with (there are several thousand files on my hard drive), but a list of folders is much easier, especially with folders named *Programs*, *Books*, *Articles*, *Letters*, etc.

- Some Help notes refer to folders as directories, the older name that is still used by MS-DOS.

Windows makes extensive use of the mouse, and the fundamental mouse actions of pointing, clicking, double-clicking and dragging are all important. You should refer to the appropriate *Made Simple* book for your version of Windows if you are unaccustomed to these terms. The disabled user can dispense with mouse use, and can call up visual and audible prompts.

PROBLEMS

Because there are so many variations of the PC machine, using different video cards, keyboards, mice, modems and other features, and so many programs that can reside in the memory, it is impossible to test a new operating system with every possible combination of machine and software. If you are using a straightforward 'clone' PC with straightforward business software (no games) it is likely that you will be able to run the Windows Set-up program and use Windows without problems.

The README files on the CD-ROM are intended to notify you of problems that have arisen since your version of Windows went into production, and you should check carefully for references to your machine or to software that might be running at the time when you install Windows. More recent notes are available from the Microsoft websites, and your installation CD-ROM will contain a text file that notifies you of the web address.

During the long testing stage for any version of Windows, a large number of incompatibilities are found and dealt with, but because of the almost infinite number of combinations that can exist, it is impossible to say that Windows can be installed in any machine without *some* alterations. The README files contain notes on known problems, most of which deal with machines and software that are not available in the UK. Many of these problems can be solved by obtaining up-to-date drivers from the suppliers of hardware and/or software.

PRELIMINARIES

The following descriptions refer to a 'normal' installation of Windows *Me* and Windows XP Home. Normal means that your computer is not one that features as a problem device (usually from a well-known manufacturer) in the README files, and you are not running any of the listed hardware or software that is known to cause problems. We'll devote most of this description to the *Me* installation because XP installation, though different initially, follows a similar routine and is, if anything, more automated.

- Note that you must deactivate any anti-virus programs on your computer before you try to install a new version of Windows. The reason is that Windows installation carries out the same types of actions as a virus attack, so that it will trigger any anti-virus program into protecting against the changes that Windows installation must make.

Windows *Me* installation

You can install Windows *Me* into a computer that is currently running either DOS, Windows 95 or Windows 98, even Windows 3.1. For a newly constructed machine, the installation will definitely be from DOS – even if you are installing on a new hard drive, the installing program will put MS-DOS in place and then add the remainder. Check that you have the correct version of the Windows *Me* CD-ROM for the installation you are going to make. The upgrade version is suitable only if you already use Windows (preferably Windows 98) and the full version is needed if you are working from DOS, particularly on a new hard drive.

- You can alter any of the installed options later, for example, to add new printers to Windows, and even if you change the screen graphics card you do not need to go all the way through Set-up again in order to ensure that you have the correct files on your hard disk.

During installation, you will be prompted to insert a floppy to be made into a *Startup* disk (which used to be called a *System* disk). You can also make a Startup disk later by using the *Add/Remove programs* option of the Control Panel. This disk can be used if, for any reason, you find that Windows *Me* does not start when the computer is switched on. When you use the Startup disk the computer will start in MS-DOS, so that you will need to use only MS-DOS commands until you can start Windows *Me*. This allows you to use FDISK and FORMAT commands to prepare a hard drive for use with the MS-DOS tracks that allow the system to be booted from the hard drive. You can also use diagnostics programs in the event of a hard drive that refuses to work. The system disk will also set up a temporary CD-ROM driver so that you can install Windows *Me* from the CD.

Insert the Windows *Me* CD. This will start automatically so that you can use the mouse to point to menu items and the ENTER or RETURN key to confirm your choice of action.

Once you have opted to continue the Set-up action, the screen will divide. The column on the left is called the *Explorer Bar*, and it will become a familiar feature of Windows *Me*. During installation, it will stay on screen during the actions that use a Windows display, and it will at this point show a set of icons with the labels:

Preparing to run set-up

Collecting Information about your computer

Copying Windows *Me* files to your computer

Restarting your computer

Setting up hardware and finalizing settings

You will also see the display of *Estimated time remaining* which at the start will be 30–60 minutes. This estimate will become more precise as installation proceeds. As each process is executed, the text in this bar will become yellow.

The main installation process then starts with a search for drives. This is followed by a quick check of the C:\ drive, after which the Windows *Me* Set-up Wizard is prepared. The *License agreement* will appear, and you need to click the box marked *Accept* to continue (you need to scroll the box to see all of the text).

The next input that you need to provide is the 25-character *Product key*. This consists of five sets each of five letters and digits that are typed into five boxes. This key will be printed on a label on the CD case, and you should take a secure note of this code in case you lose it. It's not exactly something that you can commit to memory.

- If you lose this code you will be unable to reinstall Windows or to alter details of your present installation.

The program called the *Set-up wizard* will carry out some checks for existing files and for available disk space. You are then asked to establish your location, and you should find the name *United Kingdom* from the large list of countries – this is normally automatic when you are using a CD-ROM bought in the UK.

You now have to prepare a Startup disk (you can bypass this, but it is much better to make the disk now). You will need a formatted 1.4 Mbyte floppy. When you proceed, the action will be to collect files, and ask you to insert the floppy. When you do so you are reminded that this will delete any present content, and you are also reminded to prepare a label for the floppy. This floppy can be used to get your computer running if for any reason (such as hard drive damage) your computer fails to start some day.

You will then be asked to remove the Startup disk and click *OK* to continue. The file copying action (from CD-ROM to Windows folders) will start, and will continue for ten or more minutes. A set of messages, 17 in all, will appear during this process, and you can read these to find what advantages Windows *Me* will have for you. You are invited to take the *Discover Windows Me Tour*, when Windows is up and running, to learn more.

When files have been copied you are reminded that you should register your copy. This can be done online (if you have a modem) or by post. Incidentally, several manufacturers feature online registration and I have yet to find one for which this method has worked.

The next step involves restarting the computer, and if you are not present to click the *Restart Now* button, the process will start after a 15-second interval. Following this there will be a lot of disk activity, and you will see the display return to a DOS screen (black screen with white lettering) at intervals. This takes some time, typically 10–20 minutes, and ends with the *Welcome to Windows Me* display. You need to keep the CD-ROM in its drive when you run this display, because the files are read from the CD rather than being placed on the hard drive. You are again reminded to register. That's it!

During installation, you can opt to save your existing System files if there is any possibility that you might want to return to things as they were. This is recommended if you have space on your hard drive, and if you have more than one hard drive you can specify which drive is used to store these files. The recovery files are called **W9XUNDO.DAT** and **W9XUNDO.INI**. Following this step, you are asked to make a *Startup* floppy which can be used to gain control of the PC if the hard drive fails. You should create this floppy at this point because you may not remember later. It's like insurance, better to have it and not need it than need it and not have it.

- For details of using Windows *Me* see the books on Windows *Me* from Newnes.

STARTUP DISK USE

If at some subsequent time you find that your hard drive fails, you will have to use the Startup disk. The *Multi-Config Start Menu* allows you to boot up your computer from the new Windows *Me* Startup disk using a boot menu that allows you to load drivers for the most common CD-ROM drives or optionally to perform a normal clean boot. After you have made your selection, the CONFIG.SYS file will load the appropriate CD-ROM driver (if selected) and then a 2 Mbyte RAMDrive. The RAMDrive (a portion of memory addressed like a drive) is used to store all the diagnostic tools necessary to check and remedy the most common problems. Because RAMDrive behaves like a drive, it will use a drive letter, usually D, so that your CD-ROM drive will for this time use the next available letter, usually E.

- Real-Mode CD-ROM support makes use of generic drivers that allow you the use of the CD-ROM under DOS when Windows cannot be used. Not all CD-ROM drives are supported by this action, and if yours does not work with these drivers, you must use the ones that came with your CD-ROM drive by running the installation files on the floppy that came with it.
- The RAMDrive is only temporary and will disappear when you restart your computer normally.

Me FEATURES

Windows *Me* contains support for digital photography or scanner files. This allows uploading with save, preview, rotate and print actions without the need to use any other applications. You will, of course, need to use other applications if you want to edit your image files or to use OCR on images of printed documents.

Another pair of useful new features are *System File Protection* and *System Restore*. System File Protection makes it much more difficult to erase or change important files, and System Restore tracks any changes made to System files so that you can restore the system to an earlier configuration if problems arise.

Updating by way of the Web has been made easier, and can be automatic if desired. You can also make use of the *Help and Support Centre*, the replacement for the older Windows type of System Information utility.

The Help system of Windows *Me* is outstandingly good, and in my opinion this alone would justify the upgrade. Figure 10.1 shows the appearance of the Help screen as it first appears.

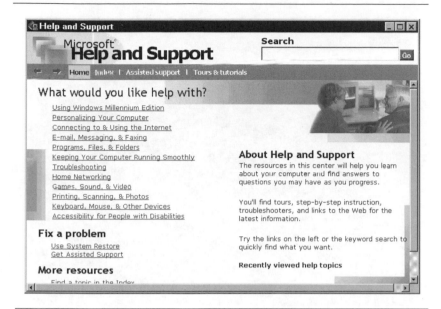

Figure 10.1   The first Help screen of Windows *Me*

When you look at Windows *Me* for the first time and start Explorer, it looks reassuringly similar to the appearance of Windows 98. Explorer is now more tightly integrated with Internet Explorer, and the Favourites menu has been reorganized so that you need to click on chevrons to see the full menu.

The most obvious change is to the Windows *Media Player* (Figure 10.2). This is now much more oriented to MP3 use, so that you do not need to download additional software to play MP3 music files. This introduces a new term – *skins*. Skins are files that determine a set of options for Media Player appearance, playlist, etc. Windows *Me* places an icon for Media Player on the foot of the screen.

Another noticeable change is the Start – Shut Down action, which has a different form of panel. The options are now Shut Down or Restart, with Shut Down the default. Restart can be used by selecting it from the drop-down list.

The Accessories set now includes eleven games, and of the familiar contents (to users of previous versions) NotePad, WordPad, Paint and Calculator are unchanged from the Windows *Me* versions. The Accessories set now includes the new item of *System Restore*. System Information now brings up a Help and Support panel.

Figure 10.2   The default appearance of Media Player, which caters for sound or video

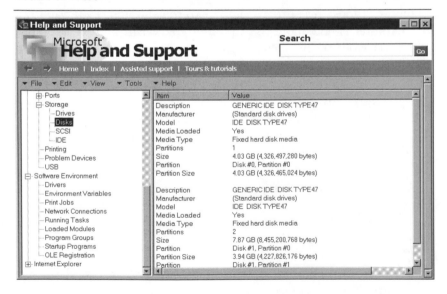

Figure 10.3   A typical display from *Help and Support*

Help and Support (Figure 10.3), takes longer to use than the older System Information of Windows 98. Each time you click on a different section, it takes time for refreshing the system information. If you use the *Problem Devices* section you may see a list with each item noted as Error Code 22. This does not imply that your computer has problems, only that the specified device is currently disabled.

Note that the Control Panel is greatly extended, but the default view shows only the commonly needed items. This same philosophy applies also to menus which can be personalized, meaning that each menu will hide the items that you don't often use. You can gain access to the less-used parts by clicking the down-pointing chevron at the foot of the menu. If you don't like this action you can revert to seeing the whole of each menu by clicking Start – Settings – Taskbar and Start Menu – General and then clear the Use Personalized Menus check box.

Installing Windows XP Home Edition upgrade

Before you even think of installing Windows XP Home, take a look (if you can) at the website:

www.microsoft.com/hcl

which contains a long list of hardware that has been approved for use with XP. This list is split into types, and you will need to know the manufacturer and type designation of each piece of hardware. It's most unlikely that your monitor, motherboard, keyboard or mouse will be a problem, so you should look in particular for modem, printer and scanner, since these seem to cause the majority of problems. If your hardware does not appear on the list this does not mean that it cannot be used, but there is a chance that you might have to download new drivers for the device.

Problems are usually caused by older hardware or software, and you will have considerable difficulty if your modem is one of the hardware items that is not recognized. If this happens, do not try to install XP until you have checked with the modem manufacturer that you can download new software, or that there is a procedure for ensuring that the modem is recognized. Note that the list provided by

Microsoft is not exhaustive, and some items that do not appear on the list may also cause problems.

- This hardware/software check is not an attempt by Microsoft to be awkward, simply a way of ensuring that everything runs smoothly. If Microsoft manufactured all PCs and PC hardware and software there would be no need for such checking, but because other manufacturers are so heavily involved there has to be some system for ensuring that what you buy to add to your machine will work correctly.

If you are about to install XP, make certain that you have made all the hardware changes to your computer that you intend to make for some time, because if you activate XP and then change the hardware you will need to activate XP again on the computer if you want to continue using XP. This alone is a good reason for not using XP on a machine that you are likely to upgrade in future. If you do not activate XP immediately, you can use it for a month (with daily warnings about activation) and make hardware changes, then activate it. The examples shown here have occurred during an upgrade installation from a computer running Windows *Me*, and you will find the procedure differs in some ways if you are installing from scratch, using a full version of XP Home Edition.

- Note that hardware changes mean internal fixed hardware such as graphics card, a network, hard drives, CD-ROM/DVD and RAM, but not modems or devices connected through the USB ports.
- As a last resort, you can uninstall XP and revert to Windows *Me* or whatever earlier system was running before XP. This is not exactly a comfort if you installed XP as the first and only operating system.

The installation of Windows XP Home Edition is started by inserting the disc into your CD-ROM drive, and Figure 10.4 shows the first screen display that appears. This offers the choices of *Install Windows XP*, *Perform additional tasks*, *Check compatibility*, and Exit. The additional tasks are more specialized, and you can usually ignore them when you make your first installation. Details of these tasks are illustrated in Figure 10.6, later.

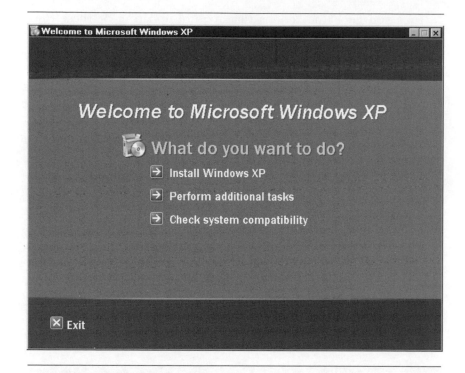

Figure 10.4   The introductory installation screen

The important first step is to check compatibility, because you need to know at this stage if any hardware or software on your computer is likely to cause problems later. This check is rigorous, and some items that trigger a listing as a problem may turn out to work perfectly, because the checking turns up anything that might be a problem. For example, your modem might trigger a warning because it is using a driver for an earlier version of windows, but in the course of Windows XP installation a more suitable driver might be located and used.

- When you use the *Check compatibility* or the *Install Windows XP* option, you are given the choice of downloading additional Set-up files from a Microsoft website. You can ignore this if you like, but I strongly advise carrying this out, because this ensures that the most up-to-date information is contained in the Set-up files, and this can avoid hardware and software problems that have been dealt with since the installation disc was issued. In my case, the download took about four minutes. This download is needed each time you click the actions that require updating of these files, because they cannot be stored on the CD and are not retained in memory after being used. At the time when this is done, the modem is still supported by the previous version of Windows, so it does not matter whether or not Windows XP can use it.

Figure 10.5 shows the Upgrade Advisor list that appeared on my computer after the compatibility check stage. Where an item is marked as not currently present, this can be because it is connected by USB and not switched on, or that it has been removed from the computer but has left a driver on the hard drive. This points to a failure of earlier versions of Windows, that so much software can be left on the hard drive after a device or software has been uninstalled.

This list needs to be checked over carefully. In the example, a device known as 'r' appears, and I haven't the faintest idea what it might be. Not shown in the illustration is a reference to a tape drive, though no tape drive has ever been fitted on this computer. This indicates that some tape drive software has remained on the hard drive which is now in its third computer.

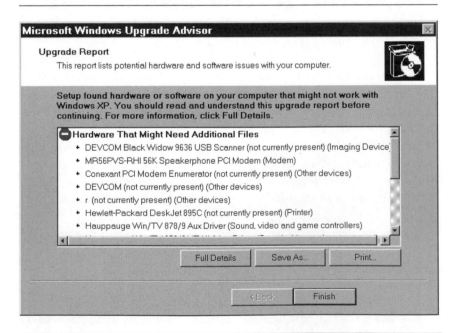

Figure 10.5   A typical Upgrade Advisor list

- I also had warnings that the ASPI Layer driver could not be loaded, but the checking continued when the warning box was deleted. This seems to have been triggered by Adaptech software that I once used for the CD writer drive.

Figure 10.6 shows the additional tasks list. The most important part of this for many users will be the option to transfer files and settings from an older computer, but you should also look at the release notes. This panel is also important if you are setting up a small-scale network at home.

So far, nothing has been done that affects your computer, and you are still running on your previous operating system (unless this is an installation of the full version of XP on to a new hard drive). You can make an exit from any of the panels that have appeared up to now, and return to the state your computer was in before you put in the XP installation disc.

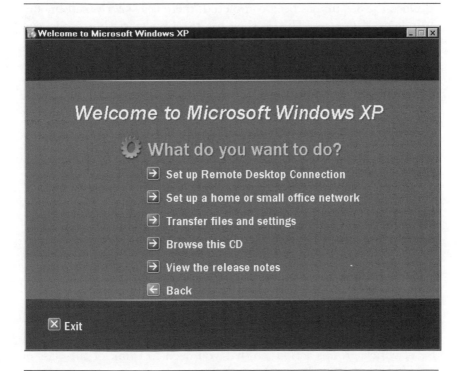

Figure 10.6   The *Additional Tasks* panel

To start the installation in earnest, go back to the initial panel (Figure 10.4) and click Install Windows XP. You will be asked again if you want to download new Setup files, and you ought to take this step to ensure that you are using the most recent version of Setup. Once the files have been downloaded, the Setup action starts, and you have nothing to do with the procedure, which continues automatically (though watch out for warnings such as the ASPI layer warning noted earlier, because these will hold up installation until you acknowledge them). The installation is lengthy, at least an hour unless your system is very fast, and at times you may feel that nothing very much is happening. Mostly, however, you will be aware of the hard drive working steadily, and the progress is shown as a list of main steps at the left-hand side of the screen, with details of progress on subsidiary steps shown as a bar display under the list. The main part of the screen lists the new features and facilities of XP. Your computer will be rebooted several times in the course of the automatic set-up actions.

Once the Set-up has been completed, there is a *Welcome* screen, and Windows XP starts. This is slow for the first start, but when you subsequently start, you will find that the start is much faster than it was for older versions. The first screen display (Figure 10.7) shows the menu that can be summoned by using the Start button. This is so very different in presentation from earlier versions of Windows that you should consider running the *Tour Windows XP* item that is offered as a way of becoming familiar with the system.

- Note that there are now separate *Log off* and *Turn off Computer* buttons, replacing the *Shut Down* action of earlier versions.

Figure 10.8 shows the appearance of the new Windows Explorer. This is more familiar if you have used an earlier version of Windows, and, as in the earlier versions, you can customize it to your preferred version. I detest icons as a display, and prefer to see a list of filenames because it allows me to see a much larger set of files on one panel.

In general, the guiding principles of XP have been to make use easier, trying to avoid long and confusing lists. This can take some time to become used to, as, for example, the much reduced Control Panel which groups actions so that you need to think of the class of item before you can choose in detail. There is a new Internet Explorer, version 6.0, with improved security, including the option to set up a

Figure 10.7 The new Start button menu, which appears after installation

personal Firewall against hacking. The new option to write CDs is reached through the Media Player rather than through a new menu, and all of this is a good reason for taking the Tour before you start to use XP seriously.

- You have the option, once XP is installed, of converting all of your files to the more advanced NTFS format, replacing the FAT32 system used for earlier Windows versions. There are many advantages to using NTFS, such as the ability to use more memory, large files and much larger hard drive partitions or using large hard drives with just one partition. If, however, there is any possibility that you might need to revert to an earlier version of Windows you must not convert, because though files can be converted from FAT32 to NTFS there is no conversion available in the reverse direction. If you want to use NTFS, convert only after using XP for some time. Partitian magic can convert NTFS to FAT32 files.

Figure 10.8   Windows Explorer display of XP

Installing a printer

- The installation of a printer takes much the same form in any version of Windows, and the illustration here uses Windows *Me* as an example; the steps are much the same for XP provided that you have not been asked to download new drivers. My H-P 895Cxi printer was correctly recognized by XP and worked with no problems.

With Windows *Me* installed, but the computer switched off, this is a good time to connect up a printer. There are two cable connections that you have to make. One is the usual mains power supply connection, and the normal pattern is to use a standard three-pin plug at one end, and a Eurosocket at the other. Note that a few printers have the mains cable permanently fixed at the printer end, so that if you find that the mains supply is just a few inches further away than the cable will reach you will need to use an extension socket.

- Note that a few printers have a fixed cable and no switch at the printer end. These will have mains power whenever the cable is plugged in, and are usually arranged to go into a standby condition if they are not used for several minutes. You should not attempt to break the cable to connect a switch, and the best way to connect a printer of this type is by way of a socket strip fed from the auxiliary mains outlet of your computer. That way, the printer will always be switched off fully when the computer is switched off.

The other connection is the printer data cable, with the DS25 connector at the computer and the standard Centronics connection at the printer end. These cables are usually one metre long, and though you can buy longer cables, you should try to locate the printer so that this cable length will be adequate. Some printers now use the USB type of connection, which can be made with the computer switched on and running.

Modern printers using the Centronics connection will need a *bi-directional* printer cable which can pass information back from the printer to the computer so that the printer can be completely driven by software. This type of software can, for example, give you an indication of how much ink remains in an inkjet cartridge. If your printer needs this type of cable, make sure that it is connected before you start the software installation for your printer, and make sure the CMOS-ROM has been set up with ECP port enabled.

- Note that if you have a printer that uses a bi-directional type of cable you should not attempt to connect and use a second printer that uses this type of cable. You should also avoid the use of printer switching boxes.
- Another point to watch is that the Centronics plug at the printer end of the cable must be inserted as far as it will go, and secured with the wire loops that are provided. Some printers are very easily upset if this plug is not fully home or if it is disturbed during printing.

Self-test

Almost every printer is capable of carrying out a self-test and printing a page without the need for any intervention by the computer. Find out from your printer manual how this is done – the usual action is to press a set of buttons simultaneously. For some printers that have no control panel on the printer itself you cannot carry out this action. A few printers need their data cable to be disconnected before a self-test can be run.

It is important to print a self-test sheet if the printer can do so. If a printer can produce a perfect copy of its test page (usually a sample of fonts) then a mechanical or electrical fault is unlikely to be the cause of the problem, which is more likely to arise from incorrect settings either at the printer or at the software. Remember, for example, that when you use the Windows printer manager the printer will not necessarily start printing immediately – it may wait until a queue forms or a 'print now' instruction is issued.

Printer port

Your printer is connected to the computer through a port, and the usual system in the past has been to use a Centronics parallel port, something that we have already dealt with. New printers are also likely to be fitted with a USB connector, and if you are determined to use this method you will have to heed the advice in the printer manual.

The usual port that is provided on all computers is labelled LPT1 (line printer 1) and it is unusual to find that this is not installed – but it's the unusual that so often causes problems. Problems are more likely to arise if you are using a printer on another port, such as LPT2, LPT3, or LPT4.

Your port settings should appear briefly on the screen when your computer is switched on, but this display is often hidden if the video monitor has not warmed up in time or if the screen display is quickly replaced by the *Loading Windows* notice. If you have any doubts about the port setting, you need to know how to bring up the CMOS-RAM display. This always requires some key or key combination to be pressed just as the computer is starting, and you may see a screen message such as:

Press Delete key to run SETUP

This varies from one computer to another, so that only the manual or the guide for the motherboard can be of assistance here. If you do not press the key(s) at the correct time there will be no action.

Once you can see the CMOS set-up screen you can check the LPT1 settings. This will show an address and the usual code here is either 03BCh or 0378h, and an IRQ number which is normally 7. If this appears, then the port is correctly installed as LPT1 for your printer.

The reason for the different address codes is that some video cards and video chipsets make use of the address code 3BCh for their own purposes. These makes are Matrox, ATI mach64, STBLMB Horizon, STB2MB Powergraph, or an Aries integrated PCI system. If you have any of these, the LPT1 port will be forced to use the address of 0378h which is normally allocated to LPT1 on older machines.

- If you install other ports (for a second printer or for parallel port peripherals such as a scanner) the address for LPT2 will be 0278 and the IRQ number is 5. There may be problems in installing an LPT3 port if you have any of the video cards or chipsets noted above, because this port would normally use the 03BCh address. You should always use the Windows *Add Hardware* option of Control Panel if you put in other ports, so that conflicts can be avoided. Windows 2000 will detect potential problems like this in the course of installation.

Drivers

A printer is not necessarily made useful simply by connecting it up to a port. Before your can print anything much you need to install printer drivers for Windows. Once the Windows driver is installed, you can print from any Windows application, such as word processors, spreadsheets, or accounts programs. One Windows driver is all that you need for one printer, but if you use MS-DOS programs you will need a separate printer driver for each application that you use running under MS-DOS.

- Some printers provide only the Windows drivers; others provide the Windows drivers with some MS-DOS drivers as well. Do not confuse a Windows driver with a Windows printer – a Windows printer is a laser printer that makes use of the Windows memory of your computer instead of requiring additional memory to be installed inside the printer.

Installing your driver software for Windows can be very straightforward if your printer is a model that was in production before your version of Windows was released, because this makes it almost certain that it will be listed in the built-in Windows driver set. Even if your printer is one that Windows does not list, however, the printer manufacturer will have provided a floppy or a CD-ROM with printer drivers. If all else fails, printer drivers can be downloaded from the Internet.

Driver installation starts with the correct printer. You need to know the name of the manufacturer and the precise model number of the printer. For example, if you are installing a Hewlett-Packard Deskjet 895Cxi, it is not good enough to use the driver for any Deskjet model – you must look for the precise phrase if you want to have full control over the printer.

With everything connected up and switched on, get to the Printers window of Windows *Me* in the usual way by clicking on the *Start* button, then on *Settings* and *Printers*. The Windows Printer panel includes an icon labelled *New Printer*. Click on this icon to start a wizard which will install your new printer.

A pair of lists will appear, Figure 10.9, one on the left-hand side of printer manufacturers and another on the right-hand side of models corresponding to the manufacturer whose name you have clicked. Once you have clicked manufacturer and model, you can proceed to the next part of the installation which will ask you to insert the CD-ROM (or floppies) that you used to install Windows. The driver software will be read from this source, and you can opt to print a trial page to ensure that the driver software will operate your printer correctly.

A slightly different procedure is needed if your printer is one that is not listed. This is likely if the printer is a very new type that was not being manufactured when Windows *Me* was issued, and you then need to use the software supplied by the printer manufacturer. In this case, you ignore the list, insert the floppy containing the drivers and click the button marked *Have Disk*. You will then be guided by messages on the screen so that the driver is installed from the disk, and you will usually be asked to opt for printing a test page.

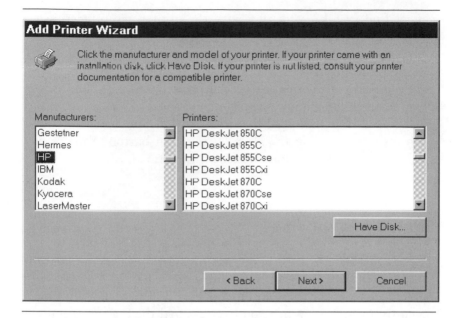

Figure 10.9   Installing a printer – this routine is the one used by Windows *Me*

If you cannot find your printer listed and there is no disk of driver software (for a second-hand printer, perhaps), your options are more limited. One is to make use of an emulation or a substitution. Despite the huge number of makes and models of printers that you see advertised, there are remarkably few manufacturers of the basic mechanisms or *engines* as they are called. An inkjet printer of uncertain origin will probably use an engine from either Canon or Hewlett-Packard, so that installing a driver for a model from one of these manufacturers will allow you to get printing, even if some actions are not supported.

- You can usually get the printer to provide text, but you may find problems with graphics and colour if you are not using the correct driver. It's easier to find a suitable driver for monochrome printers.

Finding what model to emulate is not quite so easy. If there is any paperwork with your printer it may refer to an emulation such as the H-P DeskJet 500C or the IBM ProPrinter. Laser printers can often make use of a driver from the Hewlett-Packard LaserJet series. If you cannot find useful information with the printer, try contacting the manufacturer, either by post or (much better) over their Internet website. You can also try news groups on the Net to find if anyone else in the world has experience of your problems. It's highly likely that you will get information on the printer, where to find drivers, what to watch for and how to sort out trouble.

Once you have downloaded a driver to a floppy, you can proceed with installation using the *Have Disk* option button. You are now ready to print out data from Windows as required.

Startup menu (*Me*)

The Startup menu is a list of options for starting the computer. You can go to this menu either by holding down the *left-Ctrl key* or by holding down the F8 key while you boot. This should bring up a menu (in MS-DOS). When you have entered the Startup menu you can use ordinary number keys for menu options, some of which are used for troubleshooting, others for starting in MS-DOS.

You can use key 6 to run MS-DOS in Safe mode, which means that none of the CONFIG.SYS or AUTOEXEC.BAT file commands will be used. This is useful if you suspect that one of these commands is causing problems (as, for example, a faulty network command might) that prevent Windows *Me* from loading correctly.

The 3 key will start Windows *Me* in Safe mode, in which only the bare minimum of services operate. This is enough to allow you to sort out many of the type of problems (usually with networks) that might prevent Windows *Me* from loading correctly. You should restart after sorting out the problems.

There are also the options of using key 1, for normal start (seldom needed, since this is the default if you do not press the F8 key), and for logging the start steps using the C:\BOOTLOG file. This is of interest to specialists only.

You can also start in MS-DOS by using the Startup floppy that will be made during Windows *Me* set-up.

When you leave Windows *Me* one of the options that you will see is to go to MS-DOS. This allows you to use MS-DOS in the normal way, and if you have retained your Windows 3.1 files, you can use CD to get to their directory and type WIN to start up Windows 3.1 in the usual way. You cannot, however, go from this to Windows *Me* without rebooting.

Memory and program problems

Programs (or applications, as they are often called) are the main source of trouble for the PC user. The programs need not be troublesome in themselves, but the way that they use memory, interact with other programs and require response from the user all add up to potential trouble, particularly for the user who believes that reading manuals or books would be a waste of time. This section, then, is devoted to the memory problems that can arise simply from the use of modern programs in upgraded machines (new wine in old bottles?), and we need to start with some basic ideas and recollections about programs and memory.

The main (RAM) memory of a computer behaves like a set of switches, each of which can be set to be on or off, and each remaining as it is set only for the time during which power is applied to the computer. A set of eight of these switch-like units is called one byte of memory. This size of memory unit is important, because this is the unit into which memory is organized, even if the computer works with larger units of two (16-bit) or four (32-bit) bytes at a time. One byte of memory is sufficient to store any character that can be represented in ASCII code, and memory sizes are always measured in units of kilobytes (1024 bytes) or megabytes (1 048 576 bytes). The use of the prefixes kilo and mega in this way is peculiar to computing, normally kilo means 1000 and mega means 1 000 000, and the reason for the difference is that the memory switches can be set one of two ways, so that numbers have to be stored in twos. 1024 is 2 to the power 10, so that this is preferred to the use of 1000 for computing purposes.

The microprocessor of the computer can gain access to any byte of memory by a very simple system of numbering each byte and using the number, called the address number, as a reference. In order to gain access to memory, the microprocessor must place signals corresponding to the address number on to a set of lines called the address bus, and there must be memory physically present which responds to that address. It's all very simple and logical so far, but this is where the problems start. The original 8088/8086 processors that were used on the original IBM PC machines (and the many clones that were constructed later) were capable of addressing 1 Mbyte (1024 Kbytes) of memory, an amount which at the time was thought to be ridiculously excessive. This does not mean, however, that all of this 1 Mbyte of memory can be RAM that can be used by programs. The machine needs some memory to be present in permanent (ROM) form, and some address numbers need to be reserved for this section of the memory. The microprocessor chip is made so that when it is first switched on or reset, it will try to read memory at a specific address, number 104.8560. This is built into the chip and cannot be altered, so that any computer using the Intel (or compatible) chips must provide for the BIOS program to start at this address. The remainder of the routines can be elsewhere as long as the start is at this fixed address.

A further complication is added by the use of the graphics card. The video signal depends on using memory, and the PC type of machine reserves memory addresses for this purpose, the video memory, with the RAM chips for this placed on the video graphics card itself. The amount that is needed depends on the type of video card that is being used, with SVGA requiring 2 Mbytes or more, EGA and VGA requiring a minimum of 256 Kbytes. Finally, the MS-DOS operating system, certainly in versions prior to 4.0, can use only 640 Kbytes of RAM for programs.

The later Pentium and Athlon class of machine uses a processor which can address very much more memory than the chips used in the original PC and XT machines, and the usual limit is 1024 Gbytes. This makes no difference as far as running MS-DOS programs is concerned, because they cannot use more than 640 Kbytes of memory, but Windows *Me* and XP can make full use of up to 512 Mbytes. Windows XP can use much more memory (up to 2048 Gbytes) when the NTFS filing system is used.

Your installed programs add another dimension to all this. When a program is installed in the approved way, it leaves entries into a database inside Windows called the *Registry*. If these entries are incorrect you can expect problems with some programs, notably Windows itself and all of the *Microsoft Office* set, though some older programs will run perfectly without problems because they use older methods. This is why you can encounter so many difficulties if you try to transfer all your programs from one hard drive to another. There are programs, such as *Drive Image* (from PowerQuest), that make this task easier by ensuring that registry entries and links between programs are correctly made on the new copy.

- Some programs of this type may not work on Windows XP because they might otherwise be able to bypass the need to reactivate when a hard drive is changed.

Stability is an eternal problem, and if you want to do things like playing a DVD, creating a CD-R, listening to a CD and looking at an Internet website all at the same time you will find that this sorts out machines in no uncertain way. It is this sort of combination of actions that explains why some processors are priced at £200 or more, and have to be used with equally high-performing chipsets and peripherals. The improved stability of Windows XP is another pressing reason for using this operating system.

Chapter 11

Sundry hardware items

So far in this book we have concentrated on the aspect of assembling the main hardware of a PC, assuming that the other items such as monitor, keyboard and mouse were either available from an older machine or were being purchased separately. These items are not available in DIY pack form, so they have to be purchased at some stage, and this chapter is concerned with points that you need to know so that you can buy wisely.

The monitor

The monitor is the display device that is the main output for the computer, showing the effect of your inputs. At one time computers did not use monitors, and relied entirely on printed output. When monitors were first provided on large computers they were used only for checking that the computer was working correctly, hence the name, and the main output of the computer was to a printer. Microcomputers from the beginning used monitors as a way of interactive computing that showed immediately the effect of each keystroke. In this book, we are mainly concerned with the monitor for a desktop machine rather than the built-in monitor of a laptop.

The cathode-ray tube (CRT) is the basis of the monitor for all desktop machines in the lower (less than £400) price range. The first monitors were monochrome (black/white) and of around 10 inches (diagonal) screen size – one of the attractive features of the original IBM PC was the very clear display on a monochrome monitor. Colour monitors, whose resolution is always inferior to that of a monochrome monitor, were introduced in the mid-1980s, and are now standard. All colour monitors currently used for PC machines are of the RGB type, meaning that separate red, green and blue signals are sent from computer to monitor.

The *resolution* of a monitor measures its ability to show fine detail in a picture, and is usually quoted in terms of the number of dots that can be distinguished across the screen and down the screen – the figures differ because the screen is not square, with a ratio of width to height of 4:3 (as for pre-widescreen television). A figure of 640 × 480 is now regarded as the absolute minimum standard; this is considerably better than can be obtained on a domestic TV receiver and is one of the reasons why a TV receiver makes a totally unsatisfactory monitor, the other being that it cannot use the VGA rates unless an adapter card is used. Resolutions of 1280 × 1024 or more can be obtained (at a price) with a colour monitor, but for the highest possible resolution only a monochrome monitor is satisfactory.

The reason that colour monitors have lower resolution than monochrome monitors is that each element on the screen is made up of a red dot, a green dot and a blue dot. This makes the overall size of each element or pixel on the screen larger than the single dot of a monochrome display.

- The dot size of a colour monitor is often quoted as a measure of resolution. This is misleading, because the dot size has to be compared to the screen size – a dot size of 0.25 mm looks good on a 17-inch screen but would be hopelessly large on a 5-inch screen. You should look for the dots per screen size figure, such as 1024 × 768, as a guide to resolution.

The price of a monitor is always much higher than that of a TV receiver of comparable size. This is because a monitor must use a more expensive precision-made CRT, with a closer dot spacing and a finer wire mesh to guide the three beams of cathode rays to the correct positions on the screen (Figure 11.1). Now that TV tubes are being made with flatter and squarer screens, the prices of monitor tubes are dropping because the differences in production methods are fewer. This trend will accelerate if we ever adopt a higher resolution TV system in the UK.

The screen size of a monitor is often questioned, because a screen quoted as 17 inches will neither be 17 inches wide nor 17 inches deep. TV receiver tubes were originally circular, so that the size of a tube was quoted as the diameter of its usable face. When it became possible to manufacture rectangular tube faces, the equivalent measurement was the diagonal, and this has always been used for TV receivers. The same system has been applied to monitors, but there are a few on the market whose diagonal measurement is less than the claimed size – do not assume that a Brand X 15-inch monitor will be larger than a Brand Y 14-inch monitor.

The price of monitors has currently dropped recently to such an extent that it has become quite common to see 17-inch monitors as part of a low-cost computer package, and 19-inch monitors are now available at a price that formerly bought only a 15-inch type. The larger monitors are particularly useful if you want to use the higher resolutions (800 × 600 or higher) and several screen windows. LCD slim flat-screen monitors are now appearing in larger numbers, but at the time of writing are still prohibitively expensive for the home user.

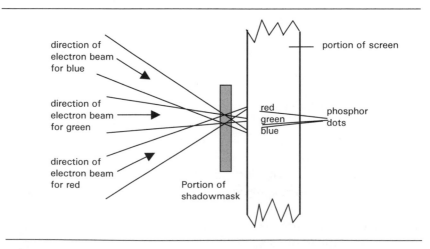

Figure 11.1   How a colour monitor tube uses three electron beams to produce colour displays

If you are replacing an old monitor with one that is intended to be used with a modern graphics board, look for one that can cope with SVGA (800 × 600 or higher) and which will make use of the standard Microsoft driver software, or which comes with good driver software of its own. Remember that driver software is one of the main sources of problems with monitors and printers, and not all drivers are of good quality, nor are the problems that they cause obvious. If you find, to quote a well-documented example, that your Internet connection keeps dropping out, this may be caused by one particular driver for ATI graphics boards, and an updated version should be downloaded. For more details of this problem, see the website:

http://support.microsoft.com/support/kb/articles/q175/1/48.asp

A good monitor should have more picture controls than a TV receiver. In addition to brightness and contrast, controls for picture position (often only side to side) and size should be present to allow for changes as the display card is switched to different resolution figures. In particular, if you alternate between using DOS and Windows, you will usually see the picture shift and change size when you switch the operating system.

Monitors that are separate from the computer use a CRT display almost exclusively, but monitor screens that are part of the computer, particularly in the smaller laptop sizes, are mostly LCD types. LCD displays, which do not emit light but can be used with transmitted or reflected light, are also used for overhead projector display so that computer output can be displayed to a large audience. Colour LCD panels are now standard for computer output. Larger LCD panels can be bought for use with a desktop computer, but these are currently still expensive, though excellent display quality can be obtained. All LCD displays suffer from the disadvantage that they provide a clear view only from the front, but the most recent types have a more acceptable angle of visibility.

Keyboards

The modern type of keyboard has 102 keys, laid out (Figure 11.2) in logical groupings. The function keys are set across the top of the

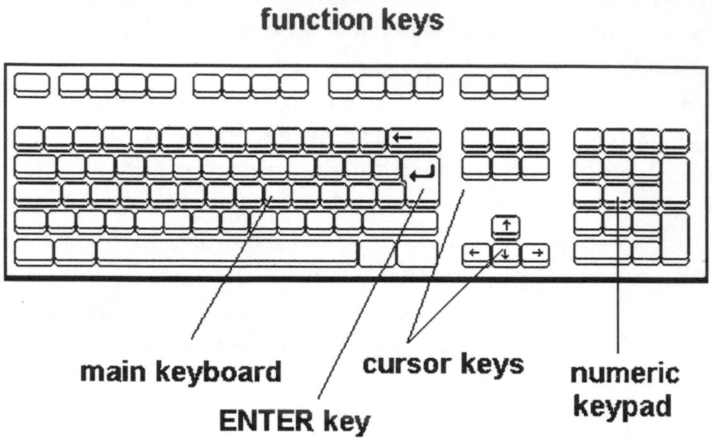

function keys

main keyboard   **cursor keys**   numeric

ENTER key   **keypad**

Figure 11.2 A typical 102-key layout. Some keyboards incorporate three extra Windows keys

keyboard, with the Esc key isolated to the left. The cursor movement keys are separated from the number keypad, as also are the Insert, Home Page Up, Page Down, Delete and End keys. The Ctrl keys are duplicated so that they can be used with either hand, making it easier to press Ctrl with any other key. Some keyboards use 105 keys; the added keys are provided for some Windows actions (such as Start button).

What you regard as a good keyboard is very much an individual preference. Most users like a keyboard to have a positive click action to the keys, but without excessive noise, and keyboards of the cheap and rubbery variety are universally disliked. IBM keyboards are very highly regarded by typists. Most anonymous keyboards are of a reasonable standard, and those branded with the name Cherry are highly regarded. Since the keyboard is your main communication with the computer, a good keyboard is important.

Though keyboards of the 102-key variety all look very similar, there are subtle differences. Some nameless clone machines come with US keyboards, which are easily detected because of the absence of the £ symbol (on the upper 3 key). Though a US keyboard can be used without difficulty, the absence of the £ sign can be irritating, though you can usually get the symbol by holding down the Alt key and typing the number 156 on the separate keypad, then releasing the

Alt key. An alternative is the use of Windows *Character Map*. If you seldom need to use a £ sign, there is no problem.

If you are using an older version of Windows, the Euro symbol, €, can be obtained by downloading a font called *Eurocollections* from a website in Holland – www.xs4all.nl. Look for the file euro13tt.zip which can be down loaded and unpacked (using WinZip or other zip utility) to give the TTF TrueType font that you can add in to your Windows fonts. Users of Windows *Me* and Windows XP will find the standard Euro symbol in the set that appears when you use Insert – Symbol and specify (normal text) for the symbol set, then look for the *Currency Symbols* set. When the time comes (as it must, since politicians always get their own way) you can use the hot key combination Alt-Ctrl-4 to provide the symbol instead. Modern keyboards place a Euro symbol on the E key.

A point that often causes confusion is the provision of an Alt key on the left of the spacebar and a key marked Alt Gr on the right-hand side. The Alt Gr key is intended to be used on machines that make use of the German character set and a lot of PC software will allow you to make use of either the Alt or Alt Gr key interchangeably. This is not always true, however. If you are accustomed to switching between Windows programs by using the Alt and Tab keys together you will find that the Alt Gr key cannot be substituted for the Alt key. *Microsoft Word for Windows* 97 also ignores the Alt Gr key (and also the right-hand Ctrl key) for many of its actions (though it can be used for some accented letters, so that Alt-Gr – e gives é). The main use of this Alt Gr key is to provide the third character on keys that display more than two character symbols. On UK keyboards the only character of this kind is the split bar which is usually shown also on the sloping front of the key next to the number 1 on the top row. One curious effect is that the solid bar and the split bar key symbols usually appear the other way around on the screen.

Keyboards should be kept covered when not in use, because dust can gather at an alarming rate. This can cause keys to jam, and when this happens you will see an error message appear when you try to boot up the machine. The message is *Keyboard error* followed by a code number which shows which key is causing the error; for example, 0E indicates that the Alt key is jammed down.

Another factor to consider is how keyboards age. Some keyboards do not change at all in the course of their life, others alter quite noticeably. One of my keyboards (a US layout) started life with a pleasant click action, but has deteriorated so that keys now stick closed or jam open at times. The other keyboard has remained good, and an old Amstrad keyboard (pensioned off after four years and a million words typed) remains as good as new. My favourite, which is now being used on its third machine, is an old IBM keyboard.

Never be tempted to spray WD40 or any other silicone lubricant on to a keyboard whose keys have started to become sticky. Using a spray virtually guarantees that some of the liquid, which is one of the best insulators known, will get into contacts, ensuring that the keyboard will never work again. You might be able to release one sticky key by careful lubrication using a drop of silicone oil on a piece of wire, but don't depend on it.

The *Control Panel* of Windows *Me* allows several keyboard actions to be controlled. When the *Keyboard* option is double-clicked, the first keyboard panel, labelled *Speed*, appears. This allows you to alter the character repeat (or typematic) settings, with separate adjustments for *Repeat Delay* (on a *Long* to *Short* scale) and *Repeat Rate* (on a *Slow* to *Fast* scale). There is a test area so that you can try out the effect of changes before closing down the Control Panel. You can also alter the *Cursor Blink Rate* (on a *Slow* to *Fast* scale) using this panel.

The other panels are concerned with *Language*, which for most users will be set to *British English*, and for *Keyboard Type*, which also remains set as it is unless you change to another keyboard.

The keyboard connector is constructed so that it can be inserted only in the correct position, and you should always turn the computer so that the socket is visible when you insert the plug. Do not use force when inserting the plug, and never pull the cable to remove the plug. Note that early Amstrad computers used a keyboard plug that is incompatible with modern designs and also with other PC machines of the same age. Some very recent keyboards use the USB type of connection with both an input (linked to the computer) and an output (linked to the mouse).

The mouse

The mouse is an essential part of the modern computer, and is the natural accompaniment to Windows. Mice exist as two-button or three-button types, with more elaborate models from Microsoft and

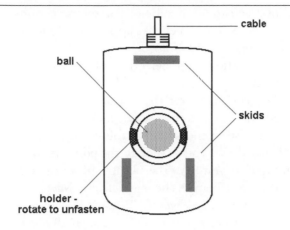

Figure 11.3   Typical underside view of a mouse

others, and with a variety of connectors. The illustration (Figure 11.3) shows the underside of a typical mouse.

The mouse can be connected in three different ways, each of which requires a mouse with the correct cable termination, and a matching connector on the computer. Computers that use the modern ATX type of motherboard and casing will normally provide a mouse port with the PS/2 type of connector specifically intended for the PS/2 type mouse. Another option, used mainly on older motherboards and cases is to fit the mouse cable with a serial connector that is plugged into the serial port. The third option that is now widely available is the USB fitting, plugging into a port on the (USB) keyboard or (unusually) to the computer directly. Adapters are available for DIN and PS/2 so that one variety of connector can be used with the other.

Connecting the mouse has no effect unless a suitable mouse driver is present and is run each time the computer is started. The MS-DOS driver is MOUSE.COM and this can be placed in the AUTOEXEC. BAT file if you need to use the mouse under MS-DOS. For Windows 95 onwards, the mouse software is run automatically when Windows starts. You can find the mouse driver for Windows by using Control Panel – System – Device Manager, select *Mouse* and use the *Properties* button followed by the *Driver* tab to display the driver. For example, you may find that the driver is given as C:\WINDOWS\SYSTEM\ MSMOUSE.VXD or the MOUSE.DRV file in the same folder.

Windows allows you to alter some of the mouse actions by using Control Panel – Mouse. The panel that appears has four tabs labelled as *Buttons*, *Pointers*, *Motion* and *General*.

The *Buttons* panel allows the selection of right-handed or left-handed use, with the default of right-handed (which I prefer even for left-hand use). You can also alter the double-click speed in a range *Slow* to *Fast*, and there is a test area (an animated Jack-in-the-box image) that you can use to check the double-click action.

The *Pointers* panel allows you to specify the pointers that the mouse controls, assuming that you have the pointer files in place. First you can select a pointer scheme, choosing from *None*, *3D Pointers*, *Animated hourglass*, *Windows Standard*, *Windows Standard (extra large)* and *Windows Standard (large)*. The three sizes of the *Windows Standard* scheme allow for using pointers that match the resolution, because the normal size (used for 640×480 displays) looks much too small on higher resolution displays. The *3D pointers* and *Animated hourglass* can be used if you have installed these files when you installed Windows. You can also select pointers for the various purposes that are used, listed as *Normal select*, *Help select*, *Working in background*, *Busy*, *Precision select*, *Text select*, *Handwriting*, *Unavailable*, *Vertical resize*, *Horizontal resize*, *Diagonal resize 1*, *Diagonal resize 2*, *Move* and *Alternate select*. The defaults can be left as they are unless you have a pressing need to change one or more, assuming that you have files for alternative pointers.

The *Motion* panel has an adjustment for *Pointer speed*, using a *Slow* to *Fast* scale, and you can also specify a *Pointer trail*, used for slow LCD screens on which the mouse pointer normally disappears when the mouse is moved. If you are using such a screen, you can click the box marked *Show pointer travel*, and specify the length of trail (mouse-tail) on the scale *Short* to *Long*.

The *General* panel shows the current type of mouse, and provides for a choice of manufacturer and model for other mouse options. The *Manufacturers* list contains *Standard Mouse Types*, *Compaq*, *Kensington*, *Logitech*, *Microsoft*, *Texas Instruments* and *Toshiba*. The *Models* list contains *Inport adapter mouse*, *Standard bus adapter mouse*, *Standard PS/2 mouse* and *Standard serial mouse*.

The main problem you are likely to encounter with a mouse is sticky or erratic pointer movement, caused by dirt in the mechanism. Turn the mouse over and remove the circular cover that holds the ball (Figure 11.4). Remove the ball and clean it, using a clean, moist cloth

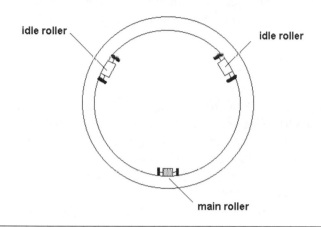

Figure 11.4   The mouse rollers that detect the movement

– you can use spectacle lens cleaner fluid or windscreen-cleaning fluid if you prefer. You must also clean the small rollers that make contact with the ball when it is in place. These are most easily cleaned by wrapping a piece of clean cloth at the tips of tweezers, moistening this and wiping it across each roller, wiping each roller several times while turning the roller slightly. Allow a few minutes for any moisture to dry and then reassemble the ball into the mouse casing and make sure that it is locked in place. You should also clean the skids or pads under the mouse, because any build-up of dirt on these can raise the body of the mouse sufficiently to make the contact between the ball and the mousepad intermittent.

If the mouse movement is erratic from the start, check that the correct driver is being used. For a machine using Windows and a standard type of mouse, it is most unlikely that the driver would be at fault, but if you have changed to another mouse or you are using a machine which has an unorthodox arrangement this is a possible cause of trouble.

- Another type of problem that you may encounter is that the mouse will move the pointer easily in one direction, but needs much more mouse movement to shift the pointer in the opposite direction. This cannot be cured by cleaning the mouse rollers (though you should try it), and usually requires you to buy another mouse. At current prices this is not a financial burden.

The standard mouse uses two buttons, but there are some three-button types, though the third button is not normally used by Windows software. A more recent Microsoft mouse design, the *Intellimouse*, uses scroll wheels to permit the scrolling action to be carried out from the mouse. A scroll-wheel type of mouse is very useful if you work with long text documents.

There are other options for pointing devices, and one is the *trackball*. The trackball (Figure 11.5) looks like an inverted mouse, and consists of a heavy casing that remains in one place on the desk. This carries a ball, larger than the usual mouse type, that can be moved with the fingers, and a button either side of the ball. The action of ball movement and button clicking follows the same pattern as the use of the mouse, and some users prefer it, particularly for graphics applications. The price of a trackball is usually rather higher than that of a comparable mouse, and you need to check that its software will be compatible with the version of Windows that you will use.

Graphics tablets are another form of pointer that, as the name suggests, are particularly suited to graphics work. A graphics pad or tablet looks like a rectangle of plastic with a stylus, and the movement of the pointer on the monitor screen is controlled by the movement of the stylus over the graphics tablet. This means that every

Figure 11.5   A typical trackball

point on the monitor screen corresponds to a point on the graphics tablet, so that the larger the tablet you use the more precisely you can control the screen pointer. The stylus can be pressed to provide the click action of a mouse. Graphics tablets are expensive, particularly in the larger sizes.

Scanners

A scanner (Figure 11.6) is a device that reads documents by using an image sensor strip, and stores a digitized image as a file. This can be used as a form of copier, for editing graphics, for fax transmissions, or for reading text into a word processor without retyping. Scanners can be hand-held, flatbed or roller-feed types, and you can also buy specialized types for scanning photographic negatives or slides.

Scanners either use an interface card (often a SCSI type), or can be connected through the parallel port or the USB port. If you buy a parallel port scanner, it is preferable to buy an additional parallel port card as well, because it can be very inconvenient to have to disconnect the printer each time you need to use the scanner. The parallel-port type needs only connecting up, and installing its software. The card type will require you to open the computer to plug in the card, and then connect the cable between the card and the scanner. The software can then be installed.

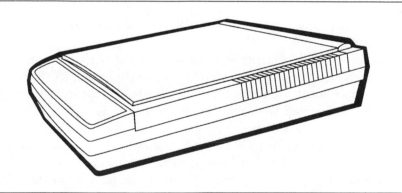

Figure 11.6   Outline of a typical flatbed scanner

- If your hard drives already use a SCSI interface, you can install a scanner that uses SCSI without the need for any additional cards. Most modern scanners can be connected through the USB port.

For copying a document, using the scanner as part of a photocopier, you need to be able to use both the scanner and the printer, so that if you are using a parallel port scanner you should have it connected to a different port. The printer and the scanner should both be switched on and the printer loaded with paper. Select the *Copy* action on the scanner software and specify the number of copies needed. If your printer is a good colour inkjet type, you can achieve very realistic colour copying in this way, and you can copy a set of photographs of normal size on one A4 sheet so that you can obtain a set of copies at a very low cost.

Graphics scanning is usually a default action, which brings up a graphics editor. When the document (usually one that contains or consists of a graphics image) is scanned, the image will appear on screen and can be edited like any other bit-mapped graphics image. The graphics software will also be able to save, load, or print the image.

The scanner can be used as the input for generating a fax message, provided that the computer is connected to a fax modem. When the software is run, the document can be scanned, and you will be asked to specify a fax number, or choose one from a list. The document will then be faxed to the recipient.

OCR means optical character recognition, and refers to software that will recognize the graphics image of a character and convert this into the ASCII code for that character. In other words, OCR allows the scanner to be used as a text reader, providing an input to a word processor.

Leading OCR software is usually bundled with a scanner, and provides for a very high standard of text recognition, so that only a spell check is usually needed on the text after recognition. Problems can be experienced with very small character sizes, with italic text, tables, or with a document received by fax. You can usually opt to vary the resolution for OCR from 200 dots per inch, suitable for large type sizes, to 400 dots per inch, suitable for smaller text.

Hand scanners were the first types available, but are not really suitable for good-quality work. Few users can hold the scanner in a fixed position and move it down a page steadily enough to allow a good image to be captured. This type of scanner would be supplied only with graphics software, and not used for copying, fax or OCR work.

Roller scanners offer, for little additional cost, very much better performance than a hand scanner. The scanner is about the size and shape of a carton of cooking foil, and when activated it will grip the document and roll it at a steady speed past the image sensors. The improvement in image quality as compared to a hand scanner is such that it can be used for all four main actions of graphics, copying, fax and OCR with good results. This type of scanner can be bought in the form of a combined scanner and keyboard. Each page of a document has to be fed in manually, and for a bound document, you may have to remove part of the casing so that the scanner can roll over the page rather than pulling the page past the scanner. Some varieties can accommodate a document feeder. The low price of flatbed scanners has now made both hand-held and rotary scanners obsolete.

A flatbed scanner holds the page steady under a lid and scans it using a system very like the scanner of a photocopier. The quality is excellent, and several models allow for colour scanning. Automatic page feed can be used, which is particularly useful when OCR is being applied to a long document. These scanners can be costly, and those at the top end of the price range can be used for professional printing tasks, such as magazine illustrations. Low-priced models, for as little as £50, are a useful addition to the computer system and provide as much as is needed for hobby and small-business needs. Scanning is an essential part of the system for reducing office paperwork, in which each incoming document is scanned into a file and made available over the office network.

- Some scanners can be fitted with an add-on for scanning photographic transparencies (slides or negatives), and in some cases you can buy the transparency unit (or tranny) at a lower price when you buy the scanner. I have tried several types of transparency adapters, but had very poor results from them, and I much prefer to have a separate transparency scanner.
- Scanning action depends on using a built-in light source. This is usually a cold-cathode type of striplamp, and it can be expensive (more than £20) to replace, despite being a mass-produced item used in photocopiers and fax machines. If your lamp fails, look on the Internet for replacement parts.

Digital camera

The digital camera (Figure 11.7) is a more recent item that is now packaged with many makes of computer, often at a considerable discount. The principle is to use a light-sensitive matrix such as is incorporated in camcorders, but with software that will read the information and compress it into a file. This file of information can then be stored in the camera, using either a memory card or (unusually) a 3½-inch disk drive.

Figure 11.7   A front and back view of a typical, modern digital camera, the Fuji 2400 Zoom (courtesy of Fuji Corp.)

Connecting the camera through a serial link or by way of the USB port to the PC allows you to download the image files from the camera to a graphics editor on the PC, so that you can edit the pictures and then print them using a colour inkjet printer. A printer of good quality is essential, and for the best results, coated paper should be used. Prices of suitable printers and paper have dropped at the time of writing.

MODERN DIGITAL CAMERAS

The first generation of digital cameras worked at maximum resolutions of 640×480, a total of 307 200 pixels, and most of them used the serial COM port for transferring their files to the hard drive of the PC. Even at this comparatively low resolution and with JPEG compression, the downloading of a set of image files to the PC's hard drive was a fairly lengthy operation, and when the modern *megapixel* (more than 1 000 000 pixels) cameras arrived, the need for faster downloading became imperative.

- Note that resolution isn't everything. Certainly the use of a camera with less than one megapixel of resolution will not be satisfactory if you want to make A4 sized prints on glossy paper. Now that cameras are being sold on the basis of having ever-increasing resolution it's time to remember that these very high resolutions are of more interest to people printing posters than those who simply want a good-looking 7×5 print with an occasional A4 enlargement.

What is much more important is the amount of *compression* that is used. Compression is needed to make files that will fit into the comparatively small command of memory that is available for a camera. There are basically two types of compression for images. Non-lossy compression provides a compressed file that can be extended without any loss of the original data, and you get back the original file exactly. Lossy compression, by contrast, removes bits of the file that are least likely to be noticed, so that when you recover data from a file compressed in this way you do not recover all that you originally had.

Non-lossy compression is very unlikely to provide a small enough file for digital camera storage purposes, so that the lossy type of compression, such as the JPEG type, is always used. The greater the amount of compression that you use, the smaller the file but the down side is that there will be more of the image lost. This is not necessarily very noticeable on some images; it amounts to a loss of fine shades of colour and of some very fine detail. If, however, you intend to make large prints of your photographs then a very compressed image will provide a noticeably inferior picture. The effect of lossy compression is also very noticeable if you edit and save a file a few times, because some more is lost each time you do this.

A few cameras allow you to store the raw pixel image file, or one that has been subjected to non-lossy conversion, but on the amount of memory that is supplied as standard this allows for only a few shots, possibly as few as two or three. At the other end of the scale, most cameras will permit large compression factors (such as ×24) to be used, and they label this degree of packing as *coarse*, with the minimum amount of packing (around ×4 to ×6) called *fine*. If you want to make good-looking enlarged images, it is much more important to use fine packing than to have a high resolution. Storing your images at a packing of × 4 with a 2 megapixel camera is much better than storing at a normal packing of ×10 on a 3 megapixel camera.

The down side is that you need more memory in your camera. Typically, a 2 megapixel camera will come with a memory of around 8 Mbytes, which permits 12 shots at a resolution of 1280 × 960. Expanding the memory to 32 Mbytes allows you to use a compression of only 1:4 at this resolution, giving 50 shots which, blown up to A4 size, will look as good as anything you can get from a conventional film camera of the same price. Given that conventional film processing is not always of the finest quality, you can generally look forward to producing better shots than you would get with film, certainly better than you could get from any compact camera. Don't even think about parting with serious money for 32 Mbytes of memory, because you will find that prices quoted in computer magazines, at computer fairs and on the Internet are very much lower (typically by a factor of 3 to 4) than you can get in high street shops.

The methods used to download these large image files, typically 640 Kbytes or more each shot, require fast transfer, and the most popular system now is to use a USB connection. This requires a special cable, supplied with the camera and software. The software makes the computer treat the camera's memory as another drive, so that downloading consists simply of dragging the files from this new drive to another drive or folder on your hard drive.

This is a very simple and reliable scheme, and I much prefer it to methods that require you to take the memory card out of the camera and place it into a reader connected to the parallel port or by a conventional USB link. This latter method can be fast, but it inevitably wears the contacts on the memory card, and eventually the contacts will become unreliable. This might take a long time, but I always prefer to plug in a memory card and leave it in place until I need a larger one.

There's another point that's not strictly related to computing but which needs to be known much more widely. Digital cameras obviously use battery power, and the design is usually optimized to use the minimum of power for taking photographs. My experience has been that a considerable increase in supply power is needed for transferring images to the PC, and unless your digital camera uses rechargeable cells then I strongly recommend using a mains adapter to power the camera when you replay pictures to the PC. You can rely on such mains adapters costing about three times as much as you would pay for a mains supply from Maplin, but I would not like to take the risk of using a supply unit that was not approved by the camera manufacturer.

If your camera uses standard alkaline cells, don't be tempted to use the new rechargeable alkaline types, because these simply cannot provide the amount of current that a digital camera requires for replaying signals. In my experience they cannot even provide enough current to power the camera for taking photos. The cameras that permit the use of rechargeable cells will normally run on either nickel cadmium or nickel hydride types, but it is more usual to have such cameras supplied with ordinary alkaline cells, leaving you to buy rechargeables and the recharging equipment for yourself.

When you buy a digital camera, you will normally find, in addition to any drivers that it needs, some editing equipment. If you are not particularly happy with the editing program that you get with the camera remember that you can use programs such as Paint Shop Pro (PSP) to edit and print your camera files. You do not need to make use of the digital camera downloading software within Paint Shop Pro unless you have one of the older cameras that makes use of the serial port. My own preference is to ignore any other software and make use of Paint Shop Pro because it is such a well-known and well-developed program that can perform all your editing tasks and also generate drawings for other types of illustration.

The last part of work needed to produce a digital photograph is, of course, a suitable printer. You should use a printer that is stated as being suitable for photographic output, and you also need to use paper that will be suitable for your needs. You can use ordinary printing paper if you simply want to make a rough draft print to get an idea of what the final version will look like. For example, you might want to make use of the PSP facility to print a page containing quite a large number of photos in thumbnail form so that you can decide which ones you want to print at higher quality. To make your final copies, you need good glossy paper, but this does not mean paying high-street prices of the order of 50 pence or more per sheet. Shopping around should come up with packets of 50 sheets for just under £10, for example the glossy photo paper from CLP. The specification for this is 170 gsm (grams per square metre), and at the time of writing, a pack of 50 sheets is priced at £9.59 if you buy two packs. Take a look at the website:

www.clp.co.uk

for details of this and other offers on paper and other inkjet supplies.

There is little point in paying a large sum for a camera with very high resolution unless you can print to the same standard, and you should note that the quoted resolution of an inkjet printer is usually applicable to monochrome printing only. For example, a printer that claims 700 or more dots per inch in mono may deliver only 300 dots per inch in colour. This will still produce pictures that look better in colour than in monochrome, because colour printing uses more ink tones, and very good results can be achieved from printers that use more than three colour heads.

- Unless you need the 'instant' access to an image that digital cameras permit, you might be better served by a low-cost colour scanner and a conventional camera.

Working with video

Video, as far as the computer builder is concerned, means signals from broadcast TV, from video recorders, or from video cameras (*camcorders*). Most of these sources are currently analogue, meaning that the variations (amplitude and phase) of the electrical signal carry all the information on brightness and colour of each part of a picture. The disadvantage of any analogue system like this is that any form of interference that can change the amplitude or phase of the signal will cause distortion of the picture information. Interference, in this sense, can mean interfering signals, such as can be caused by lightning or by the action of electrical switches, or it can mean degradation of the signal caused by travelling through a long cable or through space.

By contrast, digital video, which has for a considerable time been used in TV studios, is almost immune from interference effects. Each part of a picture is represented by a set of numbers, and there are software routines that can check the validity of these numbers to ensure that the error rate is very low. Digital signals are now being transmitted, both for TV and radio, and digital camcorders are also available so that in future any conversion from the older analogue system to digital will not be necessary. At present, we have to live with both systems, and as far as received TV is concerned the advantages of digital in an area where clear signals are already attainable is not so overwhelming as was once thought.

Television frame structure

This is not a book on television techniques, and if you want to learn more about these topics you will need to consult more specialized works. There are, however, a few points that you need to know about the structure of TV pictures before you can fully understand the problems that arise when you work with video signals in your computer. The most important of these points concerns frames and frame structure.

At present a transmitted TV picture consists of a set of lines, and the variation of brightness and colour of each point in the lines make up the picture. One complete set of lines is termed a *frame*, and in a moving picture there are differences from one frame to the next. In the European systems, the frames are repeated at the rate of 25 per second, but in the US system repetition rate is higher, 30 frames per second. This is just one of the reasons why US video tapes cannot normally be played on British machines.

When the modern system of TV transmission was being devised in the 1930s, it was important to have the picture information repeated at a fairly high rate, 50 sets of lines per second in the UK system. Unfortunately, it was not possible to transmit 50 complete frames per second (because of bandwidth considerations) and a system called *interlace* was introduced. For an interlaced picture, half of the lines of one frame are sent in 1/50th of a second and the other half are sent in the next 1/50th of a second so that the full frame takes up one 25th of a second. These half-frame units are called *fields*.

Interlacing is less relevant to digital pictures, and is not used at all on modern computer monitors because these are connected by cable and there is no problem of bandwidth as is found on transmitted pictures. The concept of a frame, however, as one complete picture unit, is important in all forms of video work, digital or analogue.

By using the frame as a unit, digital editors can allow perfect slow motion and still picture extraction, and also the ability to make a movie image from a set of stills. In addition, the idea of a frame also provides for the enormous amount of data compression that can be employed on a digital picture.

For example, a conventional analogue TV transmission of a still picture means that all the information of this picture is being transmitted 25 times per second, taking up a considerable amount of bandwidth. For the duration of that still picture, all the information apart from that of the first frame is redundant. The digital equivalents would therefore transmit the frame information, hold it in memory and use it for as long as the picture remains unchanged.

Even when the picture changes, the change is not necessarily very large. For example, a person may walk across a landscape scene so that the landscape background remains unchanged and only the image of the person is shifted from one frame to the next. Once again, an analogue system would have to transmit all the information, redundant or otherwise, but the digital system can hold the unchanging background information and concentrate on sending only as much as changes from one frame to the next.

All digital video then makes use of compression techniques that remove redundancy and also remove features that are almost unnoticeable. The removal of some parts of the picture means that this type of compression is lossy, even if the loss is not particularly noticeable. It is only by using lossy compression that we can achieve the low bandwidth that is now used for digital TV. The down side of lossy compression is that any editing action will repeat the losses. To edit a video picture, you have to undo the compression to work on the picture elements, and when you recompress it you will lose still more of the picture. After several edits, the degradation in the picture may be noticeable. This is one of the problems of working with digital video, and its effects are that very large files may be needed if you want to carry out editing on uncompressed files. You need to be aware that the consumer versions of Windows such as Windows *Me* and Windows XP Home impose a limit of 2 Gbytes on file sizes, though the professional versions such as Windows NT, Windows 2000 and Windows XP Pro will permit much larger files.

COLOUR

Until about 1952 television was available only in monochrome (black and white). Experiments with colour transmission had been tried on several occasions, but bitter experience convinced everyone that a colour system would be useless unless it was completely compatible with the black and white system. All broadcast colour systems therefore use a set of colour signals that are transmitted alongside the signals for the black and white image, and which add colour to that image. This does not add as much bandwidth as might be expected because colour is not visible in fine detail and so only patches of colour information need to be sent.

The original US system, NTSC named after the National Television Standards Committee, sends colour signals using a system that alters the amplitude and the phase of a radio signal, the subcarrier. This system originally had many problems caused by alterations in the subcarrier when the signal was reflected, and this gave rise to the nickname *never twice the same colour*. The system has been greatly improved since the early days but still relies on the same principles.

The early problems of the NTSC system led European nations to consider other possibilities, and the two solutions both involved sending one set of colour signals on even numbered fields and another set on the odd number fields, so that the colour information for one frame was the average of the colour information for the two fields of an interlaced picture. This reduced the vertical resolution of the colour picture, but since fine detail is not visible in colour, this made little difference to the perceived picture which still had the same fine detail in monochrome. The two European systems are the German PAL and the French SECAM. These differ in the way that the signals are transmitted, and the PAL system is used in Britain and over most of Europe, with SECAM used in France, French colonies and the former Soviet Union.

- These differences between European and US colour standards are another reason why video cassettes are not interchangeable between the two countries. Some video recorders and TV receivers, however, can display NTSC videos on a receiver that is primarily intended for PAL reception.

ANALOGUE SOURCES

Analogue sources include the analogue camcorder, VHS recorder, or live analogue TV. The most likely reason that you will have for working with digital video signals is the use of an analogue camcorder, and that is what we shall concentrate on in this book. You should, however, remember that these other sources can be treated in the same way.

If you have an analogue camcorder, it is likely that you have a store of tape cassettes of your treasured moving images. Some users transfer these files to VHS tape and reuse the camcorder cassettes, but this is not the best way to treat them because:

1. You get the best image quality only on a fresh camcorder tape.
2. The transfer from camcorder tape to VHS invariably causes a degradation of the image, even if you are using an S-VHS camcorder and a good VHS recorder.
3. Each time you play a VHS tape, the image quality will deteriorate. This might not be noticeable on a movie that you look at once a year (why then bother to buy it?) but it will gradually affect home movies that you show frequently.
4. Making another copy means repeating the painful business of linking the camera to the VHS recorder, setting up the recorder and then controlling both until all the video has been copied.

There is another option, to digitize the moving images and store them on your hard drive or on a CD. The latter option also allows for making VCDs (video CDs) that can be played either on your computer or through a DVD player on your main TV. We'll deal with VCDs later. Like a CD, a VCD can be copied digitally, making a perfect copy with no need to make electrical connections.

It would be great if such digitized images were of really high quality, like DVD images, but that's not possible, because DVDs are not made from VHS or camcorder video tape but from professional video tape or from film. The VHS process greatly reduces the resolu-

tion of a TV image, and the circuits that deliver the video information to a home TV receiver are also far from perfect, so that what
appears on the screen from DVD can be noticeably sharper that
anything you can get either from transmitted pictures or those from
VHS video tape. The nearest you can get to such high quality is to
make movies with an S-VHS camera and play back direct from the
camera to the TV receiver (not on to VHS tape), or to use a digital
camcorder with either direct playback, or storage on VCD or DVD.

Why not wait until DVD recorders become reasonably inexpensive? This is certainly an option but it's not necessarily the most
sensible option. Using a DVD recorder will certainly allow you to
make recordings from video without taking up vast amounts of your
hard drive, but the quality of these recordings will be no better than
the quality of video tape from which they arise. In fact, using a DVD
recorder makes no sense at all unless you have digital picture inputs,
either from the digital camcorder or from digital TV. Even pictures
from a digital camcorder are likely to have reduced resolution in
terms of a number of lines vertically and the number of pixels horizontally; some have a resolution that is about half of the 640 by 480
that you might expect. Digital TV uses compression methods that
make the copy on DVD inferior to anything you can buy on a manufactured DVD disc. You could certainly expect to make much longer
playing videos in this way, but how often would you really need this?
If you have edited down your videos correctly then very few of them
are likely to last as long as one hour, and one hour is what you can get
on to the VCD. Instead of paying several hundred pounds for a
recordable DVD machine, why not just use the equipment you
already have and make VCDs?

● The other clinching argument is that there are two main
  competing forms of DVD recording, and no one knows which will
  become predominant. Do you want to end up with the one that is
  no longer supported?

We'll look briefly at the use of digital camcorders later, but for now
we'll concentrate on getting the best out of that stack of old analogue
camcorder tapes without the need to load them into the camera and
wire up to the TV each time you want to see them.

There are three steps in transferring video signals from an analogue
camcorder to VCDs. These are:

1. Digitizing the video signals, usually to AVI (audio-video inter-lace) files.
2. Editing and conversion to MPEG-1 files.
3. 'Burning' these MPEG-1 files to a blank CD-R in the format needed for DVD replay.

- Some hardware video capture cards allow you to carry out the first two steps together, producing MPEG-1 files directly from the camcorder input. This requires very fast processing, and such cards are expensive. I'll assume that if you had that much spare cash you would already have gone to a digital camcorder, and, like me, you have a stack of analogue tapes at hand and you want to keep the cost of conversion down. After all, if you invest in an expensive capture card, you'll have to replace it later with one for digital camcorder input when eventually you change to a digital camcorder.

The first part of the solution is to install a TV capture card. There are several models available, and they are nearly all suitable for the task of downloading video signals from a camcorder, digitizing the signals, and storing as a file. Some cards specialize in capture only, and a few of this type, as noted above, will store the digitized file with MPEG compression, so that it takes up minimal space on your hard drive (amounting to only about 10 Mbytes per minute of film running time). Others will digitize the signals and store either the raw digital video in AVI format (at up to 430 Mbytes per minute), or you can opt for some compression system such as Indeo 5 to reduce the size of files. Do not assume, however, that you will be able to use compression on the files as the images are captured – more of that later.

For my own experiments into digitized video I used the low-cost Hauppauge (pronounced hop-hog) WinTV Go! card. This caters for video input or a TV signal from an aerial so that you can view and record TV programmes directly. I have used only the video input portion, and have tried both the supplied software and others, noted later.

Some care is needed regarding your computer resources. If you store raw video, you can be sure that the quality will be maintained throughout any editing actions, but the amount of hard drive space is discouraging, about 25 Gbytes for a one-hour film, and this does not allow for the creation of a temporary film while you are editing. Furthermore, Windows does not permit such large files, and the limit is 2 Gbytes (less for older versions of Windows).

The way that video capture software gets around this is to split a long video into segments that are each of 2 Gbytes or less, but for your home movies it's most unlikely that you'll want to get into such complications – most of your efforts will consist of fairly short clips (and you might want to edit a lot of longer ones down to a more manageable size). You should also be using a computer with a fairly large memory and a fast processing speed. I have been working with 384 Mbytes of memory and a modest processor speed of 850 MHz.

One point that does make a considerable difference as far as video processing is concerned is the use of separate hard drives, one containing your Windows files and other programs, and another used only for the digital file data (though you can keep other data such as text files and still picture files on it as well). The important point is to separate the program material from the streaming video material. If you have only one hard drive this should be configured to a maximum possible working speed, and divided into two partitions, one of which is used for your video files but not for any program files. An ideal specification for hard drives is a rotational speed of 7200 rpm and the use of at least an ATA-100 data transfer system with DMA.

Another option that software for capture cards will offer is compressed image files, either at the point of capture or later during editing. This is not usually MPEG compression, and the most common type that you will find offered is Intel's Indeo system. This is very effective in reducing file size, but it needs to be used with care, because too much compression will make motion look very jerky. This is not a feature of the compression system, it simply means that your computer is not up to carrying out the compression in the time available between frames of video information. If you capture using VirtualDub (see later), you can see the percentage figure for processor use on the screen, and if this is 100% or close to 100%, then you will have problems with jerky motion caused by frames being repeated to replace a frame that could not be captured in time. On a machine with only an 850 MHz clock rate, none of the high-compression options could be used without this problem arising.

- Incidentally, if you are comparing image files looking for jerky motion, use a small image because uncompressed files can also look jerky if they are played full screen (due to limitations on how fast the computer's graphics system will cope). Some software asks you to choose a quality setting on a 0 to 100 scale, but this is not the same as setting the compression, and you may find that a setting of 95 will still produce a lot of compression (more than 10 to 1).

Some software may offer compression systems that do not degrade the image, such as Brooktree YUV411. These certainly preserve quality, but the amount of compression is only twofold so that your files will need some 218 Mbytes per minute of playing. The other Brooktree system, Brooktree ProSumer Video 32, gives a compression of about 7:1, but on my system produced problems with flickering colour bands between pictures. The Hauppage software options are for *File* and *Format*, and in the *File* menu you should set for *No Compression*. In the *Format* menu, as well as the 352 × 288 picture option you need for European PAL broadcasts (as distinct from US NTSC), you can specify the *BTYUV* option which gives the same 218 Mbytes as the Brooktree (abbreviated to BT) *YUV411* option, and the *YUV9* option works at around 170 Mbytes per minute.

- **Brooktree** refers to the makers of the chipset that many capture cards use.

Audio is another matter. The default is usually CD quality, but this is usually completely inappropriate for camcorder tape digitization. Most camcorders offer mono sound of about 11 kHz upper frequency limit, so that using 24 kHz, 16-bit sampling and mono settings will be perfectly satisfactory (do not be tempted to save bandwidth by using 8-bit sampling for sound). If you are simply storing the files for replay on the PC you can compress the audio, but if you want to make VCDs that will play on a DVD player you *must not* use compressed audio. The reason is that you need to convert your video to MPEG files, and the MPEG compression system cannot work with an audio file that is already compressed (though it can work with a video file that is already compressed by a standard method like Indeo). There are utilities which will compress the audio parts of the file so that you can convert to MPEG.

Software for digitizing the video is not hard to come by. Even the cheapest interface cards will supply some form of capture software, often allowing you to capture video, stills, or separate audio. You will in any case need to load driver software for your interface card no matter what software you use to capture video. If you don't want to make use of the capture software that comes with the interface card there is a reasonable choice of other types. One obvious one is the Microsoft Movie Maker that is built into Windows *Me* and later. Another is an excellent shareware program called *VirtualDub* which allows editing of the resulting files and a huge variety of filter effects that can suppress noise, brighten the image and many other effects.

Microsoft's Movie Maker is very impressive because, by recording separate video and sound files, it allows you to add a sound commentary to the existing sound, or to replace the existing sound. It also performs a very impressive degree of compression without causing the video to appear jerky when the picture moves. If you are making video files purely to replay on the computer then this system has a lot going for it, and it contains capture software that is of very good quality. The overwhelming snag is that the final system is not compatible with AVI or MPEG and though it is possible to convert from the Microsoft WMA type of file to MPEG, software for this purpose cannot be offered because of a veto imposed by Microsoft. Because the file format is not compatible with MPEG, you cannot record these files on to a CD and expect to be able to play them in a DVD player. For me that rules out the use of this otherwise useful program.

VirtualDub can be downloaded from the site http://www.virtualdub.org/index. The program installs into any modern version of Windows in the usual way, and you can run it from the desktop or from an icon on the toolbar as you choose. VirtualDub is an advanced editing program, but this does not require you to have to learn the more advanced methods simply to capture and work with video files. When you launch VirtualDub the first screen you see is a simple one with a few menu items of *File*, *Edit*, *Video*, *Audio*, *Options*, *Tools* and *Help*. Figure 11.8 illustrates this (editing) screen with a video file being edited.

The file menu contains the item *Capture AVI*, and this is the one to click for capturing your video. When you do so a new menu appears containing the items of *File*, *Audio*, *Video*, *Capture* and *Help*. You can capture the video simply by pressing the F7 key and starting the camcorder, and the capture stops when you press the Esc key. The

Figure 11.8 VirtualDub being used for editing

audio menu allows you to specify audio compression and also the audio quality in terms of sampling rate and number of bits. For making VCD discs you will want to avoid audio compression, but you will wish to set sampling rate and number of bits appropriate for the source of your sound. The video menu has a considerably larger number of options and the one that is of most interest is the compression set, which allows you to specify various types and extent of compression.

The *Format* item in the *Video* menu allows you to set the video dimensions, and for the PAL TV system used in the UK this should be 352×288. Once you have set the sound sampling rate and number of bits, video compression (if any) and the video format then you can start experimenting with video capture. Since the purpose of this book is to show what can be done rather than to go into fine detail of using software, we'll leave it at that. Once you have captured some digital video, you can also use VirtualDub to edit it, cutting out unwanted portions, and using the filter options to correct picture faults. Much of this has to be learned by trial and error, and one of the useful things about video CDs is that you can burn the files on to CD-RW, try them out on a DVD player, then you erase and try other ideas. This lets you work on what can be a very steep learning curve at very little expense. Learning to make digital videos with CD-R discs is rather an expensive way of making coasters. This way, you can store the files on your hard disk, try them out on the CD-RW, and if they look OK you can save them to CD-R. This way there is no waste.

We're leaping ahead of ourselves, however. After you used the capture card what you have is a file that is still in the AVI format, taking up a large amount of space on your hard drive. You can still edit this file and you can, if you have enough space on the hard drive, join one to another provided that you remain below the 2 Gbyte limit. A file in the AVI format can be played back in Windows media player, but not from a DVD drive, and to make a VCD that will play back on the DVD player, we need to convert that the AVI file into an MPEG file. Once again this is a job that needs software, and though there are some excellent commercial offerings, my personal preference is for a short, neat and simple program called simply AVI2VCD. Starting this program brings up a simple panel that asks you to browse for the AVI file, and to provide the target file name and folder for the MPEG file. The conversion is not rapid, and you will have plenty of time to make and drink coffee before your MPEG file is finished. One oddity I have found is that the program tries to call up my modem, but if I close the dial-up networking panel then the conversion to MPEG goes ahead in a straightforward way.

- All of this indicates that if you are serious about working with analogue video files then it makes a lot of sense to buy a capture card that will do the MPEG conversion in one go, so saving a considerable amount of hard drive space and also quite a lot of time. The down side is that fast conversion needs costly hardware and is useful only if your computer is fast.
- If you use the Hauppage card, you can download MPEG compression software that works with the card. This requires a computer whose processor rate must be more than 500 MHz.

MPEG editing

These processes are fairly straightforward, but you always have the awkwardness of working with very large AVI files. One way around this is to convert each file from AVI to MPEG just after capture, and then delete the AVI version. You can then use an MPEG editor to join files together, and to carry out other editing actions, notably actions such as making smooth dissolves and other transitional effects between scenes.

You can edit MPG files with the Womble MPEG editor, which, at the time of writing, costs only US$45 for MPEG-1 work (much more expensive for MPEG-2). You can download a sample version, which will carry out most of the actions other than saving an edited file, from the website: http://www.womble.com.

The advantage of this is that you are working with files that are smaller than the AVI files by a factor of about 45. This means that if you have converted, say, a large number of AVI files each lasting five minutes (and therefore each of a large size) into MPEG files, you can join them using the Womble editor into one large file that you can record as a VCD. You can also use the Womble editor for editing sound, and you can insert a still picture into the video and hold it for as long as you like, an action that can be very useful for titling. The main glory of the Womble editor, however, is its ability to intercept transitions from one scene to another and there are effects selected by name such as: *wipe horizontal, wipe vertical, wipe rotate, blend, zoom circle, keying title image, colour keying title image, beginning fade, ending fade.* Figure 11.9 illustrates the panel that provides these actions.

Figure 11.9   The Womble editor panel for transition effects

These are listed both as start and end effects, but the end effects are greyed out, and there is no indication on the Help pages how to use the set of end effects, nor how to use the *Offset* slider (which is inoperative). In this portion of Womble, a new file can be inserted anywhere in the video, allowing you to paste another portion at the end of an existing one and so make a longer piece of video. Finally, you can record the final effort in MPG format, and save it as a VCD.

VCD creation

Now you have a file that is very much smaller, about 650 Mbytes for a full hour of video. You can play this file using Windows media player, but the real aim is to put it on to VCD so that it will work on a DVD player. This obviously requires a CD writer drive, and one that has modern software. My CD writer is an ancient one, a Philips CDD 3610, but it is nevertheless suitable for creating VCDs, so that more modern CD writing drives should certainly be suitable. The Philips drive came with Adaptec software that was equally ancient and which made no provision for creating VCDs. There is good software for CD writers available from Adaptec, and many CD writers now come with the excellent Nero software. I found a package called Click'N'Burn from Starland of Plymouth and have found this very easy to use for all CD writing purposes – data, audio, or video.

The important point is that you simply cannot record the MPEG file directly on to the CD-R disk. This would not create a disk in the correct format that a DVD player will recognize, hence the need to have a special writing program. It's important to know also that you cannot make a multisession type of video CD in this way, but there's nothing wrong with burning a set of files in the order that you want to see them play, providing that it is all done in one session. In other words, you should save up your MPEG video files on the hard disk until you have enough to fill one VCD. It's so easy to select different files to play on the DVD machine that there should be no problem about mixing files with different topics.

- Incidentally, once you have recorded a VCD you can still replay your files on your PC, though not simply by clicking on the CD title. You have to use Windows Explorer to find the DAT portion of the recorded files and click on that to bring up Media Player and see the result.

Digital camcorder

Digital camcorders are rapidly superseding the older analogue type, and one result of this has been to bring the prices of analogue camcorders down considerably. This might possibly encourage you to start your video experience with analogue, using conversion to VCD, rather than learn about video with an expensive digital camcorder. On the other hand you may decide that you would like to start video work right away with the digital camcorder, and another possibility is that you have had a considerable amount of experience with an analogue camcorder and you would like to change to digital. Prices for digital camcorders now start at around £450.

Like an analogue camcorder, the digital camcorder records on tape, but instead of recording analogue images (signals whose electrical voltage carries information on intensity and colour), it records digital information in the form of a set of numbers that describes each portion of each picture frame. This digital information is not raw, it has been organized into frames and compressed and then stored on to the tape using the normal methods of video recording.

The standard for a professional digital camcorder is a 720×480 image size, considerably more than the 352×288 that is used for analogue camcorders for the European PAL standard. The compression is not the MPEG type as used for transmitted pictures and for DVDs, and the system that is used aims for a constant processing rate of 3600 Kbytes per second. For 'average' pictures, this produces the same sized files as would be achieved by a compression of raw video files by a ratio of 5:1. The advantage of this system is that it allows file processing without the need to carry out expansion and recompression, so that when you copy digital video files from your camera to your hard drive there is no loss of data.

Many types of consumer digital camcorders use the Mini-DV standard. This format was first standardized in 1995 to provide more compression than was used for the professional system, hence the use of smaller tape formats and much smaller cameras. The image resolution is of the order of 500 lines and there is little discernible loss of quality when files are copied and edited. The alternative, pioneered by Sony, is a system called digital-8 which can make use of the older type of analogue Hi-8 video cassettes. Camcorders using digital-8 can also play back the analogue Hi-8 tapes that have been made on an older analogue camcorder but when the same tapes are used for digital recording they provide only two-thirds of the capacity as marked on the tape; in other words a 60-minute Hi-8 tape will provide only 40 minutes of digital recording. Note that some Sony camcorders will not play back analogue Hi-8 tapes even though they can use them for digital recording.

The downside of this is that you need to be able to transfer the information at the same high rate. When the first digital camcorders came onto the market, all that was available on a PC machine would be the serial port or the parallel port, neither of which was ideally suited for this type of data transfer. The Apple Mac, however, had a data transfer system called Firewire or iLink (more correctly IEEE1394) which could cope with this data transfer rate. Firewire ports are now available for PC machines at a price very much lower than the earlier types, so that the digital editing of files from digital camcorders can now be carried out as easily on the PC as on the Mac. Some machines even come with a Firewire port built in. USB-2 ports may in future be used on digital camcorders.

For a machine that works under any version of Windows, the digital video from a Firewire link is stored in Microsoft's standard AVI type of file. There are, in fact, two versions of the AVI file, type 1 stores all the digital video as one single stream of data, but type 2 separates the video and audio (sound) data. Most users will work with the type one file, but the second type is very similar to the Microsoft Movie Maker type of structure in which the sound can be edited separately from the video.

The original Microsoft specification for AVI files limited their size to a maximum of 4 Gbytes and the older consumer versions of Windows will not accept a file size greater than 2 Gbytes, which corresponds to about 9.5 minutes of digital video from a digital camcorder. The FAT32 file standard available from Windows 95 onwards will permit the use of up to 4 Gbyte files. The NTFS system in Windows NT and Windows 2000 allows files that are limited only by the size of hard disk or partition.

Once captured, files can be edited in the same way as has been mentioned earlier. These files can be recorded on CD, or on DVD if you have a DVD writing drive. Another option is to output the files through the Firewire connection to the camera so that the data is recorded back on tape. This is possible only if the Firewire ports in your camcorder will accept inputs as well as outputs. Because of French customs regulations, many camcorders sold in the UK have the Firewire output facility disabled, since this avoids the need to pay customs duty in France on a machine classed as a video recorder. This is yet another example of Euro-mess, and many enterprising owners of digital cameras have found sites on the Internet that show how this restriction can be avoided. It's quite likely that by the time you read this digital camcorders sold in the UK will no longer be bound by this ridiculous restriction.

Another point to look out for is the use of OHCI. This is the standard method for exchanging control signals by way of Firewire, so that the computer can control the tape actions (record, play, fast-wind) of the digital camera. If the camcorder supports this standard system and the computer software is suitable the camcorder can be regarded as another peripheral attached to the computer and controlled completely from it, just as a still camera can be connected as if it were another drive.

One warning is important. All of this technology is moving quite fast so that what seems an excellent and expensive system today may be a rather dull and outdated one tomorrow. At the time of writing, USB-2 was beginning to appear on systems with the aim of replacing Firewire, but the effect of this was being seen more on the use of external hard drives than on camcorders and it's likely we are some time away from seeing new digital camcorders with USB-2 rather than Firewire. As always, you should be guided by what your needs, as distinct from wishes, are in the future. There is no way of making a design future-proof, but if you have not spent too much on equipment then you will leave some leeway for changes in the future.

USB peripherals

The adoption of the USB for all modern computers has allowed a great variety of add-on equipment which at one time would have required either a SCSI connection or the use of the parallel port. At one time, I used to build my computers with three parallel ports so that I did not have to share the printer port with other equipment. I still prefer to run the printer from its own dedicated Centronics port and also to use the mouse and keyboard with the PS/2 connectors, but USB is preferred for all other connections such as my scanner and digital camera. The only snag with conventional USB ports is that they are not quite fast enough for the most exacting requirements, and in this respect the adoption of USB-2 will solve even these problems.

One particularly useful way of expanding your computer is by adding a hard drive externally, using the USB connection. The drive box itself costs around £50, and the only difficulty is finding a supplier, because these do not appear to be items that are stocked by many. Try RL Supplies (01923 896996), Micro Direct (www. microdirect.co.uk), Eclipse (www.eclipse-computers.com or 08707 456 000) or AUT (www.autdirect.co.uk) or you can enquire on the Internet for anyone who has these parts. External drive boxes for either 3½-inch or 2½-inch drives are available, and for the home constructor of a normal PC you would want the 3½-inch type. You may need to wait for several weeks for delivery.

The drive box contains a power supply, and has to be plugged into the mains as well as to the USB cable to the computer. You can then put any normal hard drive into the box. If the hard drive is one that is already formatted and full of files, you can use it right away as if it were a networked drive that is part of your system. You can also put in a new unformatted drive and format this and use it as you wish.

One obvious application of this is that you can expand your hard disk provision considerably, though you need to remember that a hard drive used across an ordinary USB link will not provide the speed that you would get from an IDE drive. This points to the use of such an external drive for backup, or for storing data that you can temporarily transfer to an internal drive when you need to have rapid access.

Another application is to upgrade your PC. One of the most painful parts of upgrading occurs when you need to replace your C: drive with a larger unit. This normally requires you to take out your old drive, and connect in a new one, partition it and format it, then install Windows and all your programs on it. This is very time-consuming, and if, like me, you tend to upgrade your computer very frequently, you might consider the use of a utility called Drive Image from PowerQuest software. This allows you to copy files from one disk to another so that the files on the new disk are arranged exactly as they are on the source disk. By contrast a normal copy simply takes the files and copies on with no regard to the exact position of any file on the disk.

- At the time of writing, I cannot be sure if the use of DriveImage in this way gets around the problems of upgrading a hard drive on a machine that uses Windows XP.

If you have a new formatted drive on your external USB system, you can use drive image to transfer everything from your existing C: drive. Now when you remove the old C: drive and install the new drive that was previously in the USB housing, you will find that you can boot from this drive and use all the programs that have been transferred to it without the need for reinstallation. If you also like to alter the partitioning on the hard drives that you use, there is another product called Partition Magic, also from PowerQuest, that allows you to alter partitioning without losing data.

Obviously an external drive housing allows you to use anything that can be plugged into the standard IDE connector, and this includes CD-ROM drives and even CD-R/RW drives. Some caution is needed here, because the ordinary USB connection may not be fast enough for some purposes, and there is always a risk of losing a CD-R because you are not supplying data fast enough. You should always check with the manufacturer of an external drive housing that it can be used for this type of equipment. At the time of writing, Teac had introduced a CD rewriter which was capable of using the new USB-2 system as well as the older form of USB (at a lower speed).

Expanding IDE

An alternative to the use of an externally connected drive is an IDE expansion card. These are by no means expensive, and they allow you to connect several more hard drives into a system providing that you have the bays in which to fasten them. RL Supplies (01923 896996) offer the PCI UDMA-100 IDE controller cards at a price of only £19 plus VAT. One of these controllers allows you to add up to four additional EIDE devices which can be hard drives, zip drives, CD-RW, or

DVD. At a slightly higher price you can buy a controller card that offers RAID facilities so that your data can be duplicated in such a way that the failure of one hard drive will not cause the loss of any data. The RAID facility is an added complication that may not appeal to the home computer user but which is very useful if your computer is used for business purposes. The same firm, incidentally, offers a large range of other interface cards for such purposes as Firewire, USB expansion, or audio/video capture.

Networking

Networking within your own home can offer a use for a retired computer or a way of checking what the kids are doing on their machine(s). This applies particularly to a spare machine with a reasonable amount of hard drive space. The scheme is to connect the spare computer to the main computer in a simple network. You can arrange things so that you have access to all the drives of the spare computer from the main machine, and you can, but only if you want, have access to the drives of the main computer from the spare computer. Though the spare computer can be kept in another room, it is easier to use this system if both machines are close to each other, because both must be switched on to make use of the file-sharing actions.

This can be a very useful way of backing up files from the main computer, storing files that are not immediately required, and of providing facilities that you need only occasionally on the main computer. Remember that the spare computer need only be switched on when it is needed, and with its intermittent use the hard drive will have a long life.

- Note that this also allows a printer to be shared, or for one machine to use either its own local printer or a printer that is connected to the other machine.

Obviously, anything like this requires both hardware and software, and the software is already incorporated into the later versions of Windows (95 onwards). The hardware can, at the simplest, consist only of a cable connecting the two computers. If you are content with a leisurely rate of data transfer, or for transfer over a distance of more than a metre or so, you can use a serial cable. For much faster transfer you can use a parallel cable, but this introduces a few complications. One is that the parallel cable is not the same as is used for a printer, but is differently connected, and with the same type of D-shaped plug at each end – a printer cable has a 25-pin D-plug at one end and a Centronics flat-connection plug at the other. The other point is that this system ties up the parallel port in each computer. If the spare computer is not connected to a printer, then this is of little conse-quence since there will be a parallel port free. On the main computer, however, which will be connected to a printer, a second parallel port is desirable. The third option is to use a special form of USB cable, but this is useful only if both computers have USB ports, and an older machine might not.

If the two computers you want to link are not in the same room, and you do not feel inclined to work with long runs of cable (which can present difficulties), the options are to link through the telephone lines or through the power cables. Using the telephone lines ties up two telephone points, and the ordinary telephone services cannot be used at the same time. Connection through the power lines is comparatively easy, but needs interfaces that are to approved stan-dards – do not assume that a connector that is licensed to be used in the USA (at 115 volts) is suitable for use in the UK (at 240 volts).

If you need to buy networking cards for these methods of connecting computers you should seek assistance from a computer store that you trust. Once the hardware connections are made and both computers switched on, the Home Networking wizard of Windows *Me* or XP will set up the network for you. You do not need to have Windows *Me* or XP working on both computers, only the one that is designated as the server. The other computer, however, must be running Windows 95 or later.

At the time of writing, a system called Bluetooth, using radio signals for interconnection, was becoming available for connecting peripherals and looked likely to be usable for small-distance networking as well.

Chapter 12

Junior league upgrading

There is another form of upgrading that you might wish to consider for machines that are not exactly at the leading edge of modern computing. Though it is desirable, if you wish to use modern software, to have a machine that is constructed to modern standards with a fast processor, large hard drives and adequate memory, you may feel that you can manage on a machine of lower capability, using older software. You might also consider such a machine as a gift to a child or grandchild so that they can use educational software, and not worry too much when they find that they can't run new fast games on it. You might feel that an old machine has given you good service, and that a modest upgrade is all that you need for the foreseeable future. If these are your needs, this chapter is designed to help. Since the techniques of upgrading are covered in other chapters, this can all be brief, but a few points are repeated for emphasis.

Assessing possibilities

You need to take a look first at what has to be upgraded. Upgrading a really old machine is simply quite impossible, so that if you have an ordinary PC of the 8086 or 8088 variety, and that includes the first Amstrad models, any form of upgrading is out of the question. The absolute minimum standard for even the modest upgrading outlined in this chapter is a machine of the 386, 486, or Pentium-1 class. Let's look, to start with, at what we might be able to make use of in such a machine.

1. The case may be usable if it will take one of the Baby AT sized boards that were in use a few years ago. Figure 12.1 shows the outline of a classic Baby AT board, and if this looks as if it would fit into your casing, then it will be possible to upgrade with a new motherboard. The point here is that the older types of mother-boards had the processors soldered into place, so that there is no possibility of replacing the processor in such a motherboard.

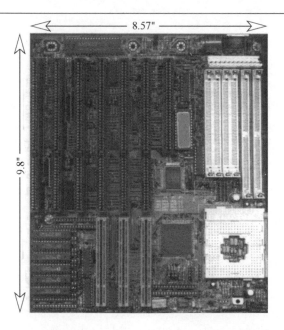

Figure 12.1   The outline of a Baby AT board

2. The 3½-inch floppy drive can be used in an upgrade machine, provided that it is of the later 1.44 Mbyte size rather than older 720 Kbyte size. If the floppy drive is of the old 5¼-inch size, take it out and sling it. If there is no provision for a 3½-inch

drive, the case cannot be used.

3. If there is a CD-ROM drive fitted, it may be usable provided that it is driven from an ATA connector, and not from a sound board or other unorthodox source. The CD-ROM will probably be a slow variety, but that's better than nothing.

4. The hard drive will probably be much too small for a modern version of Windows, and if it is connected through an interface card in one of the motherboard slots, then it is simply inappropriate for a modern machine. If you are lucky enough to have a hard drive of nearly 1 Gbyte, then it can be used.

5. Any sound board on the old machine is likely to connect through an ISA slot, but if your need for sound is modest or zero, then it's good enough.

6. A modem on an old machine is hardly worth retaining because it will be a very old and slow variety.

7. The memory on an old machine will almost certainly be in SIMM units, but if there is enough of it and it can be used in the new motherboard then you might be able to recycle it.

All of this may sound rather pessimistic, but the technology has changed so much over the last five years, and older components have become so scarce, that it is almost impossible to do an upgrade on an old computer without a large number of replacements. Whether the work is worthwhile or not depends on your need for such a machine, and how many bits and pieces you can pick up from the junk box at a computer fair. The problem with such a source of components is that you seldom have any instructions or manuals so that you are thrown back on your own experience to decide for yourself what can be used. Stallholders at computer fairs are generally very helpful over such advice, but you have to remember that there is a limit to how much help you can expect for the low price that the items cost.

You can expect then to have to buy at least a new Baby AT motherboard, and if you are upgrading a 386 or 486 machine, it makes sense to buy a motherboard that takes one of the AMD K6 processors. If you are upgrading a Pentium-1 machine, you should enquire to find if a faster Pentium chip could be fitted into the same motherboard, allowing you to reuse the old motherboard rather than buying a new one. The trouble with Pentium chips is that they went through a vogue for slot fitting, and slot-fitting motherboards are now difficult to find.

The motherboard

The motherboard is the main board that contains the microprocessor, its support chips and the main system memory. Some older machines use the full-sized AT case rather than the Baby AT size, but this is an undesirable type of board because so much of it is inaccessible underneath the power supply unit. Figure 12.2 shows an example of a Baby AT board designed to use a Socket-7 processor.

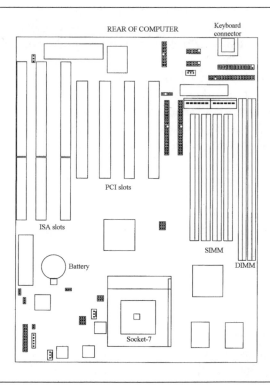

Figure 12.2   A Baby AT board for Socket-7 use

- The slots on the motherboard always face to the rear of the computer, and the keyboard connector must also be at the rear, but otherwise the position of components is not fixed, nor are the precise dimensions.

The problem is where to find a suitable Baby AT board. You will not find such boards advertised in most of the computer magazines other

than as clearance items, but you might be able to pick up such a
board, possibly with a suitable processor, from suppliers such as AUT
whose website is:

www.autonline.co.uk

At the time of writing they could offer an AT motherboard with
sound and video and modem on board and a AMD 550 MHz
processor with heatsink and fan for around £90. Figure 12.3 shows a
typical Socket-7 processor.

Figure 12.3   A typical AMD Socket-7 processor, courtesy of AMD Inc.

One of the main problems about using a motherboard that is no
longer in production is that if there is no documentation with it you
may have considerable difficulty finding out about jumper settings,
suitable chips, type of memory and so on. Once again, you may be
able to find out something from the supplier, but if not, make use of
the Internet and find if anyone has suitable information.

MOTHERBOARD PREPARATION

Jumpers are used on most Baby AT motherboards to switch actions
in or out, or to allow for options. Each jumper unit normally consists
of a row of three small pins with a bridging clip, the jumper itself,

which can be placed over two pins to provide two settings (sometimes three settings if the design provides for the jumper to be removed altogether). Jumper settings should be correct if you have bought a bare-bones system with the motherboard already installed in its case, and very often there is little chance of altering jumpers once the machine is fully assembled.

When you have read all the information on the motherboard and made notes about anything you need to watch out for, unpack the motherboard. The final wrapping will be of a material that is slightly electrically conducting, and when you take the motherboard out of this material you should lay the board down on this sheet of material to make an inspection. Touch the motherboard only at the edges at this stage, and try to keep your hands away from the metallic connections as far as possible at all times.

You will need to check any jumper settings very carefully before you place the new motherboard into the case. The small (and usually anonymous) manual or leaflet that comes with the motherboard will list the jumper settings, and these are often preset correctly, particularly if you have specified the type of processor chip you will be using. If they are not, it is not always clear what settings you ought to use, and you may need to enquire from the supplier of the board.

Another problem is that manuals usually show the pins numbered, but this numbering is not necessarily printed on the motherboard or, if it is printed, it is obscured by chips or other resident obstacles. The description that follows is of jumpers on a Socket-7 board of a few years ago. This is fairly typical of practice on Socket-7 boards, and most boards that you are likely to come across will provide for a similar list of jumpers.

TYPICAL JUMPERS

- You must always switch off the computer and allow a few minutes for voltages to decay to zero before you attempt to change jumpers. Always check jumper settings after you have made a change.

One jumper is used to control CMOS-RAM, and its default position keeps the CMOS-RAM cleared of any data. This will have to be reset to the working position before the motherboard is installed. Another jumper sets the voltage supply for DIMM memory, usually to 3.3 V, with the alternative, seldom needed, of 5 V.

Some boards have a jumper termed the *Function* jumper, and if this is used its settings are important. Typically these will allow three options labelled Normal, Configure and Recovery. In the *Normal* configuration, the BIOS uses the current CMOS-RAM settings (see later) for booting. In the *Configure* setting, the BIOS set-up will run and the screen will display a maintenance menu (this corresponds to the use of keys to activate the CMOS-RAM display). The *Recovery* option can be used only if you have inserted a floppy containing BIOS information and this data will be read and used.

A very important set of jumpers deals with CPU type and voltage. One jumper setting is for Pentium type, either P54C (dual voltage) or P55C (single voltage) types. Another set of jumpers will set the CPU (core) voltage to the required voltage within the set 2.5 V, 2.8 V, 2.9 V, 3.2 V, 3.3 V or 3.5 V. You need to set the jumpers for the type of chip and the exact voltage that your CPU chip needs.

That's easier said than done. Motherboard manuals are not always up to date, and a chip is often supplied with little or no data. A good rule is that the faster chips use lower voltages, so that if you are going to use a chip that runs at 300 MHz or more it is likely to use the lower range of voltage settings. In particular, if the chip is of the old MMX type it is likely to run at 2.8 volts, though some motherboards insist on using 3.2 volts. The sure sign of using too high a voltage is that Windows will not run correctly and even some DOS commands (like dir) will not run correctly. If reducing the core voltage restores normal operation, you can be certain that the higher voltage setting is incorrect, whatever the documentation states.

● Note that AMD K6 processors of speeds from 300 MHz to 400 MHz all specify a working voltage of 3.3 volts.

The next important settings are the internal clock speed jumpers which are set for the type of processor you are using. The settings are usually graded as 1.5×/3.5×, 2.0×, 2.5× and 3.0, and the usual default is 2.0×. You will need to check the manual for the motherboard and any leaflets that come with the processor to know how to set this. Several modern motherboards can make this setting automatically by sensing the type of CPU that is inserted, and some jumper settings work differently with different processors. These internal speed jumpers allow you to overclock the CPU.

The other clock setting is labelled *External clock* and typically allows for bus speeds of 60 MHz, 66 MHz, 75 MHz, 83 MHz and 100 MHz, often higher speeds also. The 66 MHz speed is the usual default for the slower Socket-7 chips, and 100 MHz is used for the newer, faster chips, including AMD K6. You will, once again, need to check carefully to find if you need to use a different speed.

- Remember that if you are using a 100 MHz (or faster) bus speed that your memory chips need to be of the faster type. This setting is sometimes referred to as the FSB (Front-side bus) speed. Motherboards for Pentium-3 will need to provide a 133 MHz bus speed, and must use memory that is capable of operating at this speed. This speed capability extends to the other supporting chips, but if the motherboard can use 133 MHz it's almost certain that the chips that come on the motherboard can also.
- Note that the motherboard design fixes the maximum speed of CPU that you can use. Very few motherboards using Socket-7 provide for CPU speeds above 450 MHz.

Take your time, enquire if necessary, and do not install the motherboard into the case until you are totally satisfied that the jumper settings are correct. A familiar problem is that the documentation may tell you that the setting you want is to jumper pins 1 and 2, but there is no pin numbering on the motherboard. If you come across this problem, you will often find that you can deduce pin numbers by looking at other settings which you are fairly sure have been correctly preset. You may find, for example, that pin 1 is the pin closest to the end of the motherboard that contains the expansion slots.

Once the jumper settings have been dealt with and double-checked, you can install the CPU, unless this has already been done by the supplier. Normally, if you buy a board and a CPU by mail order, the CPU will have been inserted and the jumpers set, except for the CMOS-RAM jumper. If you buy the motherboard and processor separately (at a computer fair, for example), you will have to insert the CPU for yourself and also check that the jumper settings are correct.

Socket insertion

The procedure for inserting a CPU into a Socket-7 is much the same as it is for the later Socket-A. Before inserting the CPU check that it is the type you ordered, and note which corner has an identification such as a pin missing, a notch and a white dot. Some heatsinks come with a small tube of heatsink grease (Electrolube) that helps in heat transfer, and you can order this separately from Maplin stores. Only a thin film is needed, and you should not have grease oozing out from between the fan and the chip. You can get away with omitting the grease on the slower chips such as the 166MMX type, but not on the faster chips.

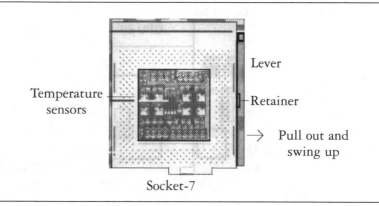

Figure 12.4   The view over an empty Socket-7 holder

Pull the lever away from the body of the Socket-7 on the motherboard and then pull it upwards (Figure 12.4). A CPU for Socket-7 has a notched corner with a white dot to identify its pin 1 position, and this needs to be placed at the corner of the socket that has a hole missing and a figure 1 stamped on the socket. The CPU should drop into place, any resistance probably indicates that it is the wrong way round. Once the CPU chip has been dropped in you can replace the lever so that the chip is locked in place.

You can then fit the cooling fan (Figure 12.5). This item clips over the top of the chip, and the clips are very strong because they have to keep the fan in very close contact with the chip. You will need to support the motherboard with your fingers to avoid excessive flexing when you press down the clips on the fan.

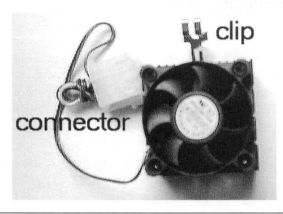

Figure 12.5   A typical fan for Socket-7 use, connecting to the PSU leads

Memory

Following these settings of jumpers and CPU insertion you will need to install memory, and on all modern Baby AT motherboards this is usually done using DIMMs. These are used in much the same way as the earlier EDO SIMMs, and the obvious difference is that the DIMM uses a much larger number of pins, 168 as contrasted with the 72 of a SIMM. A DIMM is also easier to install because it can be inserted directly and clipped in – the older SIMMs had to be inserted and then turned to lock them in place.

- By this time you will have sorted out which of the many varieties of memory chips your motherboard can use and bought the appropriate type. Be careful if your motherboard seems to accept both SIMM and DIMM units, because it may not be able to accept mixtures of both. If it can accept mixtures, you may be able to reuse some of the SIMMs from the old motherboard.

Connections are made to the DIMM just as they are to expansion cards, using an edge connector, a set of tiny metal tongues on the card which engage in springs on the holder. The DIMM is clipped in by spring-loaded holders at each end. Nowadays DIMMs come in sizes from 16 Mbytes to 256 Mbytes, and you currently can use a DIMM singly, so that you could use a single 64 Mbyte DIMM for this amount of memory.

EDO SIMMs come in sizes from 8 Mbytes per SIMM to 128 Mbytes per SIMM, and they must be installed in pairs. You are not likely to be using SIMMs except for upgrading an existing motherboard that is otherwise satisfactory. If you want to mix SIMMs and DIMMs you need to check with your motherboard documentation that this can be done. You may be able to use only one specific DIMM socket if SIMMs are present, but many modern motherboards do not accept SIMMs at all.

Motherboard insertion

Once the CPU and memory units have been inserted, the motherboard can be mounted into the casing, but don't rush into this task. Very often when a Baby AT motherboard is in place, part of it lies under the power supply unit, and because of this the PSU is often supplied separately, not connected in. The later ATX layout is much better in this respect, and nothing needs to be removed for easy access.

For installing a Baby AT board, don't connect in the PSU at this stage, and if the casing has come with its PSU fastened into place, check with the motherboard locating point to see if any of the motherboard will be covered by the PSU. If it is, as is normal, you must remove the PSU by unscrewing the three small bolts at the rear of the case and the three underneath. If your PSU uses a different number of bolts, make a note of this. A miniature socket set is useful for these bolts.

- It is particularly difficult to plug in the power connectors to the Baby AT board if the PSU is in place, and you may also have difficulties with the IDE connectors and the ports.

With the PSU laid temporarily out of the way, you can now concentrate on the motherboard mountings. Metal cases for the PC have their locating fasteners located in standardized positions, and motherboards are provided with matching location holes, so that it is very unusual to find that there are any problems in fitting a new motherboard into a new case.

Do not expect, however, that a new motherboard will have exactly as many mounting holes as there are fasteners on the casing, or that all of the mounting holes will be in the same places. Remember, though, that a motherboard should *never* be drilled because the connecting tracks on the surface are not necessarily the only tracks that exist; most boards are laminated with tracks between layers. Drilling through any of these tracks would be a very expensive mistake.

The fitting methods vary, but the most popular systems use either a brass pillar at each fixing position or a plastic clip at some positions. The brass connectors are screwed into threaded holes in a case and the motherboard is bolted in turn to the pillars; the plastic clips that fit into slots in the case are pushed into the holes in the motherboard and then slotted in place.

There should be at least one brass pillar fixing that is used to earth the motherboard electrically to the casing. Quite often, only two screwed fittings are used, with the rest being either clips or simply resting points. The motherboard must be well supported under the slots, because this is where pressure is exerted on it when cards are plugged in. If there are no supporting pillars in this region you may be able to get hold of polypropylene pillars of the correct size and glue them to the floor of the casing – do not under any circumstances glue anything to the motherboard itself.

When you have the motherboard in place, check everything again. It is remarkably easy to plug in jumpers with only one pin making contact, for example, and when you come to make other plug and socket connections this is also a hazard to look out for. If the paper-work that came with the motherboard did not have a sketch of the motherboard, this is the time to make one for yourself that shows where the board is mounted and where the jumpers are. Remember that it is often very difficult to alter jumpers once a motherboard has been fitted in place, particularly if the jumpers are underneath the power supply box.

On a Baby AT board that contains connectors for power input and for disk drives, you should consider fitting the PSU cable connectors (Figure 12.6) at this point, because they can be very difficult to reach when the PSU box is in place. In addition, you can support the moth-erboard more easily with the PSU box out, and ensure that the plugs are correctly inserted. This does not absolve you from checking these

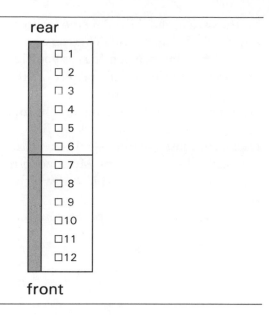

rear

front

Figure 12.6   The connector type used for the power socket on a Baby AT board

plugs again afterwards, because in the course of connecting up these plugs can (and do) work loose, causing problems with hard drive and CD-ROM use.

You now need to reinstall the PSU box if you removed it earlier. If you are fitting a PSU that came separately packaged the first requirement is to check that you have all the mounting bolts – these are usually American UNF or M5 metric types which are not easy to replace, certainly not at your local ironmonger or DIY store. The second point is that the PSU has to be slid rather carefully into the casing, ensuring that the weight of the PSU does not rest on the motherboard. This is more difficult if the older design is used with a switch at the side. The thick and stiff set of cables from the PSU makes this task of fitting more difficult than you might expect. The shape of the PSU box allows part of the motherboard to lie underneath it without touching the components on the motherboard. Once the mains switch is located, it is easy to position the PSU so that all the screw holes line up, and the bolts can be put in place, finger-tight at first.

As you tighten the bolts, check that the mains switch, if it is on the PSU box, can be operated easily. Some casing slots are a tight fit for the switch, and if the PSU mountings are a fraction out of line the switch will jam or be stiff. This can usually be avoided by moving the PSU slightly on its mountings as you tighten the bolts, but you may need to file the slot to get a perfect fit. If this is needed, take the PSU out again, and file with the outside of the slot pointing down, avoiding any filings landing on the motherboard. Tap the casing afterwards to remove any lurking filings – just one filing bridging tracks can cause puzzling symptoms that cannot be detected by any automatic checking system. Most modern casings have a main switch that is on the end of a cable and which plugs into the front of the casing.

The connections for the power connector of the Baby AT board are:

Pin	Use	Pin	Use
1	Power good	7	Earth
2	+5 V DC	8	Earth
3	+12 V DC	9	-5 V DC
4	-12 V DC	10	+5 V DC
5	Earth	11	+5 V DC
6	Earth	12	-5 V DC

Adding drives

We need to look at the installation of a hard drive first, because on a flip-lid casing it is normal to keep the hard drive in the lowest of the drive bays of a set, making it inaccessible once the floppy drive has been fitted. The tower type of AT casing often provides a bay at the back of the case for the main (or only) hard drive, making this easier to get to without removing anything else.

Do not assume that a drive will be provided with mounting brackets at exactly the same places as the drive bay, though these positions are usually standard on PC clones. An adapter will be needed if you want to put a 3½-inch hard drive into a 5¼-inch bay, but modern cases should be well provided with 3½-inch drive bays. You should enquire when you order or buy the drive what provisions are made for mounting it on the style of casing you are using. Make sure that all mounting bolts and connecting cables are supplied with the drive.

The drive bay has slots at the sides to allow for to and fro adjustment of a drive and two sets are usually provided at different heights in the bay. These should fit the hard drive in a 3½-inch bay without any problems and also fit a 5¼-inch bay using an adapter plate. Hard drives must be mounted to the bay or the adapter plate by way of small bolts fitting into their threaded mounting pads. This is important because these pads act to cushion the drive against shock. Any drive that has external access should be adjusted so that its front panel is flush with the front panel of the casing.

Under no circumstances should you consider drilling the casing of a hard drive in order to mount it in any other way. You should also handle a hard drive by its casing, not holding its weight on any other points. In particular, avoid handling the connector strips at the rear of the drive or any of the exposed electronic circuits. Read any documents that come with the hard drive to find if there are any prohibitions on the use of mounting holes – sometimes you are instructed to use only the outer set of holes.

The 5¼-inch type of hard drive, usually large capacity drives, will fit into any bay of this size with no need for adapters. The 3½-inch drives use underside mountings as well as side mountings, which makes it easier to attach them if the side fastenings are difficult to reach. If you have problems, Meccano brackets and strips can usually ensure that you get the drive unit firmly fastened. In a desperate situation, there is nothing wrong with fastening the drive to a metal plate and sticking this to the casing with self-adhesive foam pads. Maplin supply very useful side plates for fitting a 3¼-inch drive into a 5¼ inch bay.

DRIVE INSTALLATION

You will almost certainly have to replace the hard drive of an older machine. This presents two important problems. The one is that the motherboard BIOS may not be able to cope with large hard drives. The other is that you will not be able to find any small hard drives. Don't be tempted to buy a second-hand hard drive, because you have no idea what its life might be, and a hard drive failure can be frustrating and expensive. With luck you should be able to find a hard drive of modest capacity (5 Gbytes or less), which will come with software that allows the BIOS to recognize it and to make use of all, or most of, its capacity. Don't rush into buying a new hard drive unless you are quite certain that you can use it with your motherboard.

Before you start, check the drive package to make sure you have all of the mounting bolts, any adapter that is needed, cables (if not already on the computer) and instructions. Check that you have the necessary tools – a Phillips screwdriver (possible a plain-head type) and a pair of tweezers are usually needed.

The bolts are usually either 6-32 UNC × 0.31 (5/16″) or metric M4 × 0.7-6H, but some drives use M3 × 0.5. UK suppliers use millimetre sizing for the length so that the size will show 5 rather than 0.5 or 6 in place of 0.6. The frame of the drive may be stamped with M for metric or S for UNC. If you need spare UNC bolts you will need to contact a specialist supplier, but the M4 metric types can be bought from electronics suppliers such as the well-known Maplin or RS Components.

At this stage, check that any jumpers or switches are correctly set. Once the drive is in place these will be impossible to reach. Use tweezers to manipulate these devices. It is not always obvious from the accompanying instruction what settings are needed, and though drives are often set ready for use in a standard type of machine you cannot rely on this. Jumpers will quite certainly need to be set if you intend to use more than one hard drive.

Unpack the drive carefully and read any accompanying manual thoroughly, particularly to check any prohibitions on drive fastening or mounting positions. No drive should ever be mounted with its front panel facing down, but most drives can be placed flat, or on either side. Check that any adapter plate fits into the mounting bay on the casing and that all bolts and cable adapters (see later) are provided.

The hard drive is usually placed as the lowest in a set of drives on a desktop casing, and in a position nearest to the motherboard in a tower casing. Check also that the drive data cable will reach from the EIDE connector on the motherboard to the drive – you may need to put the IDE board in a different slot if the cable is short (as they often are).

Fasten the 3½-inch drive to its bay or adapter, using the small bolts that are provided to bolt into the mounting pads. Tighten these up evenly and not excessively. If an adapter is used, bolt this into its bay. Check that you can still place a floppy drive above the hard drive unit, if this is where it will be put. This latter point is important, because floppy drives may have an exposed flywheel on the underside, and the slightest contact against this flywheel will prevent the floppy drive motor from spinning. There should be no such problems if the 3½-inch floppy drive is being mounted sideways in a bay specially provided for this purpose, because such a bay is usually well clear of any others.

Installation is not a particularly skilled operation, though experience with a Meccano set as a child is helpful. Problems arise only if the mounting pads on the drive do not correspond with openings in the bay, or you have no adapter for a 3½-inch or 2½-inch drive, or an unsuitable adapter, or you manage to lose a mounting bolt. A mounting bolt that falls inside the drive casing or the computer casing can usually be shaken out or picked out with tweezers. Do *not* use a magnet to retrieve a bolt from a disk drive casing. Do *not* attempt to make use of other bolts, particularly longer bolts or bolts which need a lot of effort to tighten (because they are ruining the threads in the drive). It is better to mount a drive with only three bolts rather than to add one bolt of the wrong type.

EIDE/ATA interface

Now connect up the cables to the drive(s). There are two sets of cables required for any hard drive, the power cable and the data cable. The power cable is a simple four-strand type with a four-way connector (some drives use only two connections of the four). This connector is made so that it can be plugged in only one way round. For details of these connectors see Chapter 7.

The same power cable is used for floppy drives and for hard drives, and modern AT machines usually provide four or five plugs on the cable. The plug is a tight fit into the socket and usually locks into place. The socket for the power plug is obvious but some disk drives need an adapter which should be supplied.

The data cable, illustrated earlier, that connects to the IDE drive is of the flat 40-strand type. This plugs into the matching connector on the motherboard at one end and into the drive at the other, with no complications. Look for one strand of the cable being marked, often with a black, striped or red line, to indicate pin-1 connection. This makes it easier to locate the connector the correct way round. Do not assume that one particular way round (such as cable-entry down) will always be correct, or that a second hard drive will have its pin-1 position the same way round as your first hard drive.

And finally...

Apart from processor motherboard and memory, much of the work of upgrading an old machine follows along the same lines as for upgrading a more modern one. The difference is that even a modest upgrade of an old machine requires rather more work, particularly searching for information and for parts, than the upgrading of a more modern unit. With perseverance, however, you should be able to upgrade any of the older machines we have been talking about to something close to a 500 MHz type that can give a reasonable performance, with suitable software, even nowadays.

The question now is what software to use. If you have a complete installation of Windows 98 second edition, there's no reason why you shouldn't make use of that. I have found that Windows *Me* works very well on an older machine, even one that used a comparatively slow Pentium-1 166 chip. If you avoid any software that requires very fast processing (such as voice dictation or video editing) then you can get a good working life from your upgraded machine.

What happens at the end of its life is quite another matter, because there must be a limit to the number of the AT boards and other matching components that will still be around in a few years' time. This is why the main thrust of this book has been working with a modern ATX case and motherboard that allow for continual upgrading over the coming years.

Glossary of terms

This is a small glossary that applies particularly to terms used in Windows and MS-DOS 6.0. For a full explanation of terms used in computing, see *Collins Dictionary of Computing* by Ian Sinclair.

Active icon The Windows icon which has been clicked on and whose menu will appear on the next click.

Active printer The printer which will print out from your Windows work when you click the printer icon or use the File – Print menu. Only one printer is active at a time, though several printers can be installed.

Active window The window in which you can make entries and select items. Other windows can display on the screen but do not respond to the use of keys until you switch to one of them. Programs can, however, continue to run inside an *inactive* window, carrying out actions such as searching and sorting which do not require your attention.

Application A program or suite of programs for a particular purpose such as a spreadsheet, word processor, desktop publisher,

CAD program, etc. The same word is sometimes used to mean programs that run under MS-DOS.

Application icon   A Windows icon representing a program that appears in a Toolbar line on main screen display, normally at the top or the foot of the screen though it can be moved elsewhere. Clicking on one of these items will start the program running.

Associate   To nominate a file name extension as one created by an application, so that TXT might be associated with a word processor, SKD with a CAD program, PUB with a DTP program and so on.

Athlon   A very fast processor, particularly the later XP version, from AMD, using the same Socket-A fitting as Duron and Thunderbird chips.

Attribute   One of a set of marker bits in a file name which can make the file read-only (the R attribute), archive (A, changed but not copied), system (S, essential to operation of computer) or hidden (H, not normally appearing in a folder listing). You can use the View – Folder options of Explorer to choose whether or not to see System and/or Hidden files.

AUTOEXEC.BAT file   A file of text commands that is placed on the disk drive that the computer boots from, and which sets up various items before MS-DOS programs are run. You can usually dispense with this file if you use only Windows.

Background   1. The screen that is visible outside the current active window. 2. An inactive window or an icon whose program can be working without attention from the keyboard or mouse. A program working in the background can be sorting or searching data or exchanging text or other files with another computer.

Backup   Any system for storing data over a long period, not part of the computer system. This includes floppy disks, data tapes, detachable hard drives and writeable CDs.

Binary file   A file of coded numbers that are meaningless when printed or displayed but which convey information. A program is always in binary file form, but program control files such as CONFIG.SYS, AUTOEXEC.BAT and WIN.TNI are in ordinary readable text form.

BIOS   Acronym for basic input output system, meaning a small ROM that contains a few routines that allow elementary control over the computer, providing limited input and monitor output. The BIOS provided just enough facilities to allow the main operating system to be loaded.

Bitmap   A graphics image which is stored in the form of numbers that represent the intensity and colour of each part of the screen. A simple bitmap requires a lot of disk space, typically 100 Kbytes or more, for a screen. Other forms of file for graphics such as TIF compress this information considerably (if there are 500 consecutive red dots, for example, you need store only the information for one red dot along with the number of them).

Bluetooth   A standardized method of linking a computer with its peripherals using digital radio signals so that no connecting wires are needed.

Boot   To start up the computer either from a system disk or from a hard disk. The act of booting always checks and clears the memory.

Branch   A folder which is connected to the main (root) folder or which is a subfolder of another folder.

Built-in font   A font which is permanently contained in a printer and which can be used by any software, but mainly by MS-DOS. The view of text on the screen will not necessarily correspond to the appearance when printed unless the screen can use an identical font. You should preferably use TrueType fonts from any Windows software.

Burnproof drive   A CD-R/RW drive that will ensure that data is fed at a steady rate, so eliminating problems that lead to a recorded CD-R being useless (a coaster).

Cache   A portion of memory used for temporary storage. A set of instruction codes to the processor can be read from normal memory or from disk into fast cache memory and fed to the processor at a much higher rate than could otherwise be achieved.

Cartridge   A plug-in unit, such as the ink cartridge of an inkjet printer, the toner cartridge of a laser printer or a tape cartridge used for backup.

Cascade   A set of windows which overlap but allow each title to be displayed so that it is possible to click on the top line of any one. Also applies to menus when one menu allows another to be opened with the first still visible.

Celeron   A trademark being used for the lower cost version of Pentium chips. Modern Celeron chips use the Socket 370 fitting.

Check box   A small square box icon that can contain an X or be blank; used in Windows to switch an option on or off.

Click   The action of quickly pressing and releasing the button (usually the left-hand button) on the mouse. Clicking with the right-hand mouse button will usually bring up a menu whose content depends on the position of the cursor.

Clicking on name/icon   The action of placing a Windows cursor on a name or icon and then clicking the mouse button.

Clipboard   The temporary storage for text or graphics used by Windows to copy data from one application to another, or from one part of an application to another.

Close   To end the use of a window, either by double clicking on the control menu box, or by clicking on the control menu box and selecting *Close* from the menu.

Coaster   A CD-R disc that has not recorded correctly and so cannot be used for any computing purpose.

COM   1. Abbreviation for Communication used to indicate a serial port. The COM ports are numbered as COM1, COM2, etc. 2. An extension for a short type of program file (longer programs use the EXE extension).

Command button   The OK or Cancel word enclosed in a rectangular box and used to confirm or cancel a selection.

Communications settings   The settings of speed and other factors that are needed to make serial transfer of files possible.

CONFIG.SYS file   A file of text commands that imposes various settings on the computer before any program, even MS-DOS itself; can be loaded. Changes to the CONFIG.SYS file have no effect until the machine is rebooted. You do not need to make use of CONFIG.SYS when you work solely with Windows, but the file should not be deleted.

Confirmation message   A warning message that appears when you have chosen an action that might destroy files. You will be asked to confirm that you really intend to go ahead. Some confirmation messages can be turned off or restricted.

Control menu   The menu that is available for each Windows application, allowing you to move the window, minimize, close, expand, etc. The control menu icon is normally placed in the top left-hand corner of any window.

Control menu icon   The small icon at the left of the Windows title bar which is used to bring up the control menu (single click) or close the program (double click).

Copy   To place a copy of some selected text or images on to the Clipboard for pasting into another program or file. This leaves the original unchanged, unlike the *Cut* action.

Ctrl-Alt-Del   The key combination that can be used to escape from a Windows program that appears to have locked up. Repeating the action will reboot the computer. You can use Ctrl-Alt-Del also to find out what programs are currently running under Windows.

Cut   To select a piece of text or graphics and transfer it to the

Clipboard, removing it from the current window. Compare *Copy*.

Default   A choice that is already made for you, usually of the most likely option that will be needed. You need only confirm a default, but can make another choice if you want to.

Desktop   The full screen on which all the windows, icons and menu boxes will appear as you make use of Windows.

Desktop pattern   A pattern or colour that appears on the Windows desktop background so that you can distinguish the background more easily.

Dialog box   A box that contains messages, or which requires you to type an answer to a question that appears in the box.

Digitizer   Any device that converts information into number code form. A digital camera and a scanner are both devices that will digitize an image, and a graphics table can digitize a drawing. In this sense a keyboard is also a digitizer for alphabetical and numerical characters.

Disc   A compact disc such as a CD-ROM or DVD, whose data tracks can be used for text, sound or graphics. Multimedia programs are distributed in this form, which is also used for collections of graphics images and for other large programs. DVD has much higher storage capacity and is used primarily for video images.

Disk   A magnetic disk, usually of the floppy type – the disks of a hard drive are called *platters*.

Double clicking   The action used to select a program by placing the pointer over the program name and clicking the mouse button twice in rapid succession. This action is used much less in Windows 2000 or Windows 98 than in earlier versions.

Dragging   The action of moving an object on screen by selecting it with the pointer, then holding the mouse button down and moving the mouse so as to move the object over the screen. The object is released when the mouse button is released. Some important dragging actions make use of auxiliary keys such as Shift, Ctrl or Alt.

Drag and drop   The action of dragging a file icon to another icon such as the printer icon or a disk drive or folder icon and releasing the mouse button. When a file is dragged and dropped to the printer icon it will be printed (if it is printable and if the printer is online); when the file is dragged to a disk drive icon it will be copied to that drive. Another form of the action is to select an item such as text or a graphic and drag this to another position in a document.

Duron   The low-cost processor from AMD that uses the same design methods as the Athlon and Thunderbird. The same Socket-A is used for all of these processors, making it easy to upgrade from Duron to Athlon to Thunderbird.

ECP   A development of the Centronics parallel port allowing two-way data transfers. This type of port is used to allow modern printers to be controlled by software. See also *EPP*.

Embedding   The action of placing a drawing or an icon into a document, with the icon representing another document or drawing. A document dealing with the topic of using the mouse, for example, might have a drawing between two paragraphs on the screen. Clicking on that drawing would allow you to edit it using the program that created the drawing. See also *Linking*.

Emulation   The imitation of another device, such as an inkjet printer emulating the control codes of another type, such as a Hewlett-Packard Deskjet model.

EPP   A development of the Centronics parallel port for two-way data transfer; used mainly for interfacing the PC computer with industrial control systems.

Expansion slot   The socket (usually one of 4 to 8) within the computer which will accommodate a plug-in card that enhances the capabilities of the machine. Such slots are used for video cards, disk controller, network card and other add-on devices. The ISA slots run at a slow speed and can be used for comparatively slow devices such as sound cards. Faster cards must use the PCI slots, and fast graphics cards can use the AGP slot.

Extension   The set of up to three letters following a full stop (period) in a file name. For example, in the name MYFILE.TXT, TXT is the extension. The extension letters of a file name are used to indicate the type of file. Windows 95 onwards allows longer file names to be used, but the facility for an extension is retained.

Firewire   A system of fast data transfers using serial methods. This was developed by Apple Corp. and is now appearing in some PC applications, particularly digital camcorder interfacing.

Flash BIOS   A form of BIOS whose contents can be changed by applying abnormal voltages and inputting data under the control of a program.

Flow control   A method of ensuring that serial or parallel data sent from one computer to another is synchronized, often by sending handshaking signals to indicate ready to send and ready to receive.

Font or fount   A design of alphabetic or numerical characters, available in different sizes and styles (roman, bold, italic). Note that a font called Euro Collection can be obtained if you need to use the Euro symbol   in text, or you can use the Insert – Symbol action of Word. The Euro symbol is included in the Character Map set for Windows 98 (version 2) onwards.

Footer   A piece of text that appears at the bottom of each printed page in a document. The footer often includes the page number.

Foreground   1. The part of the screen which contains the current active window. 2. The program which is currently under keyboard control and taking most of the processor time (see also *Background*).

Graphics resolution   The measure of detail in a picture, in terms of dots per inch or dots per screen width. The higher the resolution of a picture the better the appearance, the longer it takes to print and the more memory it needs.

Handshake   See *Flow control*.

Header A piece of text that appears at the top of each printed page in a document, often used to carry book and chapter titles.

Highlight A method of marking an icon or text, using a different shading or colour.

Icon A graphics image that represents a program or menu selection which can be used (made active) by clicking the mouse button over the icon.

Inactive window A window which contains visible text or graphics but which is not currently being used by the mouse or keyboard.

Linking A form of insertion of text, graphics or other files in which the inserted material is not added to the document but retains links to its own file and to the program that created it. If you click on an icon for a linked picture, for example, you can edit the picture, and the new edited version will affect any other document linked to that icon – changing one copy changes all (in fact, there is only one copy, used by all the documents in which it is linked). Linking a graphic into a text document makes very little difference to the size of the document, unlike an embedded graphic. Once a link has been made, the file that is linked should not be moved nor renamed unless you also edit the link.

Local bus A set of connections between the processor chip and other components or cards that runs at a high clock rate and can be used for fast data transfer. The older ISA bus can be used for slower data interchange. The type of local bus used for Pentium machines is the PCI bus, but faster buses such as AGP are used for more specialized uses.

LPT An abbreviation of line printer, used to mean the parallel port (also indicated by PRN). When more than one parallel port is available, these will be numbered as LPT1, LPT2, etc.

Macro A recorded file of a set of actions, allowing the actions to be repeated by replaying the file. Many programs, such as Word for Windows or Lotus 1-2-3, contain their own macro system.

Mark   To select portions of text, graphics or complete documents or programs.

Maximize   The action of making a window expand to fill the screen. This can be done from the *Control Bar* menu, or by clicking on the up arrow at the right of the title bar.

Memory resident (or TSR)   A DOS program which is loaded and remains in the memory of the computer rather than being run and discarded as most DOS programs are. Such a program can be called into use by a key combination or it can permanently affect the machine until it is switched off. Windows uses its own version of this action, and the use of some DOS TSR programs can cause Windows error messages to appear.

MIDI   An acronym of *Musical Instrument Digital Interface*, a system for allowing a computer to control electronic musical instruments. Windows provides for such control by way of sound files, but only if a suitable sound card is added in an expansion slot of the computer, and the appropriate instruments are connected to the MIDI port.

Minimize   The action of shrinking a window and the program in it to an icon.

Modem   A device which converts computer signals into musical tones and vice versa, allowing such signals to be transmitted along telephone lines.

Motherboard   The main board of a computer, into which expansion cards, a replacement processor, and memory chips can be plugged. Most machines allow the whole motherboard to be swapped so that the machine can be upgraded.

Mouse   The small trolley whose movement on the desk controls the movement of a pointer or other indicator on the screen. The use of the mouse is central to Windows actions, though disabled users can opt for key alternatives.

MP3   A file type for compressed music files, allowing music to be downloaded over a fast Internet connection, or hundreds of music tracks to be placed on a CD-R disc.

OLE Object linking and embedding, see *Linking*, *Embedding*, *Packaging*.

Packaging The use of an icon to represent a piece of text or a drawing so that it can be embedded or linked in another document. When the document is printed, the icon is printed, but double clicking on the icon when the document is on screen will show the packaged material. Packaging also allows a program that cannot be used directly for embedding or linking to have its files represented as icons in this way.

Parallel port The connector used for printers which sends data signals along a set of cables, eight data signals at a time. Also called a Centronics port. Modern versions allow two-way communication through this port, see *ECP*, *EPP*.

Parameter A piece of information needed to complete a DOS command. For example, a COPY command would need as parameters the name of the file to be copied and the destination to which it had to be copied. Windows uses methods such as dragging and pointing in place of typing a parameter.

Parity An old and crude system of checking memory by using an additional bit as a check on the contents of a byte. At a time when memory was unreliable, parity was used on all PC machines, so that each byte of data used 9 bits rather than 8. This precaution is no longer needed, and modern computers dispense with parity, making memory cheaper. Parity is also used for serial data communications if more modern methods are not employed.

Paste To copy a piece of text or graphics from the Clipboard into a window – this does not clear the Clipboard, so that more than one Paste action can be used on the same material.

Pixel A unit of screen display, a dot, whose brightness and/or colour can be controlled. Nothing smaller than one pixel can be displayed on screen.

Platter   A disk, usually made using aluminium, coated with magnetic material and used within a hard drive for storing digital information.

PNP   Abbreviation of plug and play, a system of hardware card design that allows a card to be plugged into a modern computer and used without the need to set jumper switches.

Point size   A printer's unit of type size, equal to 1/72 inch.

Pointer   The shape on the screen that moves as you move the mouse. Windows uses several different shapes of pointers to indicate that the pointer will have a different action when it is over a different part of a window. Some programs that run under the control of Windows will use other pointer shapes in addition to these types.

Printer driver   A program that determines how the printer makes use of the codes that are sent from the computer. Using the wrong printer driver will result in very strange printed output, because different printers use different methods. Many dot matrix printers, however, use Epson codes, and many laser printers use either Hewlett-Packard Laserjet codes or the universal PostScript system (from Adobe Corp.).

Proportional font   A font in which the spacing between letters is varied according to the space needed by each letter. The alternative is a fixed-space font, as used in typewriters.

Reboot   Restarting the computer either by using the Ctrl-Alt-Del keys (a soft reboot) or by pressing the RESET key (a hard reboot). Either will wipe all programs and data from the memory.

Restore button   The button that is placed at the right-hand side of the title bar when a window has been maximized – clicking on this button will restore the former size.

Screen font   A font that appears on the screen to indicate or simulate the font that has been selected for the printer. Some screen fonts have no printer counterparts.

Scroll bars   The bars at the right-hand side and bottom of a window. Dragging the button in the scroll bar performs the action of moving the window over the text or picture, allowing a different portion to be viewed

Select   To choose an action by clicking its icon (another click needed to run it) or to mark text or graphics for cutting.

Serial port   The connector used for sending or receiving data one bit at a time. This is used mainly for connecting computers to each other, either directly or by way of a modem through telephone lines. A few printers require a serial port connection; many others allow it as an option. The serial port is referred to by the letters COM. See also *USB*.

Soft font   A font which is not built in or in cartridge form, but is sent as a file from the computer to a printer, and which needs to be loaded again after either the printer or the computer has been switched off. Such a font can be made to appear in identical forms both on screen and on paper. The TrueType fonts of Windows are soft fonts.

Sound card   An add-on card that fits into an expansion slot allowing sound inputs to be digitized, and sound outputs to be taken to amplifiers and loudspeakers (some cards incorporate a small amount of amplification). Such a card, of which SoundBlaster is typical, allows sound effects to be incorporated into Windows actions, and it can also be used in sound recording on disk or on CD.

Spool   To store printer information in memory so that it can be fed out to the printer while the computer gets on with other actions.

Swap file   Part of the hard drive used in Windows to swap data with memory so that the memory is not overloaded.

Text file   A file that contains only a limited selection of codes for the letters of the alphabet, digits and punctuation marks. Such a file will display as readable text on screen.

Tiling   An arrangement of windows in which there is no overlapping, unlike Cascade.

Title bar   The strip at the top of a window that contains the title of the application, and also the control box and minimize/maximize arrows.

TrueType font   A form of soft font packaged with Windows and with Windows applications which presents the same appearance on the screen as on paper, allowing you to be much more certain that what you see is what you eventually get. The extension letters TTF are used for font files.

USB   The Universal Serial Bus, a fast data connection intended for use by all peripherals such as monitor, keyboard, mouse, printer, scanner, etc. Versions of Windows prior to Windows 98 did not (except for a few late releases) cater for USB use. USB-2 is a much faster version suitable for digital video.

Vector font   A font that consists of a set of instructions to draw lines, as distinct from a bitmap, which is a pattern of dots. A vector font can be easily scaled to any size.

Virtual machine   Referring to the use of memory organized by Windows so that each application can be run in its own portion of memory, as if it were running in a separate PC.

Virtual memory   The use of a hard disk by Windows as if it were part of the memory of the computer.

Windows application   A program that has been designed to run within Windows, and which will not run unless Windows is being used. All such programs present the same pattern of controls (the *user interface*) making them easier to learn.

Abbreviations and acronyms

AGP   Accelerated Graphics Port, a very fast (66 MHz or more) slot for graphics cards of the AGP type.

ANSI   American National Standards Institute, the title is used for a number code system that follows the ASCII set for numbers 32 to 127, and specifies characters for the set 128 to 255.

ASCII   American Standard Code for Information Interchange, the number code for letters, numerals and punctuation marks that uses the numbers 32 to 127. Text files are normally ASCII or ANSI coded.

AT   Advanced Technology, the designation used by IBM in 1982 for the computer that succeeded the older PC-XT.

ATA   AT Attachment, a device intended to connect to the AT bus such as an IDE hard drive.

ATX   AT Extended, a later design of casing, power supply and motherboard that simplifies connections and component positioning, improves cooling and provides more low voltage supplies, plus facilities like standby operation.

BIOS Basic Input Output System, the program in a ROM chip that allows the computer to make use of screen, disk and keyboard, and which can read in the operating system.

CAD Computer Aided Design, a program that allows the computer to produce technical drawings to scale.

CD-ROM A form of read-only memory, consisting of a compact disc whose digital information can be read as a set of files.

CGA Colour Graphics Adapter, the first IBM attempt to produce a video graphics card.

CISC Complex Instruction Set Chip, a microprocessor which can act on any of a very large number (typically more than 300) instructions. All of the Intel microprocessors to date are of this type. See also *RISC*.

CMOS Complementary Metal-Oxide Semiconductor, a form of chip construction that requires a very low current. As applied to memory, a chip that allows its contents to be retained by applying a low voltage at negligible current.

CP/M Control, Program, Monitor, one of the first standard operating systems for small computers.

CPU Central Processing Unit, the main microprocessor chip of a computer.

CRT Cathode Ray Tube, the display device for monitors used with desktop machines.

CTS Clear To Send, the companion handshake signal to RTS in the RS-232 system.

DCE Data Communications Equipment, a device such as a computer that sends out serial data along a line.

DIL Dual In Line, a pin arrangement for chips that uses two sets of parallel pins.

DIMM Dual In-line Memory Module, a memory expansion card for modern computers that can be used singly rather than in pairs (as was needed for the earlier SIMM units).

DIP Dual In-line Package, a set of miniature switches arranged in the same form of package as a DIL chip.

DOS Disk Operating System, the programs that provide the commands that make a computer usable.

DSR Data Set Ready, another form of handshaking signal for RS-232.

DTE Data Terminal Equipment, a receiver of serial data such as a modem.

DTR Data Terminal Ready, the RS232 companion signals to DSR.

DTP Desktop Publishing, the use of a computer for composing type and graphics into book or newspaper pages.

ECP Extended Capability Port, a form of parallel port with two-way data flow, using for modern printers.

EGA Enhanced Graphics Adapter, the improved form of graphics card introduced by IBM to replace CGA.

EISA Enhanced Industry Standard Architecture, a system for connecting chips in a PC machine which allows faster signal interchange than the standard (ISA) method that has been used since the early PC/AT models.

EMS Expanded Memory System, the original standard for adding memory to the PC/XT machine, no longer used.

EPP Extended Parallel Port, a design of parallel port that allows two-way data flow and is intended for interfacing to devices other than printers.

ISDN Integrated Signals Digital Network, a system of cabling, often using fibre optics, that is used for high-speed digital links for computing and for digital sound and video links.

LCD   Liquid Crystal Display, a form of shadow display which is used on calculators and portable computers. It depends on the action of materials to polarize light when an electrical voltage is applied. Colour LCD displays are used for portable computers, and larger versions are becoming available at reasonable prices.

LCS   Liquid Crystal Shutter, an array of LCD elements used to control light and so expose the light-sensitive drum in a laser printer. The LCD bar is used as an alternative to the use of a laser beam.

LED   Light Emitting Diode, a device used for warning lights, and also as a form of light source in laser-style printers.

MCA   Micro Channel Architecture, a system proposed and used at one time by IBM as a way of connecting chips within a computer, intended to replace the AT-bus (ISA).

MDA   Monochrome Display Adapter, the first type of video card used in IBM PC machines.

MIDI   Musical Instrument Digital Interface, a standard form of port and serial data code used to allow electronic instruments to be controlled by a computer, or to link them with each other.

MS-DOS   Microsoft Disk Operating System, the standard operating system for the PC type of machine.

NLX   A type of motherboard that connects into an add-on card 'riser' to make it easy to replace a motherboard without replacing parts that are common to all motherboards.

NTSC   National Television Standards Committee, the body that drew up the specification for the colour TV system used in the USA and Japan since 1952. This system is not compatible with the European PAL or SECAM systems.

OCR   Optical Character Recognition, software that can be used on a scanned image file to convert images of characters into ASCII codes.

OS/2   An operating system devised by IBM and intended to replace PC-DOS (the IBM version of MS-DOS).

PAL   Phase Alternating Line, the colour TV system devised by Telefunken in Germany and used throughout Europe apart from France.

PCI   PC Interconnection, a fast form of local bus used for speed-critical cards such as graphics and video cards. The PCI bus has now replaced the older ISA bus for expansion cards.

PBX   Private Branch Exchange, sometimes a problem for using modems.

PSS   Packet Switch Stream, a method of transmitting digital signals efficiently along telephone lines.

RAM   Random Access Memory. All memory is random access, but this acronym is used to mean read-write as distinct from read-only memory.

RGB   Red, Green, Blue, the three primary colour TV signals. A monitor described as RGB needs to be supplied with three separate colour signals, unlike a TV monitor that can use a composite signal.

RISC   A microprocessor that can work with only a few simple instructions, each of which can be completed very rapidly.

RLL   Run Length Limited; a form of high-density recording for hard drives.

ROM   Read-Only Memory, the form of non-volatile memory that is not erased when the computer's power is switched off.

RS232   The old standard for serial communications.

RTS   Request to Send, a handshaking signal for RS-232.

SCART   The standard form of connector for video equipment, used on TV receivers and video recorders.

SCSI   Small Computer Systems Interface, a form of fast-acting disk drive interface which allows for almost unlimited expansion. Used mainly on Mac machines, but also found (in a less standardized form) for some PC devices.

SECAM   Séquence Couleur et Memoire, the French colour TV system, also used in Eastern Europe and the countries of the former USSR. This is not compatible with PAL or NTSC.

SIMM   Single Inline Memory Module, a slim card carrying memory chips, used for inserting memory, now superseded by DIMM.

SMART   Self-Monitoring and Reporting Technology, used on hard drives so that they can check and report on faults or potential faults.

TIFF   Tagged Image File Format, one method of coding graphics images that is widely used by scanners. Graphics files using this system have the TIF extension to their file names.

TSR   Terminate and Stay Resident, a form of DOS program that runs and remains in the memory to influence the computer.

TTL   Transistor-Transistor Logic, a family of digital chips. The name is often used to mean that a device will work on 0 and +5 V levels.

UPS   Uninterruptible Power Supply, a unit using batteries that will provide power to the PC for a limited time when mains power fails. The UPS will keep the computer running long enough to shut down all files and switch off, and the UPS batteries will be recharged when mains power is restored.

VDU   Visual Display Unit, another name for the monitor.

VEGA   Video Extended Graphics Association, a group of US manufacturers who have agreed on a common standard for high-resolution graphics cards.

VGA Video Graphics Array, the video card introduced by IBM for their PS/2 range of computers.

Index